A TREATISE ON PAINTING

LECTOR HOUSE PUBLIC DOMAIN WORKS

This book is a result of an effort made by Lector House towards making a contribution to the preservation and repair of original classic literature. The original text is in the public domain in the United States of America, and possibly other countries depending upon their specific copyright laws.

In an attempt to preserve, improve and recreate the original content, certain conventional norms with regard to typographical mistakes, hyphenations, punctuations and/or other related subject matters, have been corrected upon our consideration. However, few such imperfections might not have been rectified as they were inherited and preserved from the original content to maintain the authenticity and construct, relevant to the work. The work might contain a few prior copyright references as well as page references which have been retained, wherever considered relevant to the part of the construct. We believe that this work holds historical, cultural and/or intellectual importance in the literary works community, therefore despite the oddities, we accounted the work for print as a part of our continuing effort towards preservation of literary work and our contribution towards the development of the society as a whole, driven by our beliefs.

We are grateful to our readers for putting their faith in us and accepting our imperfections with regard to preservation of the historical content. We shall strive hard to meet up to the expectations to improve further to provide an enriching reading experience.

Though, we conduct extensive research in ascertaining the status of copyright before redeveloping a version of the content, in rare cases, a classic work might be incorrectly marked as not-in-copyright. In such cases, if you are the copyright holder, then kindly contact us or write to us, and we shall get back to you with an immediate course of action.

HAPPY READING!

A TREATISE ON PAINTING

LEONARDO DA VINCI,
JOHN FRANCIS RIGAUD,
JOHN SIDNEY HAWKINS

ISBN: 978-93-89539-23-3

Published: 1802

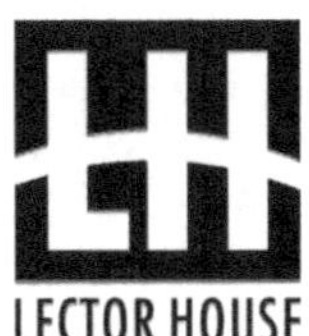

LECTOR HOUSE LLP
E-MAIL: lectorpublishing@gmail.com

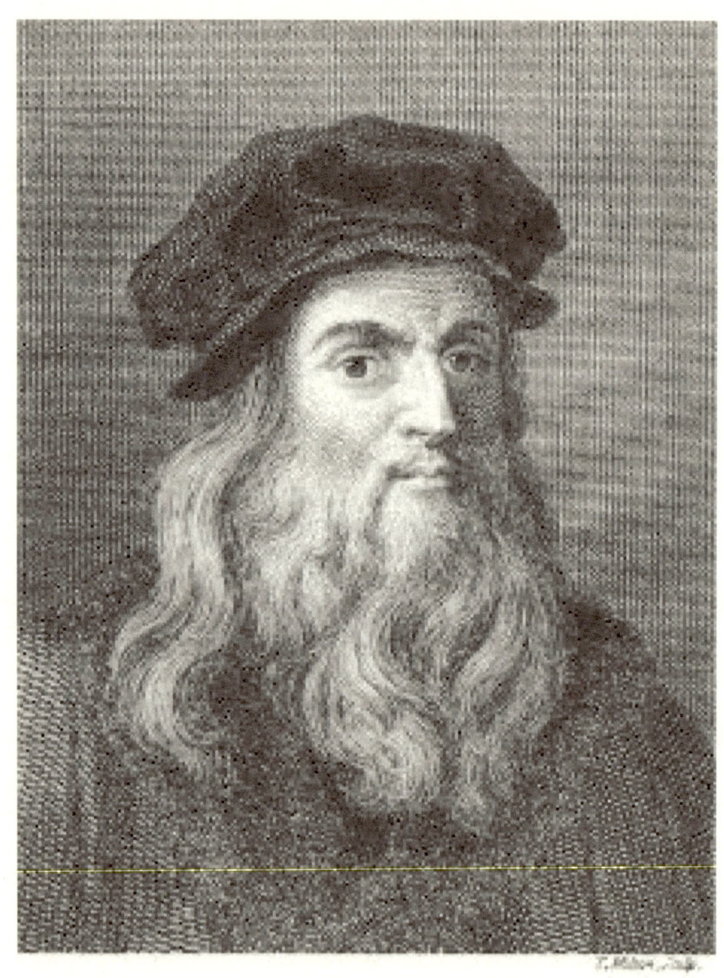

Leonardo Da Vinci.

From a picture in the Forentine Museum.

A TREATISE ON PAINTING,

BY

LEONARDO DA VINCI.

**FAITHFULLY TRANSLATED FROM THE
ORIGINAL ITALIAN,
AND NOW FIRST DIGESTED UNDER PROPER HEADS,**

BY JOHN FRANCIS RIGAUD, ESQ.

ACADEMICIAN OF THE ROYAL ACADEMY OF PAINTING AT LONDON,
AND ALSO OF THE ACADEMIA CLEMENTINA AT BOLOGNA, AND THE
ROYAL ACADEMY AT STOCKHOLM.

**ILLUSTRATED WITH TWENTY-THREE COPPER-PLATES,
AND OTHER FIGURES.**

TO WHICH IS PREFIXED

A NEW LIFE OF THE AUTHOR,

DRAWN UP FROM AUTHENTIC MATERIALS TILL NOW INACCESSIBLE,

BY JOHN SIDNEY, HAWKINS, ESQ. F.A.S.

Ars est habitus quidam faciendi verâ cum ratione.

ARISTOT. ETHIC. LIB. 6.

M.DCCC.II.

PREFACE TO THE PRESENT TRANSLATION.

THE excellence of the following Treatise is so well known to all in any tolerable degree conversant with the Art of Painting, that it would be almost superfluous to say any thing respecting it, were it not that it here appears under the form of a new translation, of which some account may be expected.

Of the original Work, which is in reality a selection from the voluminous manuscript collections of the Author, both in folio and quarto, of all such passages as related to Painting, no edition appeared in print till 1651, though its Author died so long before as the year 1519; and it is owing to the circumstance of a manuscript copy of these extracts in the original Italian, having fallen into the hands of Raphael du Fresne; that in the former of these years it was published at Paris in a thin folio volume in that language, accompanied with a set of cuts from the drawings of Nicolo Poussin, and Alberti; the former having designed the human figures, the latter the geometrical and other representations. This precaution was probably necessary, the sketches in the Author's own collections being so very slight as not to be fit for publication without further assistance. Poussin's drawings were mere outlines, and the shadows and back-grounds behind the figures were added by Errard, after the drawings had been made, and, as Poussin himself says, without his knowledge.

In the same year, and size, and printed at the same place, a translation of the original work into French was given to the world by Monsieur de Chambray (well known, under his family name of Freart, as the author of an excellent Parallel of ancient and modern Architecture, in French, which Mr. Evelyn translated into English). The style of this translation by Mons. de Chambray, being thought, some years after, too antiquated, some one was employed to revise and modernise it; and in 1716 a new edition of it, thus polished, came out, of which it may be truly said, as is in general the case on such occasions, that whatever the supposed advantage obtained in purity and refinement of language might be, it was more than counterbalanced by the want of the more valuable qualities of accuracy, and fidelity to the original, from which, by these variations, it became further removed.

The first translation of this Treatise into English, appeared in the year 1721. It does not declare by whom it was made; but though it professes to have been done from the original Italian, it is evident, upon a comparison, that more use was made of the revised edition of the French translation. Indifferent, however, as it is, it had become so scarce, and risen to a price so extravagant, that, to supply the demand, it was found necessary, in the year 1796, to reprint it as it stood, with all its errors on its head, no opportunity then offering of procuring a fresh translation.

This last impression, however, being now also disposed of, and a new one again called for, the present Translator was induced to step forward, and undertake the office of fresh translating it, on finding, by comparing the former versions both in French and English with the original, many passages which he thought might at once be more concisely and more faithfully rendered. His object, therefore, has been to attain these ends, and as rules and precepts like the present allow but little room for the decorations of style, he has been more solicitous for fidelity, perspicuity, and precision, than for smooth sentences, and well-turned periods.

Nor was this the only advantage which it was found the present opportunity would afford; for the original work consisting in fact of a number of entries made at different times, without any regard to their subjects, or attention to method, might rather in that state be considered as a chaos of intelligence, than a well-digested treatise. It has now, therefore, for the first time, been attempted to place each chapter under the proper head or branch of the art to which it belongs; and by so doing, to bring together those which (though related and nearly connected in substance) stood, according to the original arrangement, at such a distance from each other as to make it troublesome to find them even by the assistance of an index; and difficult, when found, to compare them together.

The consequence of this plan, it must be confessed, has been, that in a few instances the same precept has been found in substance repeated; but this is so far from being an objection, that it evidently proves the precepts were not the hasty opinions of the moment, but settled and fixed principles in the mind of the Author, and that he was consistent in the expression of his sentiments. But if this mode of arrangement has in the present case disclosed what might have escaped observation, it has also been productive of more material advantages; for, besides facilitating the finding of any particular passage (an object in itself of no small importance), it clearly shews the work to be a much more complete system than those best acquainted with it, had before any idea of, and that many of the references in it apparently to other writings of the same Author, relate in fact only to the present, the chapters referred to having been found in it. These are now pointed out in the notes, and where any obscurity has occurred in the text, the reader will find some assistance at least attempted by the insertion of a note to solve the difficulty.

No pains or expense have been spared in preparing the present work for the press. The cuts have been re-engraven with more attention to correctness in the drawing, than those which accompanied the two editions of the former English translation possessed (even though they had been fresh engraven for the impression of 1796); and the diagrams are now inserted in their proper places in the text, instead of being, as before, collected all together in two plates at the end. Besides this, a new Life of the Author has been also added by a Friend of the Translator, the materials for which have been furnished, not from vague reports, or uncertain conjectures, but from memoranda of the Author himself, not before used.

Fortunately for this undertaking, the manuscript collections of Leonardo da Vinci, which have lately passed from Italy into France, have, since their removal thither, been carefully inspected, and an abstract of their contents published in a quarto pamphlet, printed at Paris in 1797, and intitled, "Essai sur les Ouvrages physico-mathematiques de Leonard de Vinci;" by J. B. Venturi, Professor of Natural Philosophy at Modena; a Member of the Institute of Bologna, &c. From this pamphlet a great deal of original intelligence respecting the Author has been obtained, which, derived as it is from his own information, could not possibly be founded on better evidence.

To this Life we shall refer the reader for a further account of the origin and history of the present Treatise, conceiving we have already effected our purpose, by here giving him a sufficient idea of what he is to expect from the ensuing pages.

THE LIFE OF LEONARDO DA VINCI.

Leonardo da Vinci, the Author of the following Treatise, was the natural son of Pietro da Vinci, a notary of Vinci, in Tuscany[1], a village situated in the valley of Arno, a little below Florence, and was born in the year 1452[2].

Having discovered, when a child, a strong inclination and talent for painting, of which he had given proofs by several little drawings and sketches; his father one day accidentally took up some of them, and was induced to shew them to his friend Andrea Verocchio, a painter of some reputation in Florence, who was also a chaser, an architect, a sculptor, and goldsmith, for his advice, as to the propriety of bringing up his son to the profession of painting, and the probability of his becoming eminent in the art. The answer of Verocchio was such as to confirm him in that resolution; and Leonardo, to fit him for that purpose, was accordingly placed under the tuition of Verocchio[3].

As Verocchio combined in himself a perfect knowledge of the arts of chasing and sculpture, and was a deep proficient in architecture, Leonardo had in this situation the means and opportunity of acquiring a variety of information, which though perhaps not immediately connected with the art to which his principal attention was to be directed, might, with the assistance of such a mind as Leonardo's, be rendered subsidiary to his grand object, tend to promote his knowledge of the theory, and facilitate his practice of the profession for which he was intended. Accordingly we find that he had the good sense to avail himself of these advantages, and that under Verocchio he made great progress, and attracted his master's friendship and confidence, by the talents he discovered, the sweetness of his manners, and the vivacity of his disposition[4]. Of his proficiency in painting, the following instance is recorded; and the skill he afterwards manifested in other branches of science, on various occasions, evidently demonstrated how solicitous he had been for knowledge of all kinds, and how careful in his youth to lay a good foundation. Verocchio had undertaken for the religious of Vallombrosa, without Florence, a picture of our Saviour's Baptism by St. John, and consigned to Leonardo the office of putting in from the original drawing, the figure of an angel holding up the drapery; but, unfortunately for Verocchio, Leonardo succeeded so well,

---

[1] Vasari, Vite de Pittori, edit. Della Valle, 8vo. Siena 1792, vol. v. p. 22. Du Fresne, in the life prefixed to the Italian editions of this Treatise on Painting. Venturi, Essai sur les Ouvrages de Leonard de Vinci, 4to. Paris, 1797, p. 3, 36.

[2] Venturi, p. 3.

[3] Vasari, 23.

[4] Du Fresne.

that, despairing of ever equalling the work of his scholar, Verocchio in disgust abandoned his pencil for ever, confining himself in future solely to the practice of sculpture[5].

On this success Leonardo became sensible that he no longer stood in need of an instructor; and therefore quitting Verocchio, he now began to work and study for himself. Many of his performances of this period are still, or were lately to be seen at Florence; and besides these, the following have been also mentioned: A cartoon of Adam and Eve in the Garden, which he did for the King of Portugal[6]. This is highly commended for the exquisite gracefulness of the two principal figures, the beauty of the landscape, and the incredible exactitude of the shrubs and fruit. At the instance of his father, he made a painting for one of his old neighbours at Vinci[7]; it consisted wholly of such animals as have naturally an hatred to each other, joined artfully together in a variety of attitudes. Some authors have said that this painting was a shield[8], and have related the following particulars respecting it.

One of Pietro's neighbours meeting him one day at Florence, told him he had been making a shield, and would be glad of his assistance to get it painted; Pietro undertook this office, and applied to his son to make good the promise. When the shield was brought to Leonardo, he found it so ill made, that he was obliged to get a turner to smooth it; and when that was done, he began to consider with what subject he should paint it. For this purpose he got together, in his apartment, a collection of live animals, such as lizards, crickets, serpents, silk-worms, locusts, bats, and other creatures of that kind, from the multitude of which, variously adapted to each other, he formed an horrible and terrific animal, emitting fire and poison from his jaws, flames from his eyes, and smoke from his nostrils; and with so great earnestness did Leonardo apply to this, that though in his apartment the stench of the animals that from time to time died there, was so strong as to be scarcely tolerable, he, through his love to the art, entirely disregarded it. The work being finished, Leonardo told his father he might now see it; and the father one morning coming to his apartment for that purpose, Leonardo, before he admitted him, placed the shield so as to receive from the window its full and proper light, and then opened the door. Not knowing what he was to expect, and little imagining that what he saw was not the creatures themselves, but a mere painted representation of them, the father, on entering and beholding the shield, was at first staggered and shocked; which the son perceiving, told him he might now send the shield to his friend, as, from the effect which the sight of it had then produced, he found he had attained the object at which he aimed. Pietro, however, had too much sagacity not to see that this was by much too great a curiosity for a mere countryman, who would never be sensible of its value; he therefore privately bought for his friend an ordinary shield, rudely painted with the device of an heart with an arrow through it, and sold this for an hundred ducats to some merchants at Florence, by whom it

[5] Du Fresne. Vasari, 25.
[6] Vasari, 26. Du Fresne.
[7] Du Fresne.
[8] Vasari, 26.

was again sold for three hundred to the Duke of Milan[9].

He afterwards painted a picture of the Virgin Mary, and by her side a vessel of water, in which were flowers: in this he so contrived it, as that the light reflected from the flowers threw a pale redness on the water. This picture was at one time in the possession of Pope Clement the Seventh[10].

For his friend Antonio Segni he also made a design, representing Neptune in his car, drawn by sea-horses, and attended by tritons and sea-gods; the heavens overspread with clouds, which were driven in all directions by the violence of the winds; the waves appeared to be rolling, and the whole ocean seemed in an up-roar[11]. This drawing was afterwards given by Fabio the son of Antonio Segni, to Giovanni Gaddi, a great collector of drawings, with this epigram:

> Pinxit Virgilius Neptunum, pinxit Homerus,
> Dum maris undisoni per vada flectit equos.
> Mente quidem vates illum conspexit uterque,
> Vincius est oculis, jureque vincit eos[12].

In English thus:

> Virgil and Homer, when they Neptune shew'd,
> As he through boist'rous seas his steeds compell'd,
> In the mind's eye alone his figure view'd;
> But Vinci *saw* him, and has both excell'd[13].

To these must be added the following: A painting representing two horsemen engaged in fight, and struggling to tear a flag from each other: rage and fury are in this admirably expressed in the countenances of the two combatants; their air appears wild, and the drapery is thrown into an unusual though agreeable disorder. A Medusa's head, and a picture of the Adoration of the Magi[14]. In this last there are some fine heads, but both this and the Medusa's head are said by Du Fresne to have been evidently unfinished.

The mind of Leonardo was however too active and capacious to be contented solely with the practical part of his art; nor could it submit to receive as principles, conclusions, though confirmed by experience, without first tracing them to their source, and investigating their causes, and the several circumstances on which they depended. For this purpose he determined to engage in a deep examination into the theory of his art; and the better to effect his intention, he resolved to call in to his aid the assistance of all such other branches of science as could in any degree promote this grand object.

---

[9] Vasari, 28.

[10] Du Fresne. Vasari, 28.

[11] Du Fresne. Vasari, 28.

[12] Vasari, 28.

[13] It is impossible in a translation to preserve the jingle between the name Vinci, and the Latin verb *vincit* which occurs in the original.

[14] Du Fresne, Vasari, 28.

Vasari has related[15], that at a very early age he had, in the short time of a few months only that he applied to it, obtained a deep knowledge of arithmetic; and says, that in literature in general, he would have made great attainments, if he had not been too versatile to apply long to one subject. In music, he adds, he had made some progress; that he then determined to learn to play on the lyre; and that having an uncommonly fine voice, and an extraordinary promptitude of thought and expression, he became a celebrated *improvisatore*: but that his attention to these did not induce him to neglect painting and modelling in which last art he was so great a proficient, that in his youth he modelled in clay some heads of women laughing, and also some boys' heads, which appeared to have come from the hand of a master. In architecture, he made many plans and designs for buildings, and, while he was yet young, proposed conveying the river Arno into the canal at Pisa[16]. Of his skill in poetry the reader may judge from the following sonnet preserved by Lomazzo[17], the only one now existing of his composition; and for the translation with which it is accompanied we are indebted to a lady.

SONNETTO MORALE.

Chi non può quel vuol, quel che può voglia,
Che quel che non si può folle è volere.
Adunque saggio è l'uomo da tenere,
Che da quel che non può suo voler toglia.

Però ch'ogni diletto nostro e doglia
Sta in sì e nò, saper, voler, potere,
Adunque quel sol può, che co 'l dovere
Ne trahe la ragion suor di sua soglia.

Ne sempre è da voler quel che l'uom puote,
Spesso par dolce quel che torna amaro,
Piansi gia quel ch'io volsi, poi ch'io l'ebbi.

Adunque tu, lettor di queste note,
S'a te vuoi esser buono e a 'gli altri caro,
Vogli sempre poter quel che tu debbi.

TRANSLATION.
A MORAL SONNET.

The man who cannot what he would attain,
Within his pow'r his wishes should restrain:
The wish of Folly o'er that bound aspires,
The wise man by it limits his desires.

Since all our joys so close on sorrows run,
We know not what to choose or what to shun;
Let all our wishes still our duty meet,

---

[15] Vasari, 22.
[16] Vasari, 22 and 23.
[17] Lomazzo, Trattato della Pittura, p. 282.

Nor banish Reason from her awful seat.

Nor is it always best for man to will
Ev'n what his pow'rs can reach; some latent ill
Beneath a fair appearance may delude
And make him rue what earnest he pursued.

Then, Reader, as you scan this simple page,
Let this one care your ev'ry thought engage,
(With self-esteem and gen'ral love 't is fraught,)
Wish only pow'r to do just what you ought.

The course of study which Leonardo had thus undertaken, would, in its most limited extent by any one who should attempt it at this time, be found perhaps almost more than could be successfully accomplished; but yet his curiosity and unbounded thirst for information, induced him rather to enlarge than contract his plan. Accordingly we find, that to the study of geometry, sculpture, anatomy, he added those of architecture, mechanics, optics, hydrostatics, astronomy, and Nature in general, in all her operations[18]; and the result of his observations and experiments, which were intended not only for present use, but as the basis and foundation of future discoveries, he determined, as he proceeded, to commit to writing. At what time he began these his collections, of which we shall have occasion to speak more particularly hereafter, is no where mentioned; but it is with certainty known, that by the month of April 1490, he had already completely filled two folio volumes[19].

Notwithstanding Leonardo's propensity and application to study, he was not inattentive to the graces of external accomplishments; he was very skilful in the management of an horse, rode gracefully, and when he afterwards arrived to a state of affluence, took particular pleasure in appearing in public well mounted and handsomely accoutred. He possessed great dexterity in the use of arms: for mien and grace he might contend with any gentleman of his time: his person was remarkably handsome, his behaviour so perfectly polite, and his conversation so charming, that his company was coveted by all who knew him; but the avocations to which this last circumstance subjected him, are one reason why so many of his works remain unfinished[20].

With such advantages of mind and body as these, it was no wonder that his reputation should spread itself, as we find it soon did, over all Italy. The painting of the shield before mentioned, had already, as has been noticed, come into the possession of the Duke of Milan; and the subsequent accounts which he had from time to time heard of Leonardo's abilities and talents, induced Lodovic Sforza, surnamed the Moor, then Duke of Milan, about, or a little before the year 1489[21], to invite him to his court, and to settle on him a pension of five hundred crowns, a

---

[18] Vasari, 23. Du Fresne.
[19] Venturi, 37.
[20] Du Fresne.
[21] Venturi, 36.

considerable sum at that time[22].

Various are the reasons assigned for this invitation: Vasari[23] attributes it to his skill in music, a science of which the Duke is said to have been fond; others have ascribed it to a design which the Duke entertained of erecting a brazen statue to the memory of his father[24]; but others conceive it originated from the circumstance, that the Duke had not long before established at Milan an academy for the study of painting, sculpture, and architecture, and was desirous that Leonardo should take the conduct and direction of it[25]. The second was, however, we find, the true motive; and we are further informed, that the invitation was accepted by Leonardo, that he went to Milan, and was already there in 1489[26].

Among the collections of Leonardo still existing in manuscript, is a copy of a memorial presented by him to the Duke about 1490, of which Venturi has given an abridgment[27]. In it he offers to make for the Duke military bridges, which should be at the same time light and very solid, and to teach him the method of placing and defending them with security. When the object is to take any place, he can, he says, empty the ditch of its water; he knows, he adds, the art of constructing a subterraneous gallery under the ditches themselves, and of carrying it to the very spot that shall be wanted. If the fort is not built on a rock, he undertakes to throw it down, and mentions that he has new contrivances for bombarding machines, ordnance, and mortars, some adapted to throw hail shot, fire, and smoke, among the enemy; and for all other machines proper for a siege, and for war, either by sea or land, according to circumstances. In peace also, he says he can be useful in what concerns the erection of buildings, conducting of water-courses, sculpture in bronze or marble, and painting; and remarks, that at the same time that he may be pursuing any of the above objects, the equestrian statue to the memory of the Duke's father, and his illustrious family, may still be going on. If any one doubts the possibility of what he proposes, he offers to prove it by experiment, and ocular demonstration.

From this memorial it seems clear, that the casting of the bronze statue was his principal object; painting is only mentioned incidentally, and no notice is taken of the direction or management of the academy for painting, sculpture, and architecture; it is probable, therefore, that at this time there was no such intention, though it is certainly true, that he was afterwards placed at the head of it, and that he banished from it the barbarous style of architecture which till then had prevailed in it, and introduced in its stead a more pure and classical taste. Whatever was the fact with respect to the academy, it is however well known that the statue was cast in bronze, finished, and put up at Milan, but afterwards demolished by the French

---

[22] Du Fresne.

[23] Vasari, 30. Lettere Pittoriche, vol. ii. p. 184.

[24] Venturi, 3.

[25] Suppl. to Life of L. da Vinci, in Vasari, 65. Du Fresne.

[26] Venturi, 36; who mentions also, that Leonardo at this time constructed a machine for the theatre.

[27] Venturi, p. 44.

when they took possession of that place[28] after the defeat of Lodovic Sforza.

Some time after Leonardo's arrival at Milan, a design had been entertained of cutting a canal from Martesana to Milan, for the purpose of opening a communication by water between these two places, and, as it is said, of supplying the last with water. It had been first thought of so early as 1457[29]; but from the difficulties to be expected in its execution, it seems to have been laid aside, or at least to have proceeded slowly, till Leonardo's arrival. His offers of service as engineer in the above memorial, probably induced Lodovic Sforza, the then Duke, to resume the intention with vigour, and accordingly we find the plan was determined on, and the execution of it intrusted to Leonardo. The object was noble, but the difficulties to be encountered were sufficient to have discouraged any mind but Leonardo's; for the distance was no less than two hundred miles; and before it could be completed, hills were to be levelled, and vallies filled up, to render them navigable with security[30].

In order to enable him to surmount the obstacles with which he foresaw he should have to contend, he retired to the house of his friend Signior Melzi, at Vaverola, not far distant from Milan, and there applied himself sedulously for some years, as it is said, but at intervals only we must suppose, and according as his undertaking proceeded, to the study of philosophy, mathematics, and every branch of science that could at all further his design; still continuing the method he had before adopted, of entering down in writing promiscuously, whatever he wished to implant in his memory: and at this place, in this and his subsequent visits from time to time, he is supposed to have made the greater part of the collections he has left behind him[31], of the contents of which we shall hereafter speak more at large.

Although engaged in the conduct of so vast an undertaking, and in studies so extensive, the mind of Leonardo does not appear to have been so wholly occupied or absorbed in them as to incapacitate him from attending at the same time to other objects also; and the Duke therefore being desirous of ornamenting Milan with some specimens of his skill as a painter, employed him to paint in the refectory of the Dominican convent of Santa Maria delle Gratie, in that city, a picture, the subject of which was to be the Last Supper. Of this picture it is related, that Leonardo was so impressed with the dignity of the subject, and so anxious to answer the high ideas he had formed of it in his own mind, that his progress was very slow, and that he spent much time in meditation and thought, during which the work was apparently at a stand. The Prior of the convent, thinking it therefore neglected, complained to the Duke; but Leonardo assuring the Duke that not less than two hours were every day bestowed on it, he was satisfied. Nevertheless the Prior, after a short time, finding the work very little advanced, once more applied to the Duke, who in some degree of anger, as thinking Leonardo had deceived him, reprimanded him in strong terms for his delay. What Leonardo had scorned to urge

[28] Suppl. in Vasari, 74.
[29] Suppl. in Vasari, 63.
[30] Du Fresne.
[31] Du Fresne.

to the Prior in his defence, he now thought fit to plead in his excuse to the Duke, to convince him that a painter did not labour solely with his hands, but that his mind might be deeply studying his subject, when his hands were unemployed, and he in appearance perfectly idle. In proof of this, he told the Duke that nothing remained to the completion of the picture but the heads of our Saviour and Judas; that as to the former, he had not yet been able to find a fit model to express its divinity, and found his invention inadequate of itself to represent it: that with respect to that of Judas, he had been in vain for two years searching among the most abandoned and profligate of the species for an head which would convey an idea of his character; but that this difficulty was now at length removed, since he had nothing to do but to introduce the head of the Prior, whose ingratitude for the pains he was taking, rendered him a fit archetype of the perfidy and ingratitude he wished to express. Some persons have said[32], that the head of Judas in the picture was actually copied from that of the Prior; but Mariette denies it, and says this reply was merely intended as a threat[33].

A difference of opinion has also prevailed concerning the head of our Saviour in this picture; for some have conceived it left intentionally unfinished[34], while others think there is a gradation of resemblance, which increasing in beauty in St. John and our Saviour, shews in the dignified countenance of the latter a spark of his divine majesty. In the countenance of the Redeemer, say these last, and in that of Judas, is excellently expressed the extreme idea of God made man, and of the most perfidious of mortals. This is also pursued in the characters nearest to each of them[35].

Little judgment can now be formed of the original beauty of this picture, which has been, and apparently with very good reason, highly commended. Unfortunately, though it is said to have been in oil, the wall on which it was painted not having been properly prepared, the original colours have been so effectually defaced by the damp, as to be no longer visible[36]; and the fathers, for whose use it was painted, thinking it entirely destroyed, and some years since wishing to heighten and widen a door under it, leading out of their refectory, have given a decided proof of their own want of taste, and how little they were sensible of its value, by permitting the workmen to break through the wall on which it was painted, and, by so doing, entirely to destroy the lower part of the picture[37]. The

[32] De Piles, in the Life of Leonardo. See Lettere Pittoriche, vol. ii. p. 187.
[33] Lettere Pittoriche, vol. ii. p. 187.
[34] Du Fresne. Lettere Pitt. vol. ii. p. 186.
[35] Vasari, 31, in a note.
[36] Let. Pit. vol. ii. 183.
[37] Additions to the Life in Vasari, 53. My worthy friend, Mr. Rigaud, who has more than once seen the original picture, gives this account of it: "The cutting of the wall for the sake of opening a door, was no doubt the effect of ignorance and barbarity, but it did not materially injure the painting; it only took away some of the feet under the table, entirely shaded. The true value of this picture consists in what was seen above the table. The door is only four feet wide, and cuts off only about two feet of the lower part of the picture. More damage has been done by subsequent quacks, who, within my own time, have undertaken

injury done by the damp to the colouring has been, it is true, in some measure repaired by Michael Angelo Bellotti, a painter of Milan, who viewing the picture in 1726, made an offer to the Prior and convent to restore, by means of a secret which he possessed, the original colours. His proposition being accepted, and the experiment succeeding beyond their hopes, the convent made him a present of five hundred pounds for his labour, and he in return communicated to them the secret by which it had been effected[38].

Deprived, as they certainly are by these events, of the means of judging accurately of the merit of the original, it is still some consolation to the lovers of painting, that several copies of it made by Leonardo's scholars, many of whom were very able artists, and at a time when the picture had not been yet injured, are still in existence. A list of these copies is given by P. M. Guglielmo della Valle, in his edition of Vasari's Lives of the Painters, in Italian, vol. v. p. 34, and from him it is here inserted in the note[39]. Francis the First was so charmed on viewing the orig-

to repair it."

[38] Additions to the Life in Vasari, 53.

[39] COPIES EXISTING IN MILAN OR ELSEWHERE.

No. 1. That in the refectory of the fathers Osservanti della Pace: it was painted on the wall in 1561, by Gio. Paolo Lomazzo.

2. Another, copied on board, as a picture in the refectory of the Chierici Regolari di S. Paolo, in their college of St. Barnabas. This is perhaps the most beautiful that can be seen, only that it is not finished lower than the knees, and is in size about one eighth of the original.

3. Another on canvas, which was first in the church of S. Fedele, by Agostino S. Agostino, for the refectory of the Jesuits: since their suppression, it exists in that of the Orfani a S. Pietro, in Gessate.

4. Another of the said Lomazzo's, painted on the wall in the monastery Maggiore, very fine, and in good preservation.

5. Another on canvas, by an uncertain artist, with only the heads and half the bodies, in the Ambrosian library.

6. Another in the Certosa di Pavia, done by Marco d'Ogionno, a scholar of Leonardo's, on the wall.

7. Another in the possession of the monks Girolamini di Castellazzo fuori di Porta Lodovica, of the hand of the same Ogionno.

8. Another copy of this Last Supper in the refectory of the fathers of St. Benedict of Mantua. It was painted by Girolamo Monsignori, a Dominican friar, who studied much the works of Leonardo, and copied them excellently.

9. Another in the refectory of the fathers Osservanti di Lugano, of the hand of Bernardino Lovino; a valuable work, and much esteemed as well for its neatness and perfect imitation of the original, as for its own integrity, and being done by a scholar of Leonardo's.

10. A beautiful drawing of this famous picture is, or was lately, in the possession of Sig. Giuseppe Casati, king at arms. Supposed to be either the original design by Leonardo himself, or a sketch by one of his best scholars, to be used in painting some copy on a wall, or on canvas. It is drawn with a pen, on paper larger than usual, with a mere outline heightened with bistre.

inal, that not being able to remove it, he had a copy made, which is now, or was some years since, at St. Germains, and several prints have been published from it; but the best which has yet appeared (and very fine it is) is one not long since engraven by Morghen, at Rome, impressions of which have found their way into this country, and been sold, it is said, for ten or twelve guineas each.

In the same refectory of the Dominicans at Milan is, or was, also preserved a painting by Leonardo, representing Duke Lodovic, and Beatrix his duchess, on their knees; done no doubt about this time[40]. And at or near this period, he also painted for the Duke the Nativity, which was formerly, and may perhaps be still, in the Emperor of Germany's collection[41].

As Leonardo's principal aim, whenever he was left at liberty to pursue the bent of his own inclination, seems to have been progressive improvement in the art of painting, he appears to have sedulously embraced all opportunities of increasing his information; and wisely perceiving, that without a thorough acquaintance with anatomy, a painter could effect but little, he was particularly desirous of extending his knowledge in that branch. For that purpose he had frequent conferences on the subject with Marc Antonio della Torre, professor of anatomy at Pavia[42], and not only was present at many dissections performed by him, but made abundance of anatomical drawings from Nature, many of which were afterwards collected into a volume by his scholar Francisco Melzi[43].

Such perseverance and assiduity as Leonardo's, united as they were with such uncommon powers as his, had already formed many artists at that time of distinguished reputation, but who afterwards became still more famous, and might probably have rendered Milan the repository of some of the most valuable specimens of painting, and raised it to a rank little, if at all, inferior to that which Florence has since held with the admirers of the polite arts, had it not happened that by the disastrous termination of a contest between the Duke of Milan and the French, all hopes of further improvement were entirely cut off; and Milan, at one blow, lost all the advantages of which it was even then in possession. For about

11. Another in the refectory of the fathers Girolamini, in the monastery of St. Laurence, in the Escurial in Spain. It was presented to King Philip II. while he was in Valentia; and by his order placed in the said room where the monks dine, and is believed to be by some able scholar of Leonardo.

12. Another in St. Germain d'Auxerre, in France; ordered by King Francis I. when he came to Milan, and found he could not remove the original. There is reason to think this the work of Bernardino Lovino.

13. Another in France, in the castle of Escovens, in the possession of the Constable Montmorency.

The original drawing for this picture is in the possession of his Britannic Majesty. See the life prefixed to Mr. Chamberlaine's publication of the Designs of Leonardo da Vinci, p. 5. An engraving from it is among those which Mr. Rogers published from drawings.
[40] Vasari, 34. Du Fresne.
[41] Du Fresne.
[42] Vasari, 36. Du Fresne.
[43] Vasari, 37. Du Fresne.

this time the troubles in Italy began to break in on Leonardo's quiet, and he found his patron, the Duke, engaged in a war with the French for the possession of his dukedom; which not only endangered the academy, but ultimately deprived him both of his dominions and his liberty; as the Duke was, in 1500, completely defeated, taken prisoner, and carried into France, where, in 1510, he died a prisoner in the castle of Loches[44].

By this event of the Duke's defeat, and the consequent ruin of the Sforza family, all further progress in the canal of Martesana, of which much still remained to be done[45], was put a stop to; the academy of architecture and painting was entirely broken up; the professors were turned adrift, and the arts banished from Milan, which at one time had promised to have been their refuge and principal feat[46]. Italy in general was, it is true, a gainer by the dispersion of so many able and deeply instructed artists as issued from this school, though Milan suffered; for nothing could so much tend to the dissemination of knowledge as the mixing such men among others who needed that information in which these excelled. Among the number thus separated from each other, we find painters, carvers, architects, founders, and engravers in crystal and precious stones, and the names of the following have been given, as the principal: Cesare da Sesto, Andrea Salaino, Gio. Antonio Boltraffio, Bernardino Lovino, Bartolommeo della Porta, Lorenzo Lotto[47]. To these has been added Gio. Paolo Lomazzo; but Della Valle, in a note in his edition of Vasari, vol. v. p. 34, says this last was a disciple of Gio. Battista della Cerva, and not of Leonardo. Du Fresne mentions besides the above, Francis Melzi, Mark Uggioni Gobbo, an extraordinary painter and carver; Annibal Fontana, a worker in marble and precious stones; and Bernazzano, an excellent painter of landscapes; but omits Della Porta, and Lorenzo Lotto.

In 1499, the year before Duke Lodovic's defeat, Leonardo being at Milan, was employed by the principal inhabitants to contrive an automaton for the entertainment of Lewis XII. King of France, who was expected shortly to make a public entry into that city. This Leonardo did, and it consisted of a machine representing a lion, whose inside was so well constructed of clockwork, that it marched out to meet the King, made a stand when it came before him, reared up on its hinder legs, and opening its breast, presented an escutcheon with fleurs de lis quartered on it[48]. Lomazzo has said that this machine was made for the entry of Francis the First; but he is mistaken, that prince having never been at Milan till the year 1515[49], at which time Leonardo was at Rome.

Compelled by the disorders of Lombardy, the misfortunes of his patron, and the ruin of the Sforza family, to quit Milan, Leonardo betook himself to Florence, and his inducements to this resolution seem to have been the residence there of

---

[44] Du Fresne.
[45] Suppl. in Vasari, 64.
[46] Du Fresne.
[47] Suppl. in Vasari, 75, 76, 77, 78.
[48] Vasari, 38. Du Fresne.
[49] Du Fresne.

the Medici family, the great patrons of arts, and the good taste of its principal inhabitants[50], rather than its vicinity to the place of his birth; for which, under the circumstances that attended that event, it is not probable he could entertain much, if any predilection. The first work which he here undertook was a design for an altar-piece for the chapel of the college of the Annunciati. Its subject was, our Saviour, with his mother, St. Ann, and St. John; but though this drawing is said to have rendered Leonardo very popular among his countrymen, to so great a degree, that numbers of people went to see it, it does not appear that any picture was painted from it, nor that the undertaking ever proceeded farther than a sketch of a design, or rather, perhaps, a finished drawing. When Leonardo some years afterwards went into France[51], Francis the First was desirous of having a picture from this drawing, and at his desire he then put it into colours; but whether even this last was a regular picture, or, which is more probable, only a coloured drawing, we are not informed.

The picture, however, on which he bestowed the most time and labour, and which therefore seems intended by him as the completest specimen of his skill, at least in the branch of portrait-painting, was that which he did of Mona Lisa, better known by the appellation of la Gioconda, a Florentine lady, the wife of Francisco del Giocondo. It was painted for her husband, afterwards purchased by Francis the First, and was till lately to be seen in the King of France's cabinet. Leonardo bestowed four entire years upon it, and after all is said to have left it unfinished[52].

This has been so repeatedly said of the works of this painter, that we are here induced to inquire into the evidence of the fact. An artist who feels by experience, as every one must, how far short of the ideas of perfection he has formed in his own mind, his best performances always fall, will naturally be led to consider these as but very faint expressions of his own conceptions. Leonardo's disposition to think nothing effected while any thing remained to be done, and a mind like his, continually suggesting successive improvements, might therefore, and most probably did produce in him an opinion that his own most laboured pieces were far from being finished to that extent of beauty which he wished to give them; and these sentiments of them he might in all likelihood be frequently heard to declare. Comparing his productions, however, with those of other masters, they will be found, notwithstanding this assertion to the contrary, as eminent in this particular also, as for the more valuable qualities of composition, drawing, character, expression, and colouring.

About the same time with this of la Gioconda, he painted the portraits of a nobleman of Mantua, and of la Ginevra, a daughter of Americus Benci[53], much celebrated for her beauty; and is said to have finished a picture of Flora some years since remaining at Paris[54]; but this last Mariette discovered to be the work of Melzio, from the circumstance of finding, on a close inspection, the name of this

[50] Du Fresne.
[51] Vasari, 39. Du Fresne.
[52] Vasari, 39. Du Fresne.
[53] Vasari, 39. Du Fresne.
[54] Du Fresne.

last master written on it[55].

In the year 1503, he was elected by the Florentines to paint their council-chamber. The subject he chose for this, was the battle against Attila[56]; and he had already made some progress in his work, when, to his great mortification, he found his colours peel from the wall[57].

With Leonardo was joined in this undertaking, Michael Angelo, who painted another side of the room, and who, then a young man of not more than twenty-nine, had risen to such reputation, as not to fear a competition with Leonardo, a man of near sixty[58]. The productions of two such able masters placed in the same room, begun at the same time, and proceeding gradually step by step together, afforded, no doubt, occasion and opportunity to the admirers and critics in painting to compare and contrast with each other their respective excellencies and defects. Had these persons contented themselves simply with comparing and appreciating the merits of these masters according to justice and truth, it might perhaps have been advantageous to both, as directing their attention to the correction of errors; but as each artist had his admirers, each had also his enemies; the partisans of the one thinking they did not sufficiently value the merit of their favourite if they allowed any to his antagonist, or did not, on the contrary, endeavour to crush by detraction the too formidable reputation of his adversary. From this conduct was produced what might easily have been foreseen; they first became jealous rivals, and at length open and inveterate enemies[59].

Leonardo's reputation, which had been for many years gradually increasing, was now so firmly established, that he appears to have been looked up to as being, what he really was, the reviver and restorer of the art of painting; and to such an height had the curiosity to view his works been excited, that Raphael, who was at that time young, and studying, thought it worth his while to make a journey to Florence in the month of October 1504[60], on purpose to see them. Nor was his labour lost, or his time thrown away in so doing; for on first seeing the works of Leonardo's pencil, he was induced to abandon the dry and hard manner of his master Perugino's colouring, and to adopt in its stead the style of Leonardo[61], to which circumstance is owing no small portion of that esteem in the art, to which Raphael afterwards very justly arrived.

His father having died in 1504[62], he in consequence of that event became engaged with his half-brothers, the legitimate sons of Pietro da Vinci, in a law-suit for the recovery of a share of his father's property, which in a letter from Florence to the Governor of Milan, the date of which does not appear, he speaks of having

[55] Supp. in Vasari, 81.
[56] Suppl. in Vasari, 68.
[57] Vasari, 42. Du Fresne.
[58] Du Fresne.
[59] Du Fresne.
[60] Venturi, 37.
[61] Du Fresne.
[62] Venturi, 37.

almost brought to a conclusion[63]. At Florence he continued from 1503 to 1507[64], and in the course of that time painted, among other pictures of less note, a Virgin and Child, once in the hands of the Botti family; and a Baptist's head, formerly in those of Camillo Albizzi[65]; but in 1508, and the succeeding year, he was at Milan, where he received a pension which had been granted him by Lewis XII.[66]; and in the month of September 1513, he, in company with his scholar Francesco Melzi, quitted Milan[67], and set out for Rome (which till that time he had never visited), encouraged perhaps to this resolution by the circumstance that his friend Cardinal John de Medicis, who was afterwards known by the assumed name of Leo X. had a few months before been advanced to the papacy[68]. His known partiality to the arts, and the friendship which had subsisted between him and Leonardo, held out to the latter a well-founded expectation of employment for his pencil at Rome, and we find in this expectation he was not deceived; as, soon after his arrival, the Pope actually signified his intention of setting him to work. Upon this Leonardo began distilling oils for his colours, and preparing varnishes, which the Pope hearing, said pertly and ignorantly enough, that he could expect nothing from a man who thought of finishing his works before he had begun them[69]. Had the Pope known, as he seems not to have done, that oil was the vehicle in which the colours were to have been worked, or been witness either to the almost annihilation of the colours in Leonardo's famous picture of the Last Supper, owing to the damp of the wall, or to the peeling of the colours from the wall in the council-chamber at Florence, he probably would have spared this ill-natured reflection. If it applied at all, it could only be to a very small part of the pursuit in which Leonardo was occupied, namely, preparing varnish; and if age were necessary to give the varnish strength, or it were the better for keeping, the answer was in an equal degree both silly and impertinent; and it is no wonder it should disgust such a mind as Leonardo's, or produce, as we find it did, such a breach between the Pope and him, that the intended pictures, whatever they might have been, were never begun.

Disgusted with his treatment at Rome, where the former antipathy between him and Michael Angelo was again revived by the partisans of each, he the next year quitted it; and accepting an invitation which had been made him by Francis the First, he proceeded into France[70]. At the time of this journey he is said to have been seventy years old[71], which cannot be correct, as he did not live to attain that age in the whole. Probably the singularity of his appearance (for in his latter years he permitted his beard to grow long), together with the effect which his intense application to study had produced in his constitution, might have given rise to

[63] Venturi, 38.
[64] Venturi, 37.
[65] Du Fresne.
[66] Venturi, 38.
[67] Venturi, 38.
[68] Du Fresne.
[69] Vasari, 44. Du Fresne.
[70] Vasari, 44. Du Fresne.
[71] Du Fresne.

an opinion that he was older than he really was; and indeed it seems pretty clear, that when he arrived in France he was nearly worn out in body, if not in mind, by the anxiety and application with which he had pursued his former studies and investigations.

Although the King's motive to this invitation, which seems to have been a wish to profit by the pencil of Leonardo, was completely disappointed by his ill state of health, which the fatigues of his journey and the change of the climate produced, so that on his arrival in France no hopes could be entertained by the King of enriching his collection with any pictures by Leonardo; yet the French people in general, and the King in particular, are expressly said to have been as favourable to him as those of Rome had been injurious, and he was received by the King in the most affectionate manner. It was however unfortunately too soon evident that these symptoms of decay were only the forerunners of a more fatal distemper under which for several months he languished, but which by degrees was increasing upon him. Of this he was sensible, and therefore in the beginning of the year 1518, he determined to make his will, to which he afterwards added one or more codicils. By these he first describes himself as Leonardo da Vinci, painter to the King, at present residing at the place called Cloux, near Amboise, and then desires to be buried in the church of St. Florentine at Amboise, and that his body should be accompanied from the said place of Cloux to the said church, by the college of the said church, and the chaplains of St. Dennis of Amboise, and the friars minor of the said place; and that before his body is carried to the said church, it should remain three days in the chamber in which he should die, or in some other; he further orders that three great masses and thirty lesser masses of St. Gregory, should be celebrated there, and a like service be performed in the church of St. Dennis, and in that of the said friars minor. He gives and bequeaths to Franco di Melzio, a gentleman of Milan, in return for his services, all and every the books which he the testator has at present, and other instruments and drawings respecting his art: To Baptista de Villanis, his servant, the moiety of the garden which he has without the walls of Milan; and the other moiety of the said garden to Salay his servant. He gives to the said Francesco Meltio the arrears of his pension, and the sum of money owing to him at present, and at the time of his death, by the treasurer M. Johan Sapin; and to the same person all and singular his clothes and vestments. He orders and wills, that the sum of four hundred crowns of the sum which he has in the hands of the chamberlain of Santa Maria Nuova, at Florence, should be given to his brethren residing at Florence, with the profit and emolument thereon. And lastly, he appoints the said Gia. Francesco de Meltio, whole and sole executor[72].

This Will bears date, and appears to have been executed on the 23d of April 1518. He however survived the making of it more than a year; and on the 23d of April 1519[73], the day twelvemonth on which it had been originally made, he, though it does not appear for what reason, re-executed it; and the next day added a codicil, by which he gave to his servant, Gio. Battista de Villanis, the right which had been granted him in return for his labours on the canal of Martesana, of exact-

---

[72] Suppl. in Vasari, 79, 80.
[73] Suppl. in Vasari, 80.

ing a certain portion of all the wood transported on the Ticino[74].

All this interval of time between the making and re-execution of his will, and indeed the whole period from his arrival in France, he seems to have been struggling under an incurable illness. The King frequently during its continuance honoured him with visits; and it has been said, that in one of these Leonardo exerting himself beyond his strength, to shew his sense of this prince's condescension, was seized with a fainting fit, and that the King stooping forward to support him, Leonardo expired in his arms, on the 2d of May 1519[75]. Venturi has taken some pains to disprove this fact, by shewing[76], that though in the interval between the years 1516 and 1519, the French court passed eleven months at different times at Amboise; yet on the 1st of May 1519, it was certainly not here, but at St. Germains. History, however, when incorrect, is more frequently a mixture of true and false, than a total fabrication of falsehood; and it is therefore not impossible, or improbable, that the King might shew such an act of kindness in some of his visits when he was resident at Amboise, and that Leonardo might recover from that fit, and not die till some time after; at which latter time the Court and the King might be absent at St. Germains. This is surely a more rational supposition than to imagine such a fact could have been invented without any foundation for it whatever.

It is impossible within the limits that can here be allowed, to do any thing like justice to the merits of this extraordinary man: all that can in this place be effected is to give the principal facts respecting him; and this is all, therefore, that has been attempted. A sufficient account, however, at least for the present purpose, it is presumed has been given above of the Author, and the productions of his pencil, and it now remains therefore only to speak of those of his pen.

With what view the Author engaged in this arduous course of study, how eager he was in the pursuit of knowledge, how anxious to avail himself of the best means of obtaining complete information on every subject to which he applied, and how careful to minute down whatever he procured that could be useful, have been already shewn in the course of the foregoing narrative; but in order to prevent the necessity of interrupting there the succession of events, it has been reserved for this place to describe the contents and extent of his collections, and to give a brief idea of the branches to which they relate.

On inquiry then we learn, that Leonardo's productions of this kind consist of fourteen manuscript volumes, large and small, now in the library of the National Institute at Paris, whither they have been some few years since removed from the Ambrosian library at Milan; and of one folio volume in manuscript also, in the possession of his Majesty the King of Great Britain. Of those at Paris, J. B. Venturi, Professor of Natural Philosophy at Modena, and of the Institute of Bologna, &c. who was permitted to inspect them, says[77], that "they contain speculations in those branches of natural philosophy nearest allied to geometry; that they are

---

[74] Suppl. in Vasari, 65.
[75] Vasari, 45. Du Fresne.
[76] Venturi, 39. Suppl. in Vasari, 80.
[77] Venturi, p. 4.

first sketches and occasional notes, the Author always intending afterwards to compose from them complete treatises." He adds further, "that they are written backwards from right to left, in the manner of the oriental writers, probably with intention that the curious should not rob him of his discoveries. The spirit of geometry guided him throughout, whether it were in the art of analysing a subject in the connexion of the discourse, or the care of always generalizing his ideas. As to natural philosophy, he never was satisfied on any proposition if he had not proved it by experiment." From the extracts given from these manuscripts by Venturi himself, and which he has ranged under the different heads mentioned in the note[78], the contents of these volumes appear to be extremely miscellaneous; and it is evident, as Venturi has marked by references where each extract is to be found in the original, that from the great distance at which passages on the same subject are placed from each other, they must have been entered without any regard to method or arrangement of any kind whatever.

The volume in the possession of his Britannic Majesty is described as consisting "of a variety of elegant heads, some of which are drawn with red and black chalks on blue or red paper, others with a metal pencil on a tinted paper; a few of them are washed and heightened with white, and many are on common paper. The subjects of these drawings are miscellaneous, as portraits, caricatures, single figures, tilting, horses, and other animals; botany, optics, perspective, gunnery, hydraulics, mechanics, and a great number of anatomical subjects, which are drawn with a more spirited pen, and illustrated with a variety of manuscript notes. This volume contains what is of more importance, the very characteristic head of Leonardo, as it was sketched by himself, and now engraved by that eminent artist Mr. Bartolozzi[79]." Specimens from this volume have been published some years since by Mr. Dalton, and more recently and accurately by Mr. Chamberlaine; and though it must be confessed, that the former are extremely ill drawn, and betray the grossest ignorance of the effect which light and shadow were intended to produce, yet some of the subjects which the volume contains may be ascertained by them; and among them is also a fac simile of a page of the original manuscript, which proves this, like the other volumes, to be in Italian, and written backwards. The latter is a very beautiful work, and is calculated to give an accurate idea of Leonardo's talents as a draughtsman[80]. From these two publications it appears, that this volume also is of a very miscellaneous nature, and that it consists of manuscript entries, interspersed with finished drawings of heads and figures, and slight sketches of mechanical engines and anatomical subjects, some of which

---

[78] Sect. 1. Of the Descent of heavy Bodies, combined with the Rotation of the Earth. 2. Of the Earth divided into Particles. 3. Of the Earth and the Moon. 4. Of the Action of the Sun on the Sea. 5. Of the ancient State of the Earth. 6. Of the Flame and the Air. 7. Of Statics. 8. Of the Descent of heavy Bodies by inclined Planes. 9. Of the Water which one draws from a Canal. 10. Of Whirlpools. 11. Of Vision. 12. Of military Architecture. 13. Of some Instruments. 14. Two chymical Processes. 15. Of Method.

[79] See the Life prefixed to Mr. Chamberlaine's publication of the Designs of Leonardo da Vinci, p. 11.

[80] Fac similes of some of the pages of the original work, are also to be found in this publication.

are intermixed with the writing itself.

It has been already seen, that these volumes were originally given by the will of Leonardo to Francisco Melzi; and their subsequent history we are enabled to state on the authority of John Ambrose Mazenta, through whose hands they passed. Du Fresne, in the life prefixed to the edition which he published in Italian, of Leonardo da Vinci's Treatise on Painting, has, in a very loose way, and without citing any authority, given their history; but Venturi has inserted[81] a translation into French, from the original manuscript memoir of Mazenta; and from him a version of it into English is here given, with the addition of Venturi's notes, rendered also into English.

"It is near fifty years[82] since there fell into my hands thirteen volumes of Leonardo da Vinci in folio and quarto, written backwards. Accident brought them to me in the following manner: I was residing at Pisa, for the purpose of studying the law, in the family of Aldus Manutius the younger, a great lover of books. A person named Lelio Gavardi, of Asola, Prevost of S. Zeno, at Pavia, a very near relation of Aldus, came to our house; he had been a teacher of the *belles lettres* in the family of the Melzi of Milan, called de Vavero, to distinguish them from other families of the same name in that city. He had, at their country house at Vavero, met with several drawings, instruments, and books of Leonardo. Francisco Melzi[83] approached nearer than any one to the manner of De Vinci; he worked little, because he was rich; his pictures are very much finished, they are often confounded with those of his master. At his death he left the works of Leonardo in his house at Vavero, to his sons, who having tastes and pursuits of a different kind, neglected these treasures, and soon dispersed them; Lelio Gavardi possessed himself of as many of them as he pleased; he carried thirteen volumes to Florence, in hopes of receiving for them a good price from the Grand Duke Francis, who was eager after works of this sort; and the rather as Leonardo was in great reputation in his own country. But this prince died[84] as soon as Gavardi was arrived at Florence. He then went to Pisa, to the house of Manutius. I could not approve his proceeding; it was scandalous. My studies being finished, I had occasion to return to Milan. He gave me the volumes of Vinci, desiring me to return them to the Melzi: I acquitted myself faithfully of my commission; I carried them all back to Horatio, the chief of the family of Melzi, who was surprised at my being willing to give myself this trouble. He made me a present of these books, telling me he had still many drawings by the same author, long neglected in the garrets of his house in the country. Thus these books became my property, and afterwards they belonged to my brothers[85]. These latter having made too much parade of this acquisition, and the ease with which I was brought

---

[81] P. 33.

[82] "J. A. Mazenta died in 1635. He gave the designs for the fortifications of Livorno in Tuscany; and has written on the method of rendering the Adda navigable. Argelati Script. Mediol. vol. ii." Venturi, 33.

[83] "We shall see afterwards that this man was Leonardo's heir: he had carried back these writings and drawings from France to Milan." Venturi, 34.

[84] "This was in 1587." Venturi, p. 34.

[85] "J. Amb. Mazenta made himself a Barnabite in 1590." Venturi, 34.

to it, excited the envy of other amateurs, who beset Horatio, and obtained from him some drawings, some figures, some anatomical pieces, and other valuable remains of the cabinet of Leonardo. One of these spungers for the works of Leonardo, was Pompeo Aretin, son of the Cavalier Leoni, formerly a disciple of Bonaroti, and who was about Philip II. King of Spain, for whom he did all the bronzes which are at the Escurial. Pompeo engaged himself to procure for Melzi an employment to the senate of Milan, if he succeeded in recovering the thirteen books, wishing to offer them to King Philip, a lover of such curiosities. Flattered with this hope, Melzi went to my brother's house: he besought him on his knees to restore him his present; he was a fellow-collegian, a friend, a benefactor: seven volumes were returned to him[86]. Of the six others which remained to the Mazenta family, one was presented to Cardinal Frederic Borromeo, for the Ambrosian library[87]. My brother gave a second to Ambrose Figini, a celebrated painter of his time, who left it to his heir Hercole Bianchi, with the rest of his cabinet. Urged by the Duke of Savoy, I procured for him a third; and in conclusion, my brother having died at a distance from Milan[88], the three remaining volumes came also into the hands of Pompeo Aretin; he re-assembled also others of them, he separated the leaves of them to form a thick volume[89], which passed to his heir Polidoro Calchi, and was afterwards sold to Galeazzo Arconati. This gentleman keeps it now in his rich library; he has refused it to the Duke of Savoy, and to other princes who were desirous of it."

In addition to this memoir, Venturi notices[90], that Howard Earl of Arundel made ineffectual efforts to obtain this large volume, and offered for it as far as 60,000 francs, in the name of the King of England. Arconati would never part with it; he bought eleven other books of Da Vinci, which came also, according to appearance, from Leoni; in 1637 he made a gift of them all to the Ambrosian library[91], which already was in possession of the volume E, from Mazenta, and received afterwards the volume K from Horatio Archinto, in 1674[92].

Venturi says, this is the history of all the manuscripts of Vinci that are come into France; they are in number fourteen, because the volume B contains an appendix of eighteen leaves, which may be separated, and considered as the fourteenth

---

[86] "The drawings and books of Vinci are come for the most part into the hands of Pompeo Leoni, who has obtained them from the son of Francisco Melzo. There are some also of these books in the possession of Guy Mazenta Lomazzo, Tempio della Pittura, in 4º, Milano 1590, page 17." Venturi, 35.

[87] "It is volume C. There is printed on it in gold, *Vidi Mazenta Patritii Mediolanensis liberalitate An. 1603.*" Venturi, 35.

[88] "He died in 1613." Venturi, 35.

[89] "This is volume N, in the National Library. It is in folio, of a large size, and has 392 leaves: it bears on the cover this title: *Disegni di Macchine delle Arti secreti et altre Cose di Leonardo da Vinci, raccolte da Pompeo Leoni.*" Venturi, 35.

[90] P. 36.

[91] "A memorial is preserved of this liberality by an inscription." Venturi, 36.

[92] "This is marked at p. 1 of the same volume." Venturi, 36.

volume[93].

In the printed catalogue of the library of Turin, one does not see noticed the manuscript which Mazenta gave to the Duke of Savoy: it has then disappeared. Might it not be that which an Englishman got copied by Francis Ducci, library-keeper at Florence, and a copy of which is still remaining in the same city[94]?

The Trivulce family at Milan, according to Venturi[95], possess also a manuscript of Vinci, which is in great part only a vocabulary.

Of the volume in the possession of his Britannic Majesty, the following account is given in the life of Leonardo, prefixed to that number already published from it by Mr. Chamberlaine: "It was one of the three volumes which became the property of Pompeo Leoni, that is now in his Majesty's cabinet. It is rather probable than certain, that this great curiosity was acquired for King Charles I. by the Earl of Arundel, when he went Ambassador to the Emperor Ferdinand II. in 1636, as may indeed be inferred from an instructive inscription over the place where the volumes are kept, which sets forth, that James King of England offered three thousand pistoles for one of the volumes of Leonardo's works. And some documents in the Ambrosian library give colour to this conjecture. This volume was happily preserved during the civil wars of the last century among other specimens of the fine arts, which the munificence of Charles I. had amassed with a diligence equal to his taste. And it was discovered soon after his present Majesty's accession in the same cabinet where Queen Caroline found the fine portraits of the court of Henry VIII. by Hans Holbein, which the King's liberality permitted me lately to lay before the public. On the cover of this volume is written, in gold letters, what ascertains its descent; *Disegni di Leonardo da Vinci, restaurati da Pompeo Leoni.*"

Although no part of the collections of Leonardo was arranged and prepared by himself, or others under his direction, for publication, some extracts have been made from his writings, and given to the world as separate tracts. The best known, and indeed the principal of these, is the following Treatise on Painting, of which there will be occasion to say more presently; but besides this, Edward Cooper, a London bookseller, about the year 1720, published a fragment of a Treatise by Leonardo da Vinci, on the Motions of the Human Body, and the Manner of drawing Figures, according to geometrical Rules. It contains but ten plates in folio, including the title-page, and was evidently extracted from some of the volumes of his collections, as it consists of slight sketches and verbal descriptions both in Italian and English, to explain such of them as needed it.

Mr. Dalton, as has been before noticed, several years since published some engravings from the volume in our King's collection, but they are so badly done as to be of no value. Mr. Chamberlaine therefore, in 1796, took up the intention afresh, and in that year his first number came out, which is all that has yet appeared.

Of the Treatise on Painting, Venturi[96] gives the following particulars: "The

[93] Venturi, 36.
[94] "Lettere Pittoriche, vol. ii." Venturi, 36.
[95] P. 36. His authority is Gerli, Disegni del Vinci, Milano, 1784, fol.
[96] P. 42.

Treatise on Painting which we have of Vinci is only a compilation of different fragments extracted from his manuscripts. It was in the Barberini library at Rome, in 1630[97]: the Cav. del Pozzo obtained a copy from it, and Poussin designed the figures of it in 1640[98]. This copy, and another derived from the same source, in the possession of Thevenot, served as the basis for the edition published in 1651, by Raphael du Frêne. The manuscript of Pozzo, with the figures of Poussin, is actually at Paris, in the valuable collection of books of Chardin[99]. It is from this that I have taken the relation of Mazenta; it is at the end of the manuscript under this title: "Some Notices of the Works of Leonardo da Vinci at Milan, and of his Books, by J. Ambrose Mazenta of Milan, of the Congregation of the Priests Regular of St. Paul, called the Barnabites." Mazenta does not announce himself as the author of the compilation; he may however be so; it may also happen, that the compilation was made by the heir himself of Vinci, Francisco Melzo. Vasari, about 1567, says[100], that a painter of Milan had the manuscripts of Vinci, which were written backwards; that this painter came to him, and afterwards went to Rome, with intention to get them printed, but that he did not know what was the result. However it may be, Du Frêne confesses that this compilation is imperfect in many respects, and ill arranged. It is so, because the compiler has not seized the methodical spirit of Vinci, and that there are mixed with it some pieces which belong to other tracts; besides, one has not seen where many other chapters have been neglected which ought to make part of it. For example, the comparison of painting with sculpture, which has been announced as a separate treatise of the same author, is nothing more than a chapter belonging to the Treatise on Painting, A. 105. All this will be complete, and put in order, in the Treatise on Optics[101]. In the mean time, however, the following are the different editions of this compilation, such as it is at present:

"Trattato della Pittura di Leonardo da Vinci, nuovamente dato in Luce, con la Vita dell' Autore da Raphaele du Frêne, Parigi 1651, in fol.; reprinted at Naples in 1733, in folio; at Bologna, in 1786, in folio; at Florence, in 1792, in 4to. This last edition has been given from a copy in the hand-writing of Stephano della Bella.

"——Translated into French by Roland Freart de Chambray, Paris 1651, fol. reprinted ibid. 1716, in 12mo, and 1796, in 8vo.

---

[97] It is said, that this compilation is now in the Albani library. Venturi, 42.

[98] The sketches to illustrate his meaning, were probably in Leonardo's original manuscripts so slight as to require that more perfect drawings should be made from them before they could be fit for publication.

[99] The identical manuscript of this Treatise, formerly belonging to Mons. Chardin, one of the two copies from which the edition in Italian was printed, is now the property of Mr. Edwards of Pall Mall. Judging by the chapters as there numbered, it would appear to contain more than the printed edition; but this is merely owing to the circumstance that some of those which in the manuscript stand as distinct chapters, are in the printed edition consolidated together.

[100] Vasari, p. 37, gives the initials N. N.

[101] Which Venturi, p. 6, professes his intention of publishing from the manuscript collections of Leonardo.

"——Translated into German, in 4to. Nuremberg 1786, Weigel.

"——Translated into Greek by Panagiotto, manuscript in the Nani library at Venice.

"Another manuscript copy of this compilation was in the possession of P. Orlandi, from whence it passed into the library of Smith[102].

"Cellini, in a discourse published by Morelli, says[103], that he possessed a copy of a book of De Vinci on Perspective, which he communicated to Serlio, and that this latter published from it all that he could comprehend. Might not this be the tract which Gori announces to be in the library of the Academy of Cortona[104]?"

The reputation in which the Treatise on Painting ought to be held, is not now for the first time to be settled; its merit has been acknowledged by the best judges, though at that time it laboured under great disadvantage from the want of a proper arrangement. In the present publication that objection is removed, and the attempt has been favourable to the work itself, as it has shewn it, by bringing together the several chapters that related to each other, to be a much more complete and connected treatise than was before supposed. Notwithstanding however the fair estimation in which it has always stood, and which is no more than its due, one person has been found hardy enough to endeavour, though unsuccessfully, to lessen its credit: a circumstance which it would not have been worth while to notice, if it had not been intimated to us, that there are still some persons in France who side with the objector, which, as he was a Frenchman, and Leonardo an Italian, may perhaps be ascribed, in some measure at least, to the desire which in several instances that people have lately shewn of claiming on behalf of their countrymen, a preference over others, to which they are not entitled. Abraham Bosse, of the city of Tours, an engraver in copper, who lived in the last century, is the person here alluded to; and it may not be impertinent in this place to state some of the motives by which he was induced to such a conduct. At the time when this Treatise first made its appearance in France, as well in Italian as in French, Bosse appears to have been resident at Paris, and was a member of the Academy of Painting, where he gave the first lessons on perspective, and, with the assistance of Mons. Desargues, published from time to time several tracts on geometry and perspective, the manner of designing, and the art of engraving, some of which at least are described in the title-page, as printed at Paris for the author[105]. This man, in his lectures, having, it is said, attacked some of the pictures painted by Le Brun, the then Director of the Academy, had been very deservedly removed from his situation, and forced to quit the Academy, for endeavouring to lessen that authority, which for the instruction and improvement of students it was necessary the Director should possess, and attempting thus to render fruitless the precepts which his situation required him to deliver. As this Treatise of Leonardo had in the translation been adopted by Le Brun, who fully saw its value, and introduced

---

[102] Bibliotheca Smithiana, 4to. Ven. 1755. Venturi, 44.
[103] Libreria Nani, 4to. Ven. 1776. Venturi, 44.
[104] Gori Simbolæ literar. Flor. 1751, vol. viii. p. 66. Venturi, 44.
[105] See his Traité des Pratiques Geometrales et Perspectives, 8vo. Paris, 1665.

it into the Academy for the advantage of the students, by which means the sale of Bosse's work might be, and probably was, affected; Bosse, at the end of a Treatise on Geometry and Perspective, taught in the Royal Academy of Painting and Sculpture, published by him in octavo in 1665, has inserted a paper with this title, which in the original is given in French, but we have preferred translating it: *"What follows is for those who shall have the curiosity to be acquainted with a part of the procedings of Mons. Desargues, and myself, against some of our antagonists, and part of their skill; together with some remarks made on the contents of several chapters of a Treatise attributed to Leonardo de Vinci, translated from Italian into French by Mons. Freart Sieur de Chambray, from a manuscript taken from that which is in the library of the illustrious, virtuous, and curious Mons. le Chevalier Du Puis at Rome."*

After the explanation of his motives above given, it is not wonderful to find him asserting, that this Treatise of Leonardo was in a number of circumstances inferior to his own; nor to observe, that in a list of some of the chapters which he has there given, we should be frequently told by him that they are false, absurd, ridiculous, confused, trifling, weak, and, in short, every thing but good. It is true that the estimation of Leonardo da Vinci was in France too high for him to attack without risking his own character for judgment and taste, and he has therefore found it necessary for his purpose insidiously to suggest that these chapters were interpolations; but of this he has produced no proof, which, had it been the fact, might have been easily obtained, by only getting some friend to consult Leonardo's manuscript collections in the Ambrosian library. That he would have taken this step if he had expected any success from it, may fairly be inferred from the circumstance of his writing to Poussin at Rome, apparently in hopes of inducing him to say something to the disadvantage of the work; and his omitting to make this inquiry after the enmity he has shewn against the book, fully justifies an opinion that he forbore to inquire, because he was conscious that such an investigation would have terminated in vindicating his adversaries from his aspersions, and have furnished evidence of their fidelity and accuracy.

What the letter which he wrote to Poussin contained, he has not informed us; but he has given us, as he says, Poussin's answer[106], in which are some passages relating to this Treatise, of which we here give a translation: "As to what concerns the book of Leonard Vinci, it is true that I have designed the human figures which are in that which Mons. le Chevalier du Puis has; but all the others, whether geometrical or otherwise, are of one man, named Gli Alberti, the very same who has drawn the plants which are in the book of subterraneous Rome; and the awkward landscapes which are behind some of the little human figures of the copy which Mons. du Chambray has caused to be printed, have been added to it by one Errard, without my knowing any thing of it.

"All that is good in this book may be written on one sheet of paper, in a large character, and those who believe that I approve all that is in it, do not know me; I who profess never to give sanction to things of my profession which I know to be ill done and ill said."

Whoever recollects the difference in the course of study pursued and recom-

[106] P. 128.

mended by Leonardo (that of Nature), from that observed by Poussin (that of the antique), and remembers also the different fortunes of Le Brun and Poussin, that the one was at the head of his profession, enjoying all its honours and emoluments, while the other, though conscious of his own great powers, was toiling for a daily subsistence in comparative obscurity, may easily conceive why the latter could not approve a work which so strongly inculcates the adopting Nature as the guide throughout; and which was at the same time patronized by one whom he could not but consider as his more fortunate rival. It may however be truly affirmed, that even the talents of Poussin, great as they certainly were, and his knowledge and correctness in drawing, would have been abundantly improved by an attention to the rules laid down in this Treatise, and that the study of Nature would have freed his pictures from that resemblance to statues which his figures frequently have, and bestowed on them the soft and fleshy appearance for which Leonardo was so remarkable; while a minute investigation of Leonardo's system of colouring would have produced perhaps in him as fortunate a change as we have seen it did in the case of Raphael.

Though Bosse tells us[107], that he had seen in the hands of Mons. Felibien, a manuscript copy of this Tract on Painting, which he said he had taken from the same original mentioned before, for the purpose of translating it into French; and that on Bosse's pointing out to him some of these errors, and informing him that Mons. de Chambray was far advanced in his translation, he abandoned his design, and assigned to the Sieur de Chambray the privilege he had obtained for it; we have no intention here to enumerate or answer Bosse's objections, merely because such an undertaking would greatly exceed the limits which can here be allowed us. Most of them will be found captious and splenetic, and, together with the majority of the rest, might be fully refuted by a deduction of facts; it is however sufficient on the present occasion to say, that wherever opportunity has been afforded of tracing the means by which Leonardo procured his materials for any great composition, he is found to have exactly pursued the path which he recommends to others[108]; and for the success of his precepts, and what may be effected by them, we need only appeal to his own example.

To this enumeration of the productions of Leonardo's pen, and in contradiction to the fact already asserted, that no part of his collections was ever arranged or prepared for publication by himself, it is probable we may be told we should add tracts on Motion; on the Equilibrium of bodies; on the nature, equilibrium, and motion of Water; on Anatomy; on the Anatomy of an horse; on Perspective; and on Light and Shadow: which are either mentioned by himself in the Treatise on Painting, or ascribed to him by others. But as to these, there is great reason for supposing, that, though they might be intended, they were never actually drawn up into form. Certain it is, that no such have been ever given to the world, as those

[107] P. 134.

[108] He observed criminals when led to execution (Lett. Pitt. vol. ii. p. 182; on the authority of Lomazzo); noted down any countenance that struck him (Vasari, 29); in forming the animal for the shield, composed it of parts selected from different real animals (Vasari, p. 27); and when he wanted characteristic heads, resorted to Nature (Lett. Pitt. vol. ii. p. 181). All which methods are recommended by him in the course of the Treatise on Painting.

before noticed are the only treatises of this author that have yet appeared in print; and even they have already been shewn to be no more than extracts from the immense mass of his collections of such passages as related to the subjects on which they profess to give intelligence. If any tracts therefore in his name, on any of the above topics, are any where existing in manuscript, and in obscurity, it is probable they are only similar selections. And indeed it will be found on inspection, that his collections consist of a multitude of entries made at different times, without method, order, or arrangement of any kind, so as to form an immense chaos of intelligence, which he, like many other voluminous collectors, intended at some future time to digest and arrange, but unfortunately postponed this task so long, that he did not live to carry that intention into effect. Under these circumstances, should it happen, as perhaps it may, that any volume of the whole is confined exclusively to any one branch of science, such as hydrostatics for instance, it was not the consequence of a designed plan, but only arose from this accident, that he had then made that branch the object of his pursuit, and for a time laid aside the rest. In proof of this assertion it may be observed, that the very treatise of light and shadow above mentioned, is described as in the Ambrosian library at Milan, and as a folio volume covered with red velvet, presented by Signior Mazzenta to Cardinal Borromeo[109]; from all which circumstances it is evidently proved to be one of the volumes now existing in France[110], which were inspected and described by Venturi in the tract so often cited in the course of this life.

Although the principal of Leonardo's productions have been already mentioned, it has been thought proper, for the satisfaction of the curious, here to subjoin a catalogue of such of them as have come to our knowledge; distinguishing in it such as were only drawings, from such as were finished pictures, and noticing also which of them have been engraven, and by whom.

---

[109] Du Fresne.
[110] Venturi, 35, in a note.

CATALOGUE OF THE WORKS OF LEONARDO DA VINCI.

ARCHITECTURE.

Many *designs for plans and buildings*, made by him in his youth[111].

A *model* made by him for raising the roof of the church of St. John, at Florence[112].

The house of the family of Melzi at Vaprio, supposed by Della Valle to be designed by Leonardo[113].

MODELS AND SCULPTURE.

Some *heads of laughing women*, modelled by him in clay, in his youth[114].

Some *boys' heads* also, which appeared to have come from the hand of a master[115].

Three figures in bronze, over the gate on the north side of the church of St. John, at Florence, made by Gio. Francesco Rustici, but designed with the advice of Leonardo da Vinci[116].

A *model in clay*, in alto relievo. It is a circle of about two palms in diameter, and represents St. Jerom in a grotto, old, and much worn out by prayer. It was in the possession of Sig. Ignazio Hugford, a painter at Florence, who was induced to buy it in consequence of the great praises which in his youth he had heard bestowed on it by the celebrated Anton. Dominico Gabbiani, his master, who knew it to be of the hand of Leonardo. This model appears to have been much studied in the time of Pontormo and Rosso; and many copies of it, both drawings and pictures, are to be found throughout Florence, well painted in their manner[117].

The *equestrian statue* in memory of the Duke of Milan's father, which was not only finished and exposed to view, but broken to pieces by the French when they

[111] Vasari, 23.
[112] Vasari, 24.
[113] Suppl. in Vasari, 67.
[114] Vasari, 23.
[115] Ibid.
[116] Vasari, 45.
[117] Additions to the life in Vasari, p. 47.

took possession of Milan. It has been said by some, that the model only was finished, and the statue never cast, and that it was the model only which the French destroyed[118].

Vasari, p. 36, mentions a little *model* by Leonardo in wax, but he does not say what was its subject.

DRAWINGS.

VASARI, p. 24, says, that it was Leonardo's practice to model figures from the life, and then to cover them with fine thin lawn or cambric, so as to be able to see through it, and with the point of a fine pencil to trace off the outlines in black and white; and that some such drawings he had in his collection.

A head in chiaro oscuro, in the possession of Vasari, and mentioned by him as divine, a drawing on paper[119].

A carton of Adam and Eve in Paradise, made by him for the King of Portugal. It is done with a pen in chiaro oscuro, and heightened with white, and was intended to be worked as tapestry in silk and gold; but Vasari says it was never executed, and that in his time the carton remained at Florence, in the house of Ottaviano de Medici. Whether this carton is still existing is unknown[120].

Several ridiculous heads of men and women, formerly in Vasari's collection, drawn in pen and ink[121]. Aurelio Lovino had, says Lomazzo, a book of sketches by Leonardo, of odd and ridiculous heads. This book appears to have contained about 250 figures of countrymen and countrywomen laughing, drawn by the hand of Leonardo. Card. Silvio Valenti had a similar book, in which were caricature heads drawn with a pen, like that engraven by Count Caylus. Of these caricatures mention is made in the second volume of the Lettere Pittoriche, p. 170[122]. The passage in the Lettere Pittoriche here referred to, is part of a letter without any name or date, addressed *Al Sig. C. di C.*; but a note of the editor's explains these initials, as meaning Sig. Conte di Caylus, and supposes the author to have been the younger Mariette. The letter mentions a collection of heads from Leonardo's drawings, published by the Count; and the editor, in another note, tells us, that they are caricature heads drawn in pen and ink; that the originals were bought in Holland, from Sig. Cardin. Silvio Valenti, and that the prints of which the letter speaks, are in the famous collection of the Corsini library. The author of the Letter supposes these caricatures to have been drawn when Vinci retired to Melzi's house, that he invented them as a new sort of recreation, and intended them as a subject for the academy which he had established at Milan.

In another part of the same Letter, p. 173, 174, this collection of drawings of heads is again mentioned, and it is there said, that it might be that which belonged

---

[118] Suppl. in Vasari, 74.
[119] Vasari, 24.
[120] Vasari, 26.
[121] Vasari, 29.
[122] Additions to the life in Vasari, 61.

to the Earl of Arundel. This conjecture is founded on there being many such heads engraven formerly by Hollar. In fact, the number of the plates which he has done from drawings of this painter, are near one hundred, which compose different series. The author of the Letter adds, that, if a conjecture might be permitted, we might affirm, that this is the collection of heads of which Paul Lomazzo speaks; at least the description which he gives of a similar collection which was in the hands of Aurelio Lovino, a painter of Milan, corresponds with this as well in the number of the drawings as their subjects. It represents, like this, studies from old men, countrymen, wrinkled old women, which are all laughing. Another part of this Letter says, it is easy to believe that the collection of drawings of heads which occasioned this Letter, might be one of those books in which Leonardo noted the most singular countenances.

In p. 198 of the same Letter, Hollar's engravings are said to be about an hundred, and to have been done at Antwerp in 1645, and the following year; and in p. 199, Count Caylus's publication is said to contain 59 plates in aqua fortis, done in 1730, and that this latter is the work so often mentioned in the Letter.

Another collection of the same kind of caricature heads mentioned in Mariette's Letter[123], as existing in the cabinet of either the King of Spain or the King of Sardinia.

Four caricature heads, mentioned, Lett. Pitt. vol. ii. p. 190, as being in the possession of Sig. Crozat. They are described as drawn with a pen, and are said to have come originally from Vasari's collection of drawings. Of this collection it is said, in a note on the above passage, that it was afterwards carried into France, and fell into the hands of a bookseller, who took the volume to pieces, and disposed of the drawings separately, and that many of them came into the cabinets of the King, and Sig. Crozat. Others say, and it is more credible, that Vasari's collection passed into that of the Grand Dukes of Medici.

A head of Americo Vespucci, in charcoal, but copied by Vasari in pen and ink[124].

A head of an old man, beautifully drawn in charcoal[125].

An head of Scarramuccia, captain of the gypsies, in chalk; formerly belonging to Pierfrancesco Giambullari, canon of St. Lorenzo, at Florence, and left by him to Donato Valdambrini of Arezzo, canon of St. Lorenzo also[126].

Several designs of combatants on horseback, made by Leonardo for Gentil Borri, a master of defence[127], to shew the different positions necessary for a horse soldier in defending himself, and attacking his enemy.

A carton of our Saviour, the Virgin, St. Ann, and St. John. Vasari says of this, that for two days, people of all sorts, men and women, young and old, resorted to Leonardo's house to see this wonderful performance, as if they had been going to a solemn feast; and adds, that this carton was afterwards in France. It seems that

[123] Lett. Pitt. vol. ii. 171.
[124] Vasari, 29.
[125] Ibid.
[126] Ibid.
[127] Venturi, 42.

this was intended for an altar-piece for the high altar of the church of the Annunziata, but the picture was never painted[128]. However, when Leonardo afterwards went into France, he, at the desire of Francis the First, put the design into colours. Lomazzo has said, that this carton of St. Ann was carried into France; that in his time it was at Milan, in the possession of Aurelio Lovino, a painter; and that many drawings from it were in existence. What was the fate this carton of St. Ann underwent, may be seen in a letter of P. Resta, printed in the third volume of the Lettere Pittoriche, in which he says, that Leonardo made three of these cartons, and nevertheless did not convert it into a picture, but that it was painted by Salai, and that the picture is still in the sacristy of St. Celsus at Milan[129].

A drawing of an old man's head, seen in front, in red chalk; mentioned Lett. Pitt. vol. ii. p. 191.

A carton designed by him *for painting the council-chamber at Florence.* The subject which he chose for this purpose was, the history of Niccolo Piccinino, the Captain of Duke Philip of Milan, in which he drew a group of men on horseback fighting for a standard[130]. Mariette, in a note, Lett. Pitt. vol. ii. p. 193, mentions this carton, which he says represented two horsemen fighting for a standard; that it was only part of a large history, the subject of which was the rout of Niccolo Piccinino, General of the army of Philip Duke of Milan, and that a print was engraven of it by Edelinck, when young, but the drawing from which he worked was a bad one. In the catalogue of prints from the works of Leonardo, inserted Lett. Pitt. vol. ii. p. 195, this print is again mentioned and described more truly, as representing four horsemen fighting for a standard. It is there supposed to have been engraven from a drawing by Fiammingo, and that this drawing might have been made from the picture which Du Fresne speaks of as being in his time in the possession of Sig. La Maire, an excellent painter of perspective.

A design of Neptune drawn in his car by sea horses, attended by sea gods; made by him for his friend Antonio Segni[131].

Several anatomical drawings made from the life, many of which have been since collected into a volume, by his scholar Francesco Melzi[132].

A book of the Anatomy of man, mentioned by Vasari, p. 36, the drawings for which were made with the assistance of Marc Antonio della Torre, before noticed in the present life. It is probably the same with the preceding.

[128] Vasari, 39. In a note in Lettere Pittoriche, vol. ii. p. 174, on the before cited letter of Mariette, it is said that Bernardino Lovino was a scholar of Leonardo, and had in his possession the carton of St. Ann, which Leonardo had made for a picture which he was to paint in the church della Nunziata, at Florence. Francis I. got possession of it, and was desirous that Leonardo should execute it when he came into France, but without effect. It is known it was not done, as this carton went to Milan. Lomazzo, lib. ii. cap. 17. Lett. Pitt. vol. ii. p. 174, in a note. A carton similar to this is now in the library of the Royal Academy, at London.

[129] Vasari, p. 39, in a note.

[130] Vasari, 41. In the suppl. to the life, Vasari, 68, the subject painted in the council-chamber at Florence is said to be the wonderful battle against Attila.

[131] Du Fresne. Vasari, 28.

[132] Du Fresne.

A beautiful and well-preserved study in red and black chalk, of the *head of a Virgin*, from which he afterwards painted a picture. This study was at one time in the celebrated Villa de Vecchietti, but afterwards, in consequence of a sale, passed into the hands of Sig. Ignazio Hugford[133].

Two heads of women in profile, little differing from each other, drawn in like manner in black and red chalk, bought at the same sale by Sig. Hugford, but now among the Elector Palatine's collection of drawings[134].

A book of the Anatomy of a horse, mentioned by Vasari, p. 36, as a distinct work; but probably included in Leonardo's manuscript collections. See the account before given of them.

Several designs by Leonardo were in the possession of Sig. Jabac, who seems to have been a collector of pictures, and to have bought up for the King of France several excellent pictures particularly by Leonardo da Vinci[135].

A drawing of a young man embracing an old woman, whom he is caressing for the sake of her riches. This is mentioned, Lett. Pitt. vol. ii. p. 198, as engraven by Hollar, in 1646.

A head of a young man seen in profile, engraven in aqua fortis by Conte di Caylus, from a drawing in the King of France's collection[136].

A fragment of a Treatise on the Motions of the Human Body, already mentioned in the foregoing life.

In the Lettere Pittoriche, vol. ii. p. 199, mention is made of a print representing *some intertwisted lines upon a black ground*, in the style of some of Albert Durer's engravings in wood. In the middle of this, in a small compartment, is to be read, "Academia Leonardi Vin." Vasari, it is there said, has noticed it as a singularity.

In p. 200 of the same work, a similar print is also noticed, which differs only in the inscription from the former. In this last it is Academia Leonardi Vici. Both this and the former print are said to be extremely rare, and only to have been seen in the King of France's collection. It does not however appear from any thing in the Lett. Pitt. that they were designed by Leonardo.

The Abate di Villeloin, in his Catalogue of Prints published in 1666, speaks, under the article of Leonardo da Vinci, of a print of the taking down from the Cross; but the Lett. Pitt. says it was engraven from Eneas Vico, not from Leonardo[137].

Two drawings of monsters, mentioned by Lomazzo, consisting of a boy's head each, but horribly distorted by the misplacing of the features, and the introduction of other members not in Nature to be found there. These two drawings were in the

---

[133] Additions to the Life in Vasari, 48.
[134] Ibid.
[135] Additions to the Life in Vasari, 60.
[136] Lett. Pitt. vol. ii. p. 198.
[137] Lett. Pitt. vol. ii. p. 200.

hands of Francesco Borella, a sculptor[138].

A portrait by Leonardo, *of Artus, Maestro di Camera to Francis I.* drawn in black lead pencil[139].

The head of a Cæsar crowned with oak, among a valuable collection of drawings in a thick volume in folio, in the possession of Sig. Pagave[140].

The proportions of the human body. The original of this is preserved in the possession of Sig. Pagave. At the head and foot of this drawing is to be read the description which begins thus: *Tanto apre l'Uomo nelle braccia quanto è la sua altezza, &c.* and above all, at the head of the work is the famous Last Supper, which he proposes to his scholars as the rule of the art[141].

The Circumcision, a large drawing mentioned Lett. Pitt. vol. ii. 283, as the work of Leonardo, by Nicolo Gabburri, in a letter dated Florence, 4th Oct. 1732, and addressed *Al Sig. Pietro Mariette.* Gabburri says he saw this drawing, and that it was done on white paper a little tinted with Indian ink, and heightened with ceruse. Its owner then was Alessandro Galilei, an architect of Florence.

A drawing consisting of several laughing heads, in the middle of which is another head in profile, crowned with oak leaves. This drawing was the property of the Earl of Arundel, and was engraven by Hollar in 1646[142].

A man sitting, and collecting in a looking-glass the rays of the sun, to dazzle the eyes of a dragon who is fighting with a lion. A print of this is spoken of, Lett. Pitt. vol. ii. p. 197, as badly engraven by an anonymous artist, but it is there said to have so little of Leonardo's manner as to afford reason for believing it not designed by him, though it might perhaps be found among his drawings in the King of France's collection. Another print of it, of the same size, has been engraven from the drawing by Conte de Caylus. It represents a pensive man, and differs from the former in this respect, that in this the man is naked, whereas in the drawing he is clothed.

PAINTINGS.

A Madonna, formerly in the possession of Pope Clement the Seventh[143].

A small Madonna and Child, painted for Baldassar Turini da Pescia, who was the Datary[144] at Lyons, the colours of which are much faded[145]. It is not known where this now is.

A Virgin and Child, at one time in the hands of the Botti family[146].

---

[138] Additions to the Life in Vasari, 68.
[139] Ibid.
[140] Ibid.
[141] Ibid.
[142] Lett. Pitt. vol. ii. 198.
[143] Vasari, 28.
[144] The Datary is the Pope's officer who nominates to vacant benefices.
[145] Vasari, 44.
[146] Du Fresne.

The Virgin sitting in St. Ann's lap, and holding her little Son, formerly at Paris[147]. This has been engraven in wood, in chiaro oscuro, by an unknown artist. The picture was in the King of France's cabinet, and a similar one is in the sacristy of St. Celsus at Milan[148].

Another Virgin with her Son, St. John, and an Angel, mentioned by Du Fresne, as at Paris[149].

A Madonna and Child, in the possession of the Marquis di Surdi[150].

A Madonna and Child, painted on the wall in the church of St. Onofrio at Rome[151].

A Madonna kneeling, in the King's gallery in France[152].

An Holy Family, with St. Michael, and another Angel, in the King of France's collection[153].

A Madonna, in the church of St. Francis at Milan, attributed to Leonardo by Sorman[154].

A Virgin and Child, by Leonardo, in Piacenza, near the church of Our Lady in the Fields. It was bought for 300 chequins by the Principe di Belgioioso[155].

A Madonna, half length, holding on her knee the infant Jesus, with a lily in his hand. A print of this, engraven in aqua fortis by Giuseppe Juster, is mentioned Lett. Pitt. vol. ii. p. 196. The picture is there said to have been in the possession of Charles Patin, and was supposed by some to have been painted for Francis I.

An Herodiade, some time in Cardinal Richelieu's possession[156].

The daughter of Herodias, with an executioner holding out to her the head of St. John, in the Barberini palace[157].

An Herodiade with a basket, in which is the head of John the Baptist. A print of this in aqua fortis, by Gio. Troven, under the direction of Teniers, is mentioned Lett. Pitt. vol. ii. p. 197, and is there said to have been done from a picture which was then in the cabinet of the Archduke Leopold, but had been before in that of the Emperor.

Another picture of the same subject, but differently disposed. It is also an half length. A print from it, in aqua fortis, by Alessio Loyr, is mentioned Lett. Pitt. vol. ii. p. 197; but it is not there said in whose possession the picture ever was.

---

[147] Du Fresne. Additions in Vasari, 60.
[148] Lett. Pitt. vol. ii. 196.
[149] Du Fresne.
[150] Du Fresne. Additions to Vasari, 60.
[151] Additions to Vasari, 59.
[152] Additions to Vasari, 60.
[153] Additions to Vasari, 60.
[154] Additions in Vasari, 61.
[155] Suppl. in Vasari, 68.
[156] Du Fresne.
[157] Additions to Vasari, 59.

The angel in Verrochio's picture before mentioned[158].

The shield, mentioned by Vasari, p. 26, as painted by him at the request of his father, and consisting of serpents, &c.

A head of Medusa, in oil, in the palace of Duke Cosmo. It is still in being, and in good preservation[159].

A head of an angel raising one arm in the air, in the collection of Duke Cosmo[160]. Whether this is a picture, or only a drawing, does not appear; but as Vasari does not notice any difference between that and the head of Medusa, which he decidedly says is in oil, it is probable that this is so also.

The Adoration of the Magi: it was in the house of Americo Benci, opposite to the Portico of Peruzzi[161].

The famous Last Supper, in the Refectory of the Dominican convent of Santa Maria delle Grazie[162]. A list of the copies made from this celebrated picture has, together with its history, been given in a former page. A print has been engraven from it under the direction of Pietro Soutman; but he being a scholar of Rubens, has introduced into it so much of Rubens's manner[163], that it can no longer be known for Leonardo da Vinci's. Besides this, Mariette also mentions two other prints, one of them an engraving, the other an etching, but both by unknown authors. He notices also, that the Count di Caylus had etched it in aqua fortis[164]. The print lately engraven of it by Morghen has been already noticed in a former page.

A Nativity, sent as a present from the Duke of Milan to the Emperor[165].

The portraits of Lodovic Sforza, Duke of Milan, and Maximilian his eldest son, and on the other side Beatrix his dutchess, and Francesco his other son, all in one picture, in the same Refectory with the Last Supper[166].

The portraits of two of the handsomest women at Florence, painted by him as a present to Lewis XII[167].

The painting in the council-chamber at Florence[168]. The subject of this is the battle

---

[158] Vasari, 25.

[159] Vasari, 28.

[160] Vasari, 29.

[161] Vasari, 30. In p. 29, it is said in a note, that there is in the Medici gallery an Adoration of the Magi, by Leonardo, unfinished, which may probably be the picture of which Vasari speaks.

[162] Vasari, 30.

[163] Lett. Pitt. vol. ii. 184. The real fact is known to be, that it was engraven from a drawing made by Rubens himself, who, as I am informed, had in it altered the back-ground.

[164] Lett. Pitt. vol. ii. 195.

[165] Vasari, 30.

[166] Vasari, 33.

[167] Venturi, 4.

[168] Venturi, 37.

of Attila[169].

A portrait of Ginevra, daughter of Americo Benci[170].

The portrait of Mona Lisa, the wife of Francesco del Giocondo, painted for her husband[171]. Lomazzo has said, she was a Neapolitan, but this is supposed a mistake, and that she was a Florentine[172]. In a note of Mariette's, Lett. Pitt. vol. ii. p. 175, this picture is said to have been in the collection of Francis I. King of France, who gave for it 4000 crowns.

A small picture of a child, which was at Pescia, in the possession of Baldassar Turini. It is not known where this now is[173].

A painting of two horsemen struggling for a flag, in the Palais Royal at Paris[174].

A nobleman of Mantua[175].

A picture of Flora, which Du Fresne mentions as being in his time at Paris. This is said to have been once in the cabinet of Mary de Medicis[176], and though for some time supposed to have been painted by Leonardo da Vinci, was discovered by Mariette to have been the work of Francisco Melzi, whose name is upon it[177]. In the supplement to the life of Leonardo, inserted in Della Valle's edition of Vasari, this picture is said to have been painted for the Duke de S. Simone.

A head of John the Baptist, in the hands of Camillo Albizzo[178].

The Conception of the blessed Virgin, for the church of St. Francis at Milan[179]. This was esteemed a copy, and not worth more than 30 chequins, till an Englishman came there, who thought a large sum of money well employed in the purchase of it[180].

St. John in the Wilderness, said to be at Paris[181]. In Lett. Pitt. vol. ii. p. 197, mention is made of a print of St. John the Baptist, half length, by Sig. Jabac, who had the original picture, which was formerly in the King of France's cabinet.

Joseph and Potiphar's wife, which Mons. de Charmois, secretary to the Duke of Schomberg, had[182].

---

[169] Suppl. in Vasari, 68.
[170] Vasari, 39.
[171] Ibid.
[172] Suppl. in Vasari, 60.
[173] Vasari, 44.
[174] Du Fresne.
[175] Du Fresne.
[176] Suppl. in Vasari, 61.
[177] Ibid. 81.
[178] Du Fresne.
[179] Du Fresne. Add. to the Life in Vasari, 60.
[180] Suppl. in Vasari, 69.
[181] Du Fresne. Add. to Vasari, 60.
[182] Du Fresne.

A portrait of Raphael, in oil, in the Medici gallery. This is mentioned in Vasari, p. 47; and though not expressly there said to be by Leonardo, is so placed as to make it doubtful whether it was or not.

A Nun, half length, by Leonardo, in the possession of Abbate Nicolini[183].

Two fine heads, painted in oil by Leonardo, bought at Florence by Sig. Bali di Breteuil, ambassador from Malta to Rome. One of these, representing a woman, was in his first manner. The other, a Virgin, in his last[184].

A Leda, which Lomazzo says was at Fontainebleau, and did not yield in colouring to the portrait of Joconda in the Duke's gallery. Richardson says it was in the palace Mattei[185].

The head of a dead man, with all its minute parts, painted by Leonardo, formerly in the Mattei palace, but no longer there[186].

A picture containing a study of *two most delicate female heads*, in the Barberini palace at Rome[187].

A portrait of a girl with a book in her hand, in the Strozzi palace in Rome[188].

The Dispute of Jesus with the Doctors, half length, in the Panfili palace[189].

Five pictures in the Ambrosian library at Milan, the subjects not mentioned[190].

Some in the gallery of the archbishopric at Milan, the number and subjects equally unnoticed[191].

One picture in the sacristy of Santa Maria, near St. Celsus at Milan[192].

A small head of Christ, while a youth, mentioned by Lomazzo. Probably this may be the study for the picture of Jesus disputing with the Doctors, at the Panfili palace[193].

St. Michael with a man kneeling, in the King of France's collection[194].

A Bacchus, in the same collection[195].

---

[183] Add. in Vasari, 47.
[184] Add. to Vasari, 48.
[185] Add. in Vasari, 57.
[186] Add. to Vasari, 58.
[187] Add. to Vasari, 59.
[188] Ibid.
[189] Ibid. This is the picture lately exhibited in Brook Street, Grosvenor Square, and is said to have been purchased by the Earl of Warwick.
[190] Add. to Vasari, 59.
[191] Ibid.
[192] Ibid.
[193] Ibid.
[194] Ibid. 60.
[195] Ibid.

The fair Ferraia, in the same collection[196].

A portrait of a lady, there also[197].

A Christ with a globe in his hand[198]. A very fine picture, half length, now in the possession of Richard Troward, Esq. of Pall Mall. This was engraven by Hollar in 1650, in aqua fortis[199].

The Fall of Phaeton, in the gallery of the Grand Duke of Tuscany, of which Scannelli speaks, but it is mentioned by no one else[200].

St. Catherine with a palm-branch, in the gallery of the Duke of Modena[201].

The head of a young man armed, in the same collection, very graceful, but inferior to the St. Catherine[202].

A portrait of the Queen of Naples, which was in the Aldobrandini gallery, but afterwards to be found in a chamber of portraits in the Panfili palace. It is not equal in colouring to the Dispute of Jesus with the Doctors[203].

A portrait in profile of the Dutchess of Milan, mentioned by Richardson as being in a chamber leading to the Ambrosian library[204].

A beautiful figure of the Virgin, half length, in the palace of Vaprio. It is of a gigantic size, for the head of the Virgin is six common palms in size, and that of the Divine Infant four in circumference. Della Valle speaks of having seen this in the year 1791, and says he is not ignorant that tradition ascribes this Madonna to Bramante, notwithstanding which he gives it to Leonardo[205].

A laughing Pomona with three veils, commended by Lomazzo. It was done for Francis I. King of France[206].

The portrait of Cecilia Gallarani, mentioned by Bellincione in one of his sonnets, as painted by Leonardo[207].

Another of Lucrezia Cavelli, a celebrated performer on the lute, ascribed to him on the same authority. Copies of both this and the former may be seen at Milan[208].

Our Saviour before Pilate, in the church of S. Florentino, at Amboise. It is thought that the carton only of this was Leonardo's, and that the picture was painted by

[196] Ibid.
[197] Ibid.
[198] Ibid.
[199] Lett. Pitt. vol. ii. 197.
[200] Add. in Vasari, 60.
[201] Add. in Vasari, 61.
[202] Ibid.
[203] Ibid.
[204] Ibid.
[205] Supp. in Vasari, 67.
[206] Ibid. 68.
[207] Supp. in Vasari, 75.
[208] Ibid.

Andrea Salai, or Melzi[209].

A portrait of Leonardo by himself, half length, in the Ambrosian library at Milan[210]. Della Valle has inserted a copy of this before the Supplement to Leonardo's Life, in his edition of Vasari, for which purpose Sig. Pagave transmitted him a drawing from the original picture. But Leonardo's own drawing for the picture itself, is in the possession of his Britannic Majesty, and from that Mr. Chamberlaine has prefixed to his publication before mentioned, a plate engraven by Bartolozzi.

---

[209] Supp. in Vasari, 80.
[210] Supp. in Vasari, 81.

CONTENTS

Chapter *Page*

DRAWING.

PROPORTION.

ANATOMY.

MOTION AND EQUIPOISE OF FIGURES.

LINEAR PERSPECTIVE.

INVENTION, OR COMPOSITION.

INVENTION, OR COMPOSITION.

EXPRESSION AND CHARACTER.

LIGHT AND SHADOW.

LIGHT AND SHADOW.

CONTRASTE AND EFFECT.

REFLEXES.

COLOURS AND COLOURING.

COLOURS.

COLOURS IN REGARD TO LIGHT AND SHADOW.

COLOURS IN REGARD TO BACK-GROUNDS.

CONTRASTE, HARMONY, AND REFLEXES, IN REGARD TO COLOURS.

PERSPECTIVE OF COLOURS.

MISCELLANEOUS OBSERVATIONS.

LANDSCAPE.

MISCELLANEOUS OBSERVATIONS.

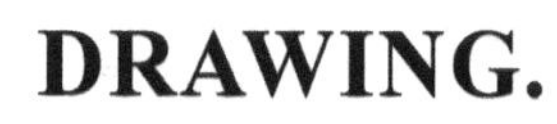

DRAWING.

PROPORTION.

CHAP. I.

WHAT THE YOUNG STUDENT IN PAINTING OUGHT IN THE FIRST PLACE TO LEARN.

THE young student should, in the first place, acquire a knowledge of perspective, to enable him to give to every object its proper dimensions: after which, it is requisite that he be under the care of an able master, to accustom him, by degrees, to a good style of drawing the parts. Next, he must study Nature, in order to confirm and fix in his mind the reason of those precepts which he has learnt. He must also bestow some time in viewing the works of various old masters, to form his eye and judgment, in order that he may be able to put in practice all that he has been taught[211].

CHAP. II.

RULE FOR A YOUNG STUDENT IN PAINTING.

THE organ of sight is one of the quickest, and takes in at a single glance an infinite variety of forms; notwithstanding which, it cannot perfectly comprehend more than one object at a time. For example, the reader, at one look over this page, immediately perceives it full of different characters; but he cannot at the same moment distinguish each letter, much less can he comprehend their meaning. He must consider it word by word, and line by line, if he be desirous of forming a just notion of these characters. In like manner, if we wish to ascend to the top of an edifice, we must be content to advance step by step, otherwise we shall never be able to attain it.

A young man, who has a natural inclination to the study of this art, I would advise to act thus: In order to acquire a true notion of the form of things, he must begin by studying the parts which compose them, and not pass to a second till he

---

[211] This passage has been by some persons much misunderstood, and supposed to require, that the student should be a deep proficient in perspective, before he commences the study of painting; but it is a knowledge of the leading principles only of perspective that the author here means, and without such a knowledge, which is easily to be acquired, the student will inevitably fall into errors, as gross as those humorously pointed out by Hogarth, in his Frontispiece to Kirby's Perspective.

has well stored his memory, and sufficiently practised the first; otherwise he loses his time, and will most certainly protract his studies. And let him remember to acquire accuracy before he attempts quickness.

CHAP. III.

HOW TO DISCOVER A YOUNG MAN'S DISPOSITION FOR PAINTING.

Many are very desirous of learning to draw, and are very fond of it, who are, notwithstanding, void of a proper disposition for it. This may be known by their want of perseverance; like boys, who draw every thing in a hurry, never finishing, or shadowing.

CHAP. IV.

OF PAINTING, AND ITS DIVISIONS.

Painting is divided into two principal parts. The first is the figure, that is, the lines which distinguish the forms of bodies, and their component parts. The second is the colour contained within those limits.

CHAP. V.

DIVISION OF THE FIGURE.

The form of bodies is divided into two parts; that is, the proportion of the members to each other, which must correspond with the whole; and the motion, expressive of what passes in the mind of the living figure.

CHAP. VI.

PROPORTION OF MEMBERS.

The proportion of members is again divided into two parts, viz. equality, and motion. By equality is meant (besides the measure corresponding with the whole), that you do not confound the members of a young subject with those of old age, nor plump ones with those that are lean; and that, moreover, you do not blend the robust and firm muscles of man with feminine softness: that the attitudes and motions of old age be not expressed with the quickness and alacrity of youth; nor those of a female figure like those of a vigorous young man. The motions and members of a strong man should be such as to express his perfect state of health.

CHAP. VII.

OF DIMENSIONS IN GENERAL.

In general, the dimensions of the human body are to be considered in the length, and not in the breadth; because in the wonderful works of Nature, which we endeavour to imitate, we cannot in any species find any one part in one model precisely similar to the same part in another. Let us be attentive, therefore, to the variation of forms, and avoid all monstrosities of proportion; such as long legs united to short bodies, and narrow chests with long arms. Observe also attentively the measure of joints, in which Nature is apt to vary considerably; and imitate her example by doing the same.

CHAP. VIII.

MOTION, CHANGES, AND PROPORTION OF MEMBERS.

The measures of the human body vary in each member, according as it is more or less bent, or seen in different views, increasing on one side as much as they diminish on the other.

CHAP. IX.

THE DIFFERENCE OF PROPORTION BETWEEN CHILDREN AND GROWN MEN.

In men and children I find a great difference between the joints of the one and the other in the length of the bones. A man has the length of two heads from the extremity of one shoulder to the other, the same from the shoulder to the elbow, and from the elbow to the fingers; but the child has only one, because Nature gives the proper size first to the seat of the intellect, and afterwards to the other parts.

CHAP. X.

THE ALTERATIONS IN THE PROPORTION OF THE HUMAN BODY FROM INFANCY TO FULL AGE.

A man, in his infancy, has the breadth of his shoulders equal to the length of the face, and to the length of the arm from the shoulder to the elbow, when the arm is bent[212]. It is the same again from the lower belly to the knee, and from the knee to the foot. But, when a man is arrived at the period of his full growth, every one of these dimensions becomes double in length, except the face, which, with the top of the head, undergoes but very little alteration in length. A well-proportioned and full-grown man, therefore, is ten times the length of his face; the breadth of his shoulders will be two faces, and in like manner all the above lengths will be dou-

---

[212] See Chap. 351.

ble. The rest will be explained in the general measurement of the human body[213].

CHAP. XI.

OF THE PROPORTION OF MEMBERS.

ALL the parts of any animal whatever must be correspondent with the whole. So that, if the body be short and thick, all the members belonging to it must be the same. One that is long and thin must have its parts of the same kind; and so of the middle size. Something of the same may be observed in plants, when uninjured by men or tempests; for when thus injured they bud and grow again, making young shoots from old plants, and by those means destroying their natural symmetry.

CHAP. XII.

THAT EVERY PART BE PROPORTIONED TO ITS WHOLE.

IF a man be short and thick, be careful that all his members be of the same nature, viz. short arms and thick, large hands, short fingers, with broad joints; and so of the rest.

CHAP. XIII.

OF THE PROPORTION OF THE MEMBERS.

MEASURE upon yourself the proportion of the parts, and, if you find any of them defective, note it down, and be very careful to avoid it in drawing your own compositions. For this is reckoned a common fault in painters, to delight in the imitation of themselves.

CHAP. XIV.

THE DANGER OF FORMING AN ERRONEOUS JUDGMENT IN REGARD TO THE PROPORTION AND BEAUTY OF THE PARTS.

IF the painter has clumsy hands, he will be apt to introduce them into his works, and so of any other part of his person, which may not happen to be so beautiful as it ought to be. He must, therefore, guard particularly against that self-love, or too good opinion of his own person, and study by every means to acquire the knowledge of what is most beautiful, and of his own defects, that he may adopt the one and avoid the other.

---

[213] Not to be found in this work.

CHAP. XV.

ANOTHER PRECEPT.

THE young painter must, in the first instance, accustom his hand to copying the drawings of good masters; and when his hand is thus formed, and ready, he should, with the advice of his director, use himself also to draw from relievos; according to the rules we shall point out in the treatise on drawing from relievos[214].

CHAP. XVI.

THE MANNER OF DRAWING FROM RELIEVOS, AND RENDERING PAPER FIT FOR IT.

WHEN you draw from relievos, tinge your paper of some darkish demi-tint. And after you have made your outline, put in the darkest shadows, and, last of all, the principal lights, but sparingly, especially the smaller ones; because those are easily lost to the eye at a very moderate distance[215].

CHAP. XVII.

OF DRAWING FROM CASTS OR NATURE.

IN drawing from relievo, the draftsman must place himself in such a manner, as that the eye of the figure to be drawn be level with his own[216].

---

[214] From this, and many other similar passages, it is evident, that the author intended at some future time to arrange his manuscript collections, and to publish them as separate treatises. That he did not do so is well known; but it is also a fact, that, in selecting from the whole mass of his collections the chapters of which the present work consists, great care appears in general to have been taken to extract also those to which there was any reference from any of the chapters intended for this work, or which from their subject were necessarily connected with them. Accordingly, the reader will find, in the notes to this translation, that all such chapters in any other part of the present work are uniformly pointed out, as have any relation to the respective passages in the text. This, which has never before been done, though indispensably necessary, will be found of singular use, and it was thought proper here, once for all, to notice it.

In the present instance the chapters, referring to the subject in the text, are Chap. xvi. xvii. xviii. xix. xx. xxvi.; and though these do not afford complete information, yet it is to be remembered, that drawing from relievos is subject to the very same rules as drawing from Nature; and that, therefore, what is elsewhere said on that subject is also equally applicable to this.

[215] The meaning of this is, that the last touches of light, such as the shining parts (which are always narrow), must be given sparingly. In short, that the drawing must be kept in broad masses as much as possible.

[216] This is not an absolute rule, but it is a very good one for drawing of portraits.

CHAP. XVIII.

TO DRAW FIGURES FROM NATURE.

Accustom yourself to hold a plummet in your hand, that you may judge of the bearing of the parts.

CHAP. XIX.

OF DRAWING FROM NATURE.

When you draw from Nature, you must be at the distance of three times the height of the object; and when you begin to draw, form in your own mind a certain principal line (suppose a perpendicular); observe well the bearing of the parts towards that line; whether they intersect, are parallel to it, or oblique.

CHAP. XX.

OF DRAWING ACADEMY FIGURES.

When you draw from a naked model, always sketch in the whole of the figure, suiting all the members well to each other; and though you finish only that part which appears the best, have a regard to the rest, that, whenever you make use of such studies, all the parts may hang together.

In composing your attitudes, take care not to turn the head on the same side as the breast, nor let the arm go in a line with the leg[217]. If the head turn towards the right shoulder, the parts must be lower on the left side than on the other; but if the chest come forward, and the head turn towards the left, the parts on the right side are to be the highest.

CHAP. XXI.

OF STUDYING IN THE DARK, ON FIRST WAKING IN THE MORNING, AND BEFORE GOING TO SLEEP.

I have experienced no small benefit, when in the dark and in bed, by retracing in my mind the outlines of those forms which I had previously studied, particularly such as had appeared the most difficult to comprehend and retain; by this method they will be confirmed and treasured up in the memory.

CHAP. XXII.

OBSERVATIONS ON DRAWING PORTRAITS.

The cartilage, which raises the nose in the middle of the face, varies in eight different ways. It is equally straight, equally concave, or equally convex, which

[217] See Chap. ci.

is the first sort. Or, secondly, unequally straight, concave, or convex. Or, thirdly, straight in the upper part, and concave in the under. Or, fourthly, straight again in the upper part, and convex in those below. Or, fifthly, it may be concave and straight beneath. Or, sixthly, concave above, and convex below. Or, seventhly, it may be convex in the upper part, and straight in the lower. And in the eighth and last place, convex above, and concave beneath.

The uniting of the nose with the brows is in two ways, either it is straight or concave. The forehead has three different forms. It is straight, concave, or round. The first is divided into two parts, viz. it is either convex in the upper part, or in the lower, sometimes both; or else flat above and below.

CHAP. XXIII.

THE METHOD OF RETAINING IN THE MEMORY THE LIKE-NESS OF A MAN, SO AS TO DRAW HIS PROFILE, AFTER HAVING SEEN HIM ONLY ONCE.

You must observe and remember well the variations of the four principal features in the profile; the nose, mouth, chin, and forehead. And first of the nose, of which there are three different sorts[218], straight, concave, and convex. Of the straight there are but four variations, short or long, high at the end, or low. Of the concave there are three sorts; some have the concavity above, some in the middle, and some at the end. The convex noses also vary three ways; some project in the upper part, some in the middle, and others at the bottom. Nature, which seems to delight in infinite variety, gives again three changes to those noses which have a projection in the middle; for some have it straight, some concave, and some convex.

CHAP. XXIV.

HOW TO REMEMBER THE FORM OF A FACE.

If you wish to retain with facility the general look of a face, you must first learn how to draw well several faces, mouths, eyes, noses, chins, throats, necks, and shoulders; in short, all those principal parts which distinguish one man from another. For instance, noses are often different sorts[219]. Straight, bunched, concave, some raised above, some below the middle, aquiline, flat, round, and sharp. These affect the profile. In the front view there are eleven different sorts. Even, thick in the middle, thin in the middle, thick at the tip, thin at the beginning, thin at the tip, and thick at the beginning. Broad, narrow, high, and low nostrils; some with a large opening, and some more shut towards the tip.

The same variety will be found in the other parts of the face, which must be drawn from Nature, and retained in the memory. Or else, when you mean to draw

[218] See the preceding chapter.
[219] See the two preceding chapters.

a likeness from memory, take with you a pocket-book, in which you have marked all these variations of features, and after having given a look at the face you mean to draw, retire a little aside, and note down in your book which of the features are similar to it; that you may put it all together at home.

CHAP. XXV.

THAT A PAINTER SHOULD TAKE PLEASURE IN THE OPINION OF EVERY BODY.

A PAINTER ought not certainly to refuse listening to the opinion of any one; for we know that, although a man be not a painter, he may have just notions of the forms of men; whether a man has a hump on his back, a thick leg, or a large hand; whether he be lame, or have any other defect. Now, if we know that men are able to judge of the works of Nature, should we not think them more able to detect our errors?

ANATOMY.

CHAP. XXVI.
WHAT IS PRINCIPALLY TO BE OBSERVED IN FIGURES.

THE principal and most important consideration required in drawing figures, is to set the head well upon the shoulders, the chest upon the hips, the hips and shoulders upon the feet.

CHAP. XXVII.
MODE OF STUDYING.

STUDY the science first, and then follow the practice which results from that science. Pursue method in your study, and do not quit one part till it be perfectly engraven in the memory; and observe what difference there is between the members of animals and their joints[220].

CHAP. XXVIII.
OF BEING UNIVERSAL.

IT is an easy matter for a man who is well versed in the principles of his art, to become universal in the practice of it, since all animals have a similarity of members, that is, muscles, tendons, bones, &c. These only vary in length or thickness, as will be demonstrated in the Anatomy[221]. As for aquatic animals, of which there is great variety, I shall not persuade the painter to take them as a rule, having no connexion with our purpose.

---

[220] Man being the highest of the animal creation, ought to be the chief object of study.

[221] An intended Treatise, as it seems, on Anatomy, which however never was published; but there are several chapters in the present work on the subject of Anatomy, most of which will be found under the present head of Anatomy; and of such as could not be placed there, because they also related to some other branch, the following is a list by which they may be found: Chapters vi. vii. x. xi. xxxiv. xxxv. xxxvi. xxxvii. xxxviii. xxxix. xl. xli. xlii. xliii. xliv. xlv. xlvi. xlviii. xlix. l. li. lii. cxxix.

CHAP. XXIX.

A PRECEPT FOR THE PAINTER.

It reflects no great honour on a painter to be able to execute only one thing well, such as a head, an academy figure, or draperies, animals, landscape, or the like, confining himself to some particular object of study; because there is scarcely a person so void of genius as to fail of success, if he apply earnestly to one branch of study, and practise it continually.

CHAP. XXX.

OF THE MEASURES OF THE HUMAN BODY, AND THE BENDING OF MEMBERS.

It is very necessary that painters should have a knowledge of the bones which support the flesh by which they are covered, but particularly of the joints, which increase and diminish the length of them in their appearance. As in the arm, which does not measure the same when bent, as when extended; its difference between the greatest extension and bending, is about one eighth of its length. The increase and diminution of the arm is effected by the bone projecting out of its socket at the elbow; which, as is seen in figure A B, Plate I. is lengthened from the shoulder to the elbow; the angle it forms being less than a right angle. It will appear longer as that angle becomes more acute, and will shorten in proportion as it becomes more open or obtuse.

CHAP. XXXI.

OF THE SMALL BONES IN SEVERAL JOINTS OF THE HUMAN BODY.

There are in the joints of the human body certain small bones, fixed in the middle of the tendons which connect several of the joints. Such are the patellas of the knees, and the joints of the shoulders, and those of the feet. They are eight in number, one at each shoulder, one at each knee, and two at each foot under the first joint of the great toe towards the heel. These grow extremely hard as a man advances in years.

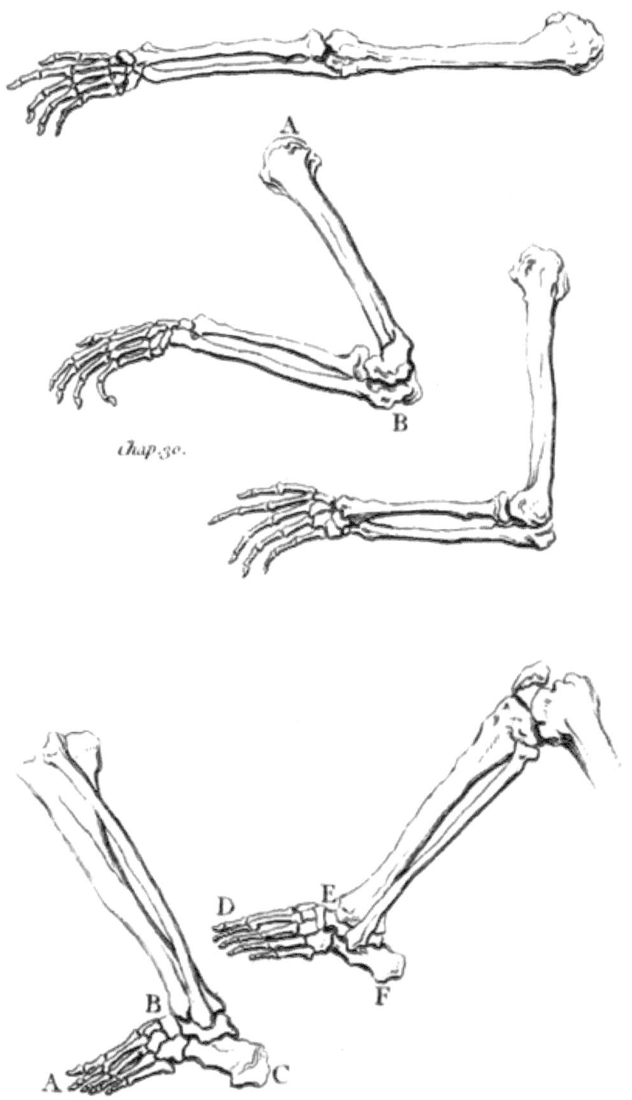

Chap. 30.

PLATE 1.

CHAP. XXXII.

MEMORANDUM TO BE OBSERVED BY THE PAINTER.

Note down which muscles and tendons are brought into action by the motion of any member, and when they are hidden. Remember that these remarks are of the greatest importance to painters and sculptors, who profess to study anatomy, and the science of the muscles. Do the same with children, following the different gradations of age from their birth even to decrepitude, describing the changes which the members, and particularly the joints, undergo; which of them grow fat, and which lean.

CHAP. XXXIII.

THE SHOULDERS.

The joints of the shoulders, and other parts which bend, shall be noticed in their places in the Treatise on Anatomy, where the cause of the motions of all the parts which compose the human body shall be explained[222].

CHAP. XXXIV.

THE DIFFERENCE OF JOINTS BETWEEN CHILDREN AND GROWN MEN.

Young children have all their joints small, but they are thick and plump in the spaces between them; because there is nothing upon the bones at the joints, but some tendons to bind the bones together. The soft flesh, which is full of fluids, is enclosed under the skin in the space between the joints; and as the bones are bigger at the joints than in the space between them, the skin throws off in the progress to manhood that superfluity, and draws nearer to the bones, thinning the whole part together. But upon the joints it does not lessen, as there is nothing but cartilages and tendons. For these reasons children are small in the joints, and plump in the space between, as may be observed in their fingers, arms, and narrow shoulders. Men, on the contrary, are large and full in the joints, in the arms and legs; and where children have hollows, men are knotty and prominent.

CHAP. XXXV.

OF THE JOINTS OF THE FINGERS.

The joints of the fingers appear larger on all sides when they bend; the more they bend the larger they appear. The contrary is the case when straight. It is the same in the toes, and it will be more perceptible in proportion to their fleshiness.

---

[222] See chap. lxxxvii.

CHAP. XXXVI.

OF THE JOINT OF THE WRIST.

The wrist or joint between the hand and arm lessens on closing the hand, and grows larger when it opens. The contrary happens in the arm, in the space between the elbow and the hand, on all sides; because in opening the hand the muscles are extended and thinned in the arm, from the elbow to the wrist; but when the hand is shut, the same muscles swell and shorten. The tendons alone start, being stretched by the clenching of the hand.

CHAP. XXXVII.

OF THE JOINT OF THE FOOT.

The increase and diminution in the joint of the foot is produced on that side where the tendons are seen, as D E F, *Plate I.* which increases when the angle is acute, and diminishes when it becomes obtuse. It must be understood of the joint in the front part of the foot A B C.

CHAP. XXXVIII.

OF THE KNEE.

Of all the members which have pliable joints, the knee is the only one that lessens in the bending, and becomes larger by extension.

CHAP. XXXIX.

OF THE JOINTS.

All the joints of the human body become larger by bending, except that of the leg.

CHAP. XL.

OF THE NAKED.

When a figure is to appear nimble and delicate, its muscles must never be too much marked, nor are any of them to be much swelled. Because such figures are expressive of activity and swiftness, and are never loaded with much flesh upon the bones. They are made light by the want of flesh, and where there is but little flesh there cannot be any thickness of muscles.

CHAP. XLI.

OF THE THICKNESS OF THE MUSCLES.

Muscular men have large bones, and are in general thick and short, with very little fat; because the fleshy muscles in their growth contract closer together, and the fat, which in other instances lodges between them, has no room. The muscles in such thin subjects, not being able to extend, grow in thickness, particularly towards their middle, in the parts most removed from the extremities.

CHAP. XLII.

FAT SUBJECTS HAVE SMALL MUSCLES.

Though fat people have this in common with muscular men, that they are frequently short and thick, they have thin muscles; but their skin contains a great deal of spongy and soft flesh full of air; for that reason they are lighter upon the water, and swim better than muscular people.

CHAP. XLIII.

WHICH OF THE MUSCLES DISAPPEAR IN THE DIFFERENT MOTIONS OF THE BODY.

In raising or lowering the arm, the pectoral muscles disappear, or acquire a greater relievo. A similar effect is produced by the hips, when they bend either inwards or outwards. It is to be observed, that there is more variety of appearances in the shoulders, hips, and neck, than in any other joint, because they are susceptible of the greatest variety of motions. But of this subject I shall make a separate treatise[223].

CHAP. XLIV.

OF THE MUSCLES.

The muscles are not to be scrupulously marked all the way, because it would be disagreeable to the sight, and of very difficult execution. But on that side only where the members are in action, they should be pronounced more strongly; for muscles that are at work naturally collect all their parts together, to gain increase of strength, so that some small parts of those muscles will appear, that were not seen before.

---

[223] It does not appear that this intention was ever carried into execution; but there are many chapters in this work on the subject of motion, where all that is necessary for a painter in this branch will be found.

CHAP. XLV.

OF THE MUSCLES.

THE muscles of young men are not to be marked strongly, nor too much swelled, because that would indicate full strength and vigour of age, which they have not yet attained. Nevertheless they must be more or less expressed, as they are more or less employed. For those which are in motion are always more swelled and thicker than those which remain at rest. The intrinsic and central line of the members which are bent, never retains its natural length.

CHAP. XLVI.

THE EXTENSION AND CONTRACTION OF THE MUSCLES.

THE muscle at the back part of the thigh shows more variety in its extension and contraction, than any other in the human body; the second, in that respect, are those which compose the buttocks; the third, those of the back; the fourth, those of the neck; the fifth, those of the shoulders; and the sixth, those of the Abdomen, which, taking their rise under the breast, terminate under the lower belly; as I shall explain when I speak of each.

CHAP. XLVII.

OF THE MUSCLE BETWEEN THE CHEST AND THE LOWER BELLY.

THERE is a muscle which begins under the breast at the Sternum, and is inserted into, or terminates at the Os pubis, under the lower belly. It is called the Rectus of the Abdomen; it is divided, lengthways, into three principal portions, by transverse tendinous intersections or ligaments, viz. the superior part, and a ligament; the second part, with its ligaments; and the third part, with the third ligament; which last unites by tendons to the Os pubis. These divisions and intersections of the same muscle are intended by nature to facilitate the motion when the body is bent or distended. If it were made of one piece, it would produce too much variety when extended, or contracted, and also would be considerably weaker. When this muscle has but little variety in the motion of the body, it is more beautiful[224].

---

[224] Anatomists have divided this muscle into four or five sections; but painters, following the ancient sculptors, shew only the three principal ones; and, in fact, we find that a greater number of them (as may often be observed in nature) gives a disagreeable meagreness to the subject. Beautiful nature does not shew more than three, though there may be more hid under the skin.

CHAP. XLVIII.

OF A MAN'S COMPLEX STRENGTH, BUT FIRST OF THE ARM.

THE muscles which serve either to straighten or bend the arm, arise from the different processes of the Scapula; some of them from the protuberances of the Humerus, and others about the middle of the Os humeri. The extensors of the arm arise from behind, and the flexors from before.

That a man has more power in pulling than in pushing, has been proved by the ninth proposition De Ponderibus[225], where it is said, that of two equal weights, that will have the greatest power which is farthest removed from the pole or centre of its balance. It follows then of course, that the muscle N B, *Plate II.* and the muscle N C, being of equal power, the inner muscle N C, will nevertheless be stronger than the outward one N B, because it is inserted into the arm at C, a point farther removed from the centre of the elbow A, than B, which is on the other side of such centre, so that that question is determined. But this is a simple power, and I thought it best to explain it before I mentioned the complex power of the muscles, of which I must now take notice. The complex power, or strength, is, for instance, this, when the arm is going to act, a second power is added to it (such as the weight of the body and the strength of the legs, in pulling or pushing), consisting in the extension of the parts, as when two men attempt to throw down a column; the one by pushing, and the other by pulling[226].

CHAP. XLIX.

IN WHICH OF THE TWO ACTIONS, PULLING OR PUSHING, A MAN HAS THE GREATEST POWER, PLATE II.

A MAN has the greatest power in pulling, for in that action he has the united exertion of all the muscles of the arm, while some of them must be inactive when he is pushing; because when the arm is extended for that purpose, the muscles which move the elbow cannot act, any more than if he pushed with his shoulders against the column he means to throw down; in which case only the muscles that extend the back, the legs under the thigh, and the calves of the legs, would be active. From which we conclude, that in pulling there is added to the power of extension the strength of the arms, of the legs, of the back, and even of the chest, if the oblique motion of the body require it. But in pushing, though all the parts were employed, yet the strength of the muscles of the arms is wanting; for to push with an extended arm without motion does not help more than if a piece of wood were placed from the shoulder to the column meant to be pushed down.

---

[225] A treatise on weights, like many others, intended by this author, but never published.

[226] See the next chapter.

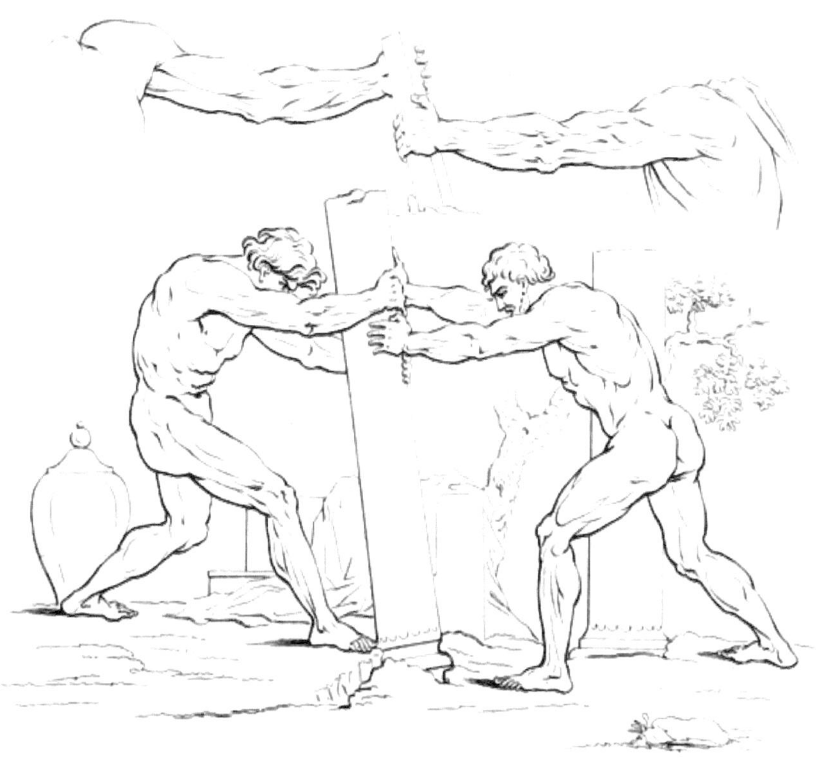

Chap. 48, 49.

PLATE 2.

CHAP. L.

OF THE BENDING OF MEMBERS, AND OF THE FLESH ROUND THE BENDING JOINT.

The flesh which covers the bones near and at the joints, swells or diminishes in thickness according to their bending or extension; that is, it increases at the inside of the angle formed by the bending, and grows narrow and lengthened on the outward side of the exterior angle. The middle between the convex and concave angle participates of this increase or diminution, but in a greater or less degree as the parts are nearer to, or farther from, the angles of the bending joints.

CHAP. LI.

OF THE NAKED BODY.

The members of naked men who work hard in different attitudes, will shew the muscles more strongly on that side where they act forcibly to bring the part into action; and the other muscles will be more or less marked, in proportion as they co-operate in the same motion.

CHAP. LII.

OF A LIGAMENT WITHOUT MUSCLES.

Where the arm joins with the hand, there is a ligament, the largest in the human body, which is without muscles, and is called the strong ligament of the Carpus; it has a square shape, and serves to bind and keep close together the bones of the arm, and the tendons of the fingers, and prevent their dilating, or starting out.

CHAP. LIII.

OF CREASES.

In bending the joints the flesh will always form a crease on the opposite side to that where it is tight.

CHAP. LIV.

HOW NEAR BEHIND THE BACK ONE ARM CAN BE BROUGHT TO THE OTHER, PLATE III. AND IV.

When the arms are carried behind the back, the elbows can never be brought nearer than the length from the elbow to the end of the longest finger; so that the fingers will not be seen beyond the elbows, and in that situation, the arms with the shoulders form a perfect square. The greatest extension of the arm across the chest is, when the elbow comes over the pit of the stomach; the elbow and the shoulder in this position, will form an equilateral triangle.

CHAP. LV.
OF THE MUSCLES.

A NAKED figure being strongly marked, so as to give a distinct view of all the muscles, will not express any motion; because it cannot move, if some of its muscles do not relax while the others are pulling. Those which relax cease to appear in proportion as the others pull strongly and become apparent.

CHAP. LVI.
OF THE MUSCLES.

THE muscles of the human body are to be more or less marked according to their degree of action. Those only which act are to be shewn, and the more forcibly they act, the stronger they should be pronounced. Those that do not act at all must remain soft and flat.

CHAP. LVII.
OF THE BENDING OF THE BODY.

THE bodies of men diminish as much on the side which bends, as they increase on the opposite side. That diminution may at last become double, in proportion to the extension on the other side. But of this I shall make a separate treatise[227].

CHAP. LVIII.
THE SAME SUBJECT.

THE body which bends, lengthens as much on one side as it shortens on the other; but the central line between them will never lessen or increase.

---

[227] It is believed that this treatise, like many others promised by the author, was never written; and to save the necessity of frequently repeating this fact, the reader is here informed, once for all, that in the life of the author prefixed to this edition, will be found an account of the works promised or projected by him, and how far his intentions have been carried into effect.

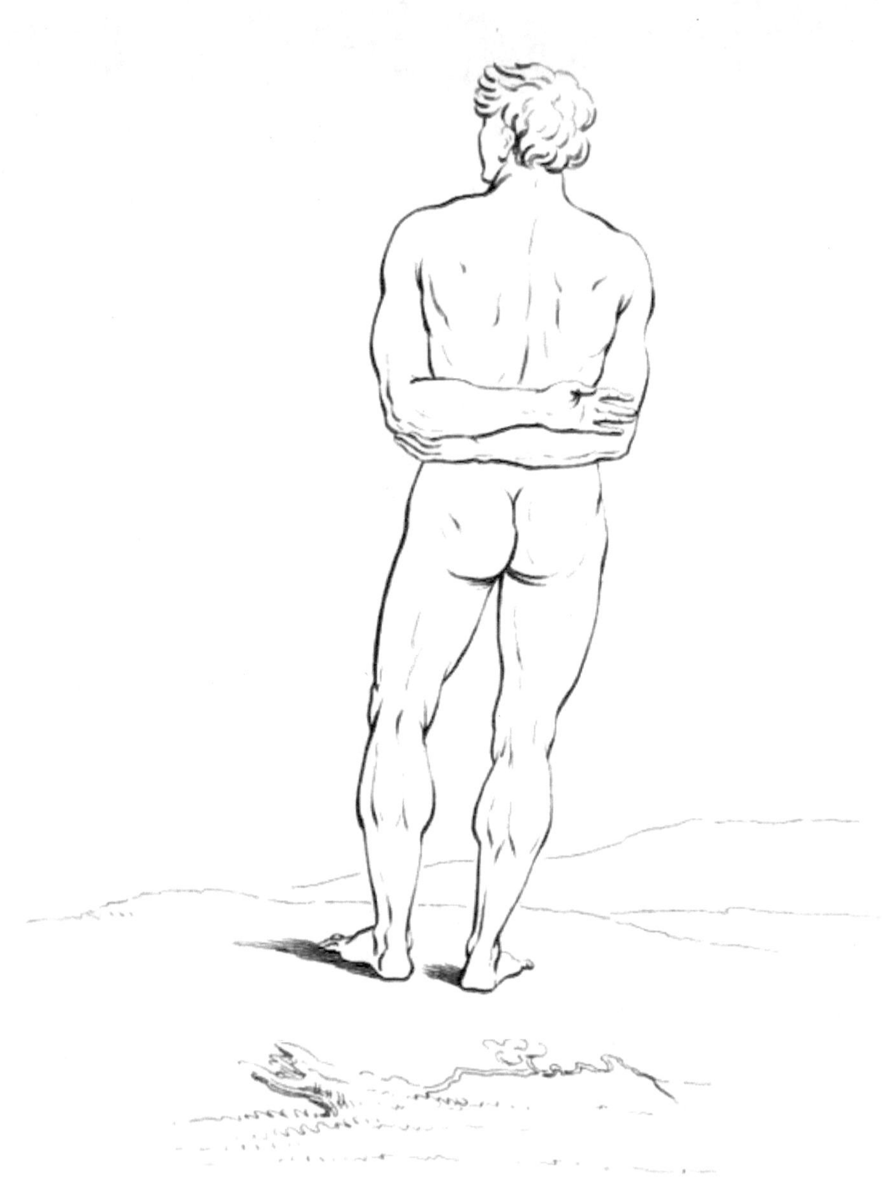

Page 18.

Chap. 54.

PLATE 3.

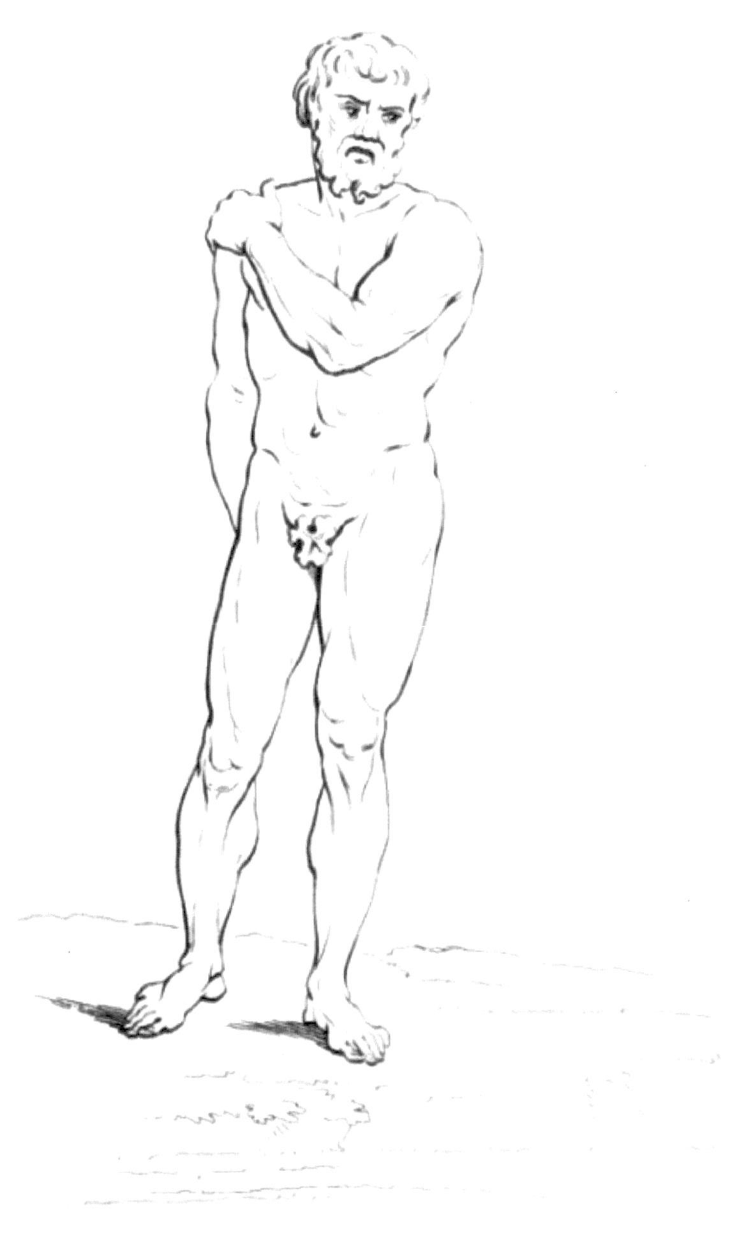

Chap. 53.

PLATE 4.

CHAP. LIX.

THE NECESSITY OF ANATOMICAL KNOWLEDGE.

THE painter who has obtained a perfect knowledge of the nature of the tendons and muscles, and of those parts which contain the most of them, will know to a certainty, in giving a particular motion to any part of the body, which, and how many of the muscles give rise and contribute to it; which of them, by swelling, occasion their shortening, and which of the cartilages they surround.

He will not imitate those who, in all the different attitudes they adopt, or invent, make use of the same muscles, in the arms, back, or chest, or any other parts.

MOTION AND EQUIPOISE OF FIGURES.

CHAP. LX.

OF THE EQUIPOISE OF A FIGURE STANDING STILL.

THE non-existence of motion in any animal resting on its feet, is owing to the equality of weight distributed on each side of the line of gravity.

CHAP. LXI.

MOTION PRODUCED BY THE LOSS OF EQUILIBRIUM.

MOTION is created by the loss of due equipoise, that is, by inequality of weight; for nothing can move of itself, without losing its centre of gravity, and the farther that is removed, the quicker and stronger will be the motion.

CHAP. LXII.

OF THE EQUIPOISE OF BODIES, PLATE V.

THE balance or equipoise of parts in the human body is of two sorts, viz. simple, and complex. Simple, when a man stands upon his feet without motion: in that situation, if he extends his arms at different distances from the middle, or stoop, the centre of his weight will always be in a perpendicular line upon the centre of that foot which supports the body; and if he rests equally upon both feet, then the middle of the chest will be perpendicular to the middle of the line which measures the space between the centres of his feet.

The complex balance is, when a man carries a weight not his own, which he bears by different motions; as in the figure of Hercules stifling Anteus, by pressing him against his breast with his arms, after he has lifted him from the ground. He must have as much of his own weight thrown behind the central line of his feet, as the weight of Anteus adds before.

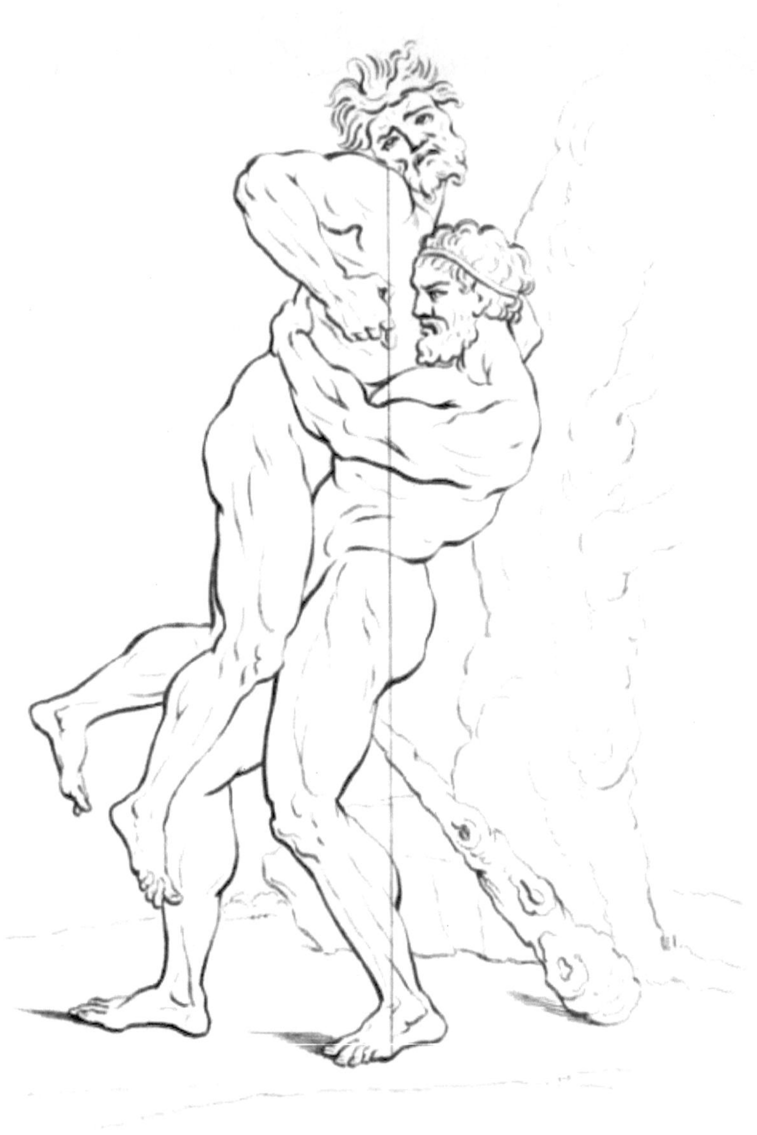

Chap. 62.

PLATE 5.

CHAP. LXIII.

OF POSITIONS.

The pit of the neck, between the two Clavicles, falls perpendicularly with the foot which bears the weight of the body. If one of the arms be thrown forwards, this pit will quit that perpendicular; and if one of the legs goes back, that pit is brought forwards, and so changes its situation at every change of posture.

CHAP. LXIV.

OF BALANCING THE WEIGHT ROUND THE CENTRE OF GRAVITY IN BODIES.

A FIGURE standing upon its feet without motion, will form an equipoise of all its members round the centre of its support.

If this figure without motion, and resting upon its feet, happens to move one of its arms forwards, it must necessarily throw as much of its weight on the opposite side, as is equal to that of the extended arm and the accidental weight. And the same I say of every part, which is brought out beyond its usual balance.

CHAP. LXV.

OF FIGURES THAT HAVE TO LIFT UP, OR CARRY ANY WEIGHT.

A WEIGHT can never be lifted up or carried by any man, if he do not throw more than an equal weight of his own on the opposite side.

CHAP. LXVI.

THE EQUILIBRIUM OF A MAN STANDING UPON HIS FEET, PLATE VI.

The weight of a man resting upon one leg will always be equally divided on each side of the central or perpendicular line of gravity, which supports him.

CHAP. LXVII.

OF WALKING, PLATE VII.

A MAN walking will always have the centre of gravity over the centre of the leg which rests upon the ground.

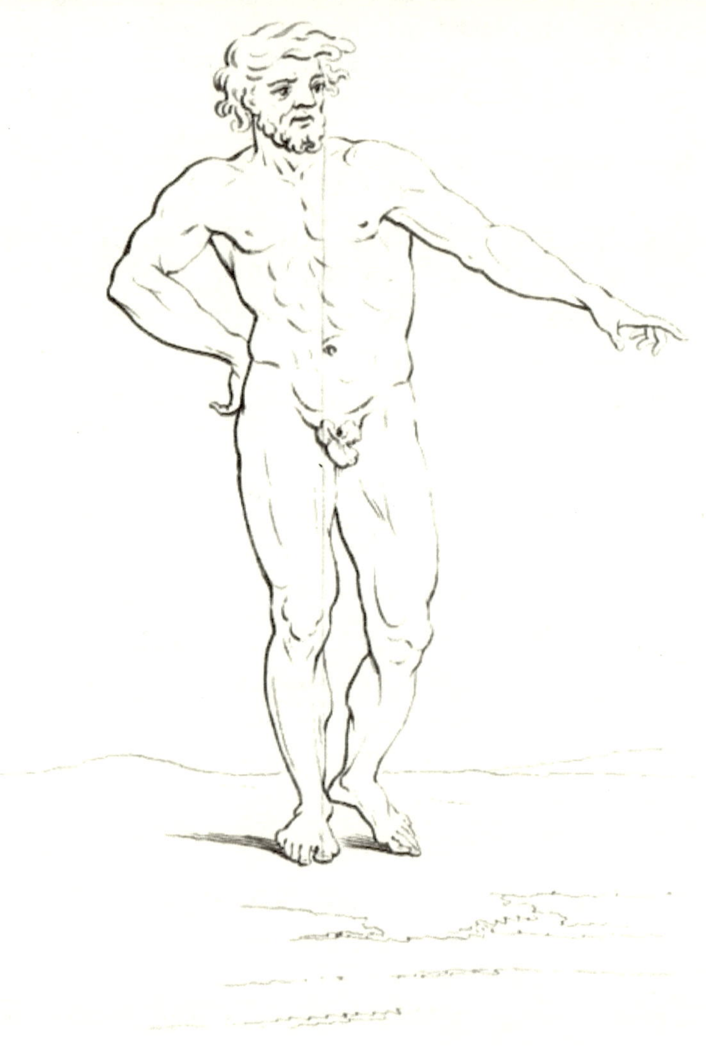

Chap. 66.

PLATE 6.

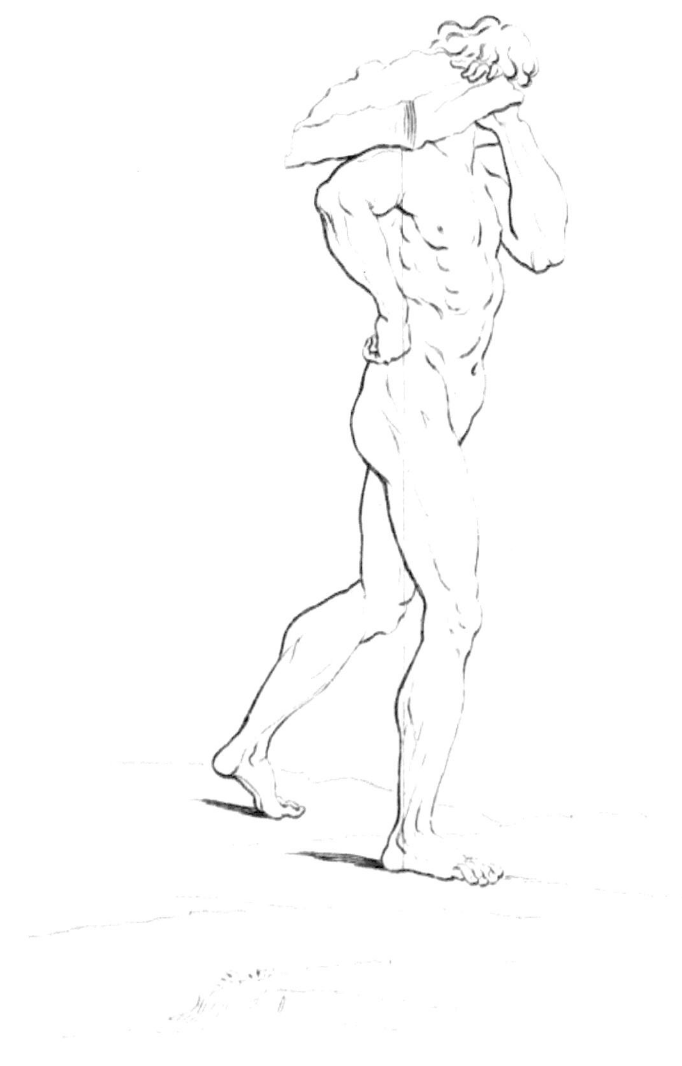

Chap. 67.

PLATE 7.

CHAP. LXVIII.

OF THE CENTRE OF GRAVITY IN MEN AND ANIMALS.

THE legs, or centre of support, in men and animals, will approach nearer to the centre of gravity, in proportion to the slowness of their motion; and, on the contrary, when the motion is quicker, they will be farther removed from that perpendicular line.

CHAP. LXIX.

OF THE CORRESPONDING THICKNESS OF PARTS ON EACH SIDE OF THE BODY.

THE thickness or breadth of the parts in the human body will never be equal on each side, if the corresponding members do not move equally and alike.

CHAP. LXX.

OF THE MOTIONS OF ANIMALS.

ALL bipeds in their motions lower the part immediately over the foot that is raised, more than over that resting on the ground, and the highest parts do just the contrary. This is observable in the hips and shoulders of a man when he walks; and also in birds in the head and rump.

CHAP. LXXI.

OF QUADRUPEDS AND THEIR MOTIONS.

THE highest parts of quadrupeds are susceptible of more variation when they walk, than when they are still, in a greater or less degree, in proportion to their size. This proceeds from the oblique position of their legs when they touch the ground, which raise the animal when they become straight and perpendicular upon the ground.

CHAP. LXXII.

OF THE QUICKNESS OR SLOWNESS OF MOTION.

THE motion performed by a man, or any other animal whatever, in walking, will have more or less velocity as the centre of their weight is more or less removed from the centre of that foot upon which they are supported.

CHAP. LXXIII.

OF THE MOTION OF ANIMALS.

THAT figure will appear the swiftest in its course which leans the most forwards.

Any body, moving of itself, will do it with more or less velocity in proportion as the centre of its gravity is more or less removed from the centre of its support. This is mentioned chiefly in regard to the motion of birds, which, without any clapping of their wings, or assistance of wind, move themselves. This happens when the centre of their gravity is out of the centre of their support, viz. out of its usual residence, the middle between the two wings. Because, if the middle of the wings be more backward than the centre of the whole weight, the bird will move forwards and downwards, in a greater or less degree as the centre of its weight is more or less removed from the middle of its wings. From which it follows, that if the centre of gravity be far removed from the other centre, the descent of the bird will be very oblique; but if that centre be near the middle of the wings, the descent will have very little obliquity.

CHAP. LXXIV.

OF A FIGURE MOVING AGAINST THE WIND, PLATE VIII.

A MAN moving against the wind in any direction does not keep his centre of gravity duly disposed upon the centre of support[228].

CHAP. LXXV.

OF THE BALANCE OF A FIGURE RESTING UPON ITS FEET.

THE man who rests upon his feet, either bears the weight of his body upon them equally, or unequally. If equally, it will be with some accidental weight, or simply with his own; if it be with an additional weight, the opposite extremities of his members will not be equally distant from the perpendicular of his feet. But if he simply carries his own weight, the opposite extremities will be equally distant from the perpendicular of his feet: and on this subject of gravity I shall write a separate book[229].

---

[228] See chap. lxiv.
[229] See in this work from chap. lx. to lxxxi.

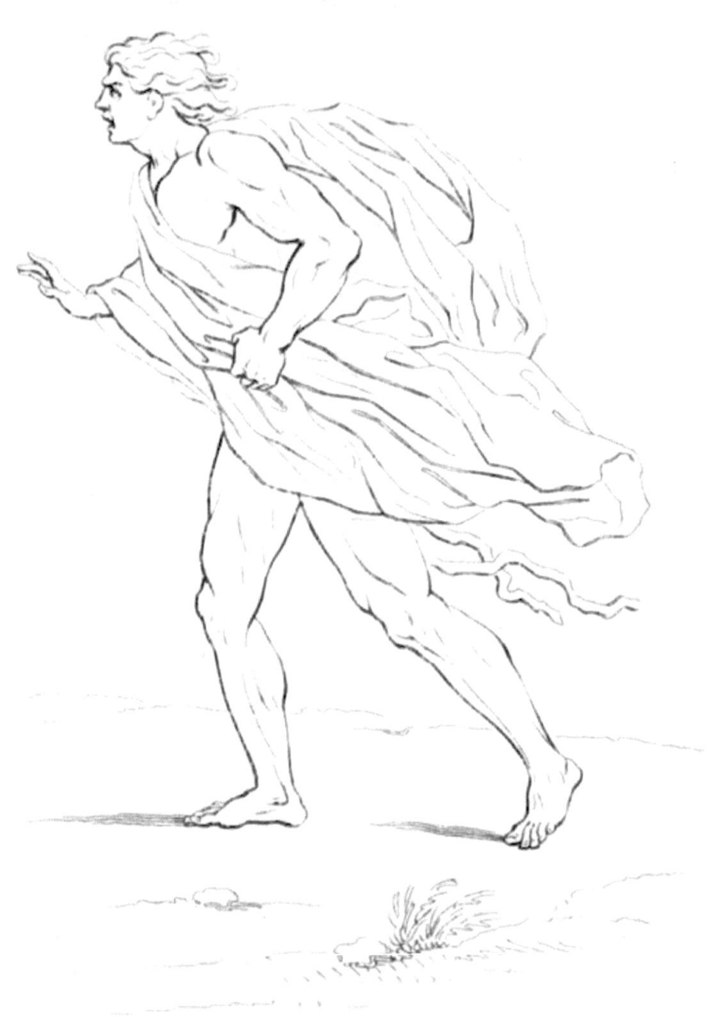

Page 29.

Chap. 74.

PLATE 8.

CHAP. LXXVI.

A PRECEPT.

THE navel is always in the central or middle line of the body, which passes through the pit of the stomach to that of the neck, and must have as much weight, either accidental or natural, on one side of the human figure as on the other. This is demonstrated by extending the arm, the wrist of which performs the office of a weight at the end of a steelyard; and will require some weight to be thrown on the other side of the navel, to counterbalance that of the wrist. It is on that account that the heel is often raised.

CHAP. LXXVII.

OF A MAN STANDING, BUT RESTING MORE UPON ONE FOOT THAN THE OTHER.

AFTER a man, by standing long, has tired the leg upon which he rests, he sends part of his weight upon the other leg. But this kind of posture is to be employed only for old age, infancy, or extreme lassitude, because it expresses weariness, or very little power in the limbs. For that reason, a young man, strong and healthy, will always rest upon one of his legs, and if he removes a little of his weight upon the other, it is only a necessary preparative to motion, without which it is impossible to move; as we have proved before, that motion proceeds from inequality[230].

CHAP. LXXVIII.

OF THE BALANCE OF FIGURES, PLATE IX.

IF the figure rests upon one foot, the shoulder on that side will always be lower than the other; and the pit of the neck will fall perpendicularly over the middle of that leg which supports the body. The same will happen in whatever other view we see that figure, when it has not the arm much extended, nor any weight on its back, in its hand, or on its shoulder, and when it does not, either behind or before, throw out that leg which does not support the body.

---

[230] See chapters lxi. lxiv.

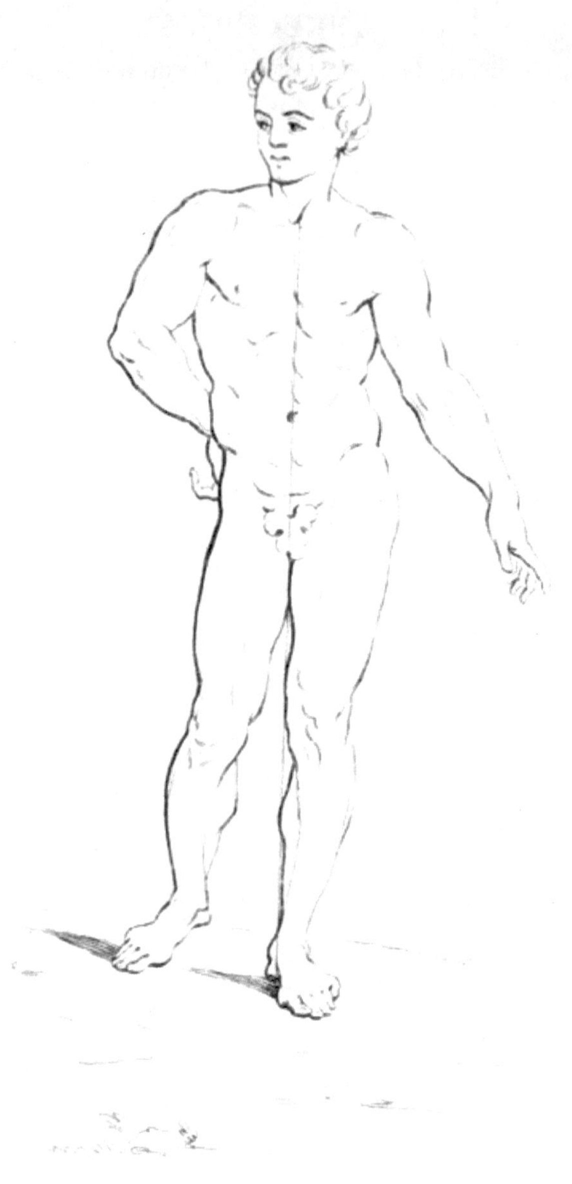

Chap. 78.

PLATE 9.

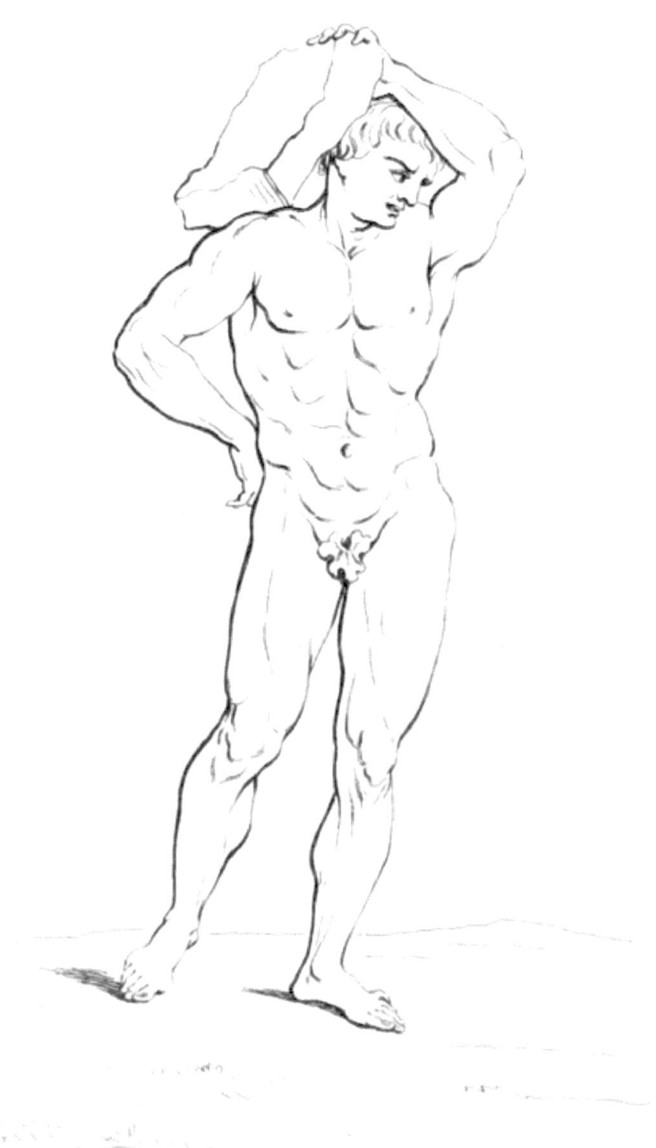

Chap. 80.

PLATE 10.

CHAP. LXXIX.

IN WHAT MANNER EXTENDING ONE ARM ALTERS THE BALANCE.

THE extending of the arm, which was bent, removes the weight of the figure upon the foot which bears the weight of the whole body: as is observable in rope-dancers, who dance upon the rope with their arms open, without any pole.

CHAP. LXXX.

OF A MAN BEARING A WEIGHT ON HIS SHOULDERS, PLATE X.

THE shoulder which bears the weight is always higher than the other. This is seen in the figure opposite, in which the centre line passes through the whole, with an equal weight on each side, to the leg on which it rests. If the weight were not equally divided on each side of this central line of gravity, the whole would fall to the ground. But Nature has provided, that as much of the natural weight of the man should be thrown on one side, as of accidental weight on the other, to form a counterpoise. This is effected by the man's bending, and leaning on the side not loaded, so as to form an equilibrium to the accidental weight he carries; and this cannot be done, unless the loaded shoulder be raised, and the other lowered. This is the resource with which Nature has furnished a man on such occasions.

CHAP. LXXXI.

OF EQUILIBRIUM.

ANY figure bearing an additional weight out of the central line, must throw as much natural or accidental weight on the opposite side as is sufficient to form a counterpoise round that line, which passes from the pit of the neck, through the whole mass of weight, to that part of the foot which rests upon the ground. We observe, that when a man lifts a weight with one arm, he naturally throws out the opposite arm; and if that be not enough to form an equipoise, he will add as much of his own weight, by bending his body, as will enable him to resist such accidental load. We see also, that a man ready to fall sideways and backwards at the same time, always throws out the arm on the opposite side.

CHAP. LXXXII.

OF MOTION.

WHETHER a man moves with velocity or slowness, the parts above the leg which sustains the weight, will always be lower than the others on the opposite side.

CHAP. LXXXIII.

THE LEVEL OF THE SHOULDERS.

THE shoulders or sides of a man, or any other animal, will preserve less of their level, in proportion to the slowness of their motion; and, *vice versâ*, those parts will lose less of their level when the motion is quicker. This is proved by the ninth proposition, treating of local motions, where it is said, any weight will press in the direction of the line of its motion; therefore the whole moving towards any one point, the parts belonging to it will follow the shortest line of the motion of its whole, without giving any of its weight to the collateral parts of the whole.

CHAP. LXXXIV.

OBJECTION TO THE ABOVE ANSWERED, PLATE XI. AND XII.

IT has been objected, in regard to the first part of the above proposition, that it does not follow that a man standing still, or moving slowly, has his members always in perfect balance upon the centre of gravity; because we do not find that Nature always follows that rule, but, on the contrary, the figure will sometimes bend sideways, standing upon one foot; sometimes it will rest part of its weight upon that leg which is bent at the knee, as is seen in the figures B C. But I shall reply thus, that what is not performed by the shoulders in the figure C, is done by the hip, as is demonstrated in another place.

CHAP. LXXXV.

OF THE POSITION OF FIGURES, PLATE XIII.

IN the same proportion as that part of the naked figure marked D A, lessens in height from the shoulder to the hip, on account of its position the opposite side increases. And this is the reason: the figure resting upon one (suppose the left) foot, that foot becomes the centre of all the weight above; and the pit of the neck, formed by the junction of the two Clavicles, quits also its natural situation at the upper extremity of the perpendicular line (which passes through the middle surface of the body), to bend over the same foot; and as this line bends with it, it forces the transverse lines, which are always at right angles, to lower their extremities on that side where the foot rests, as appears in A B C. The navel and middle parts always preserve their natural height.

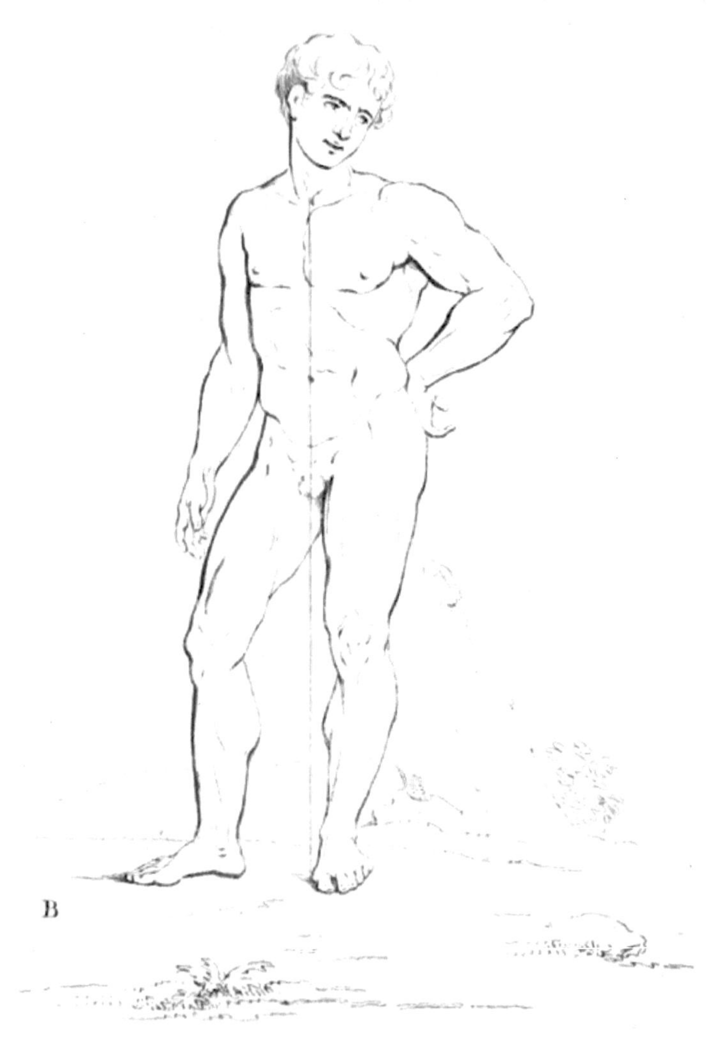

Page 35.

Chap. 84.

PLATE 11.

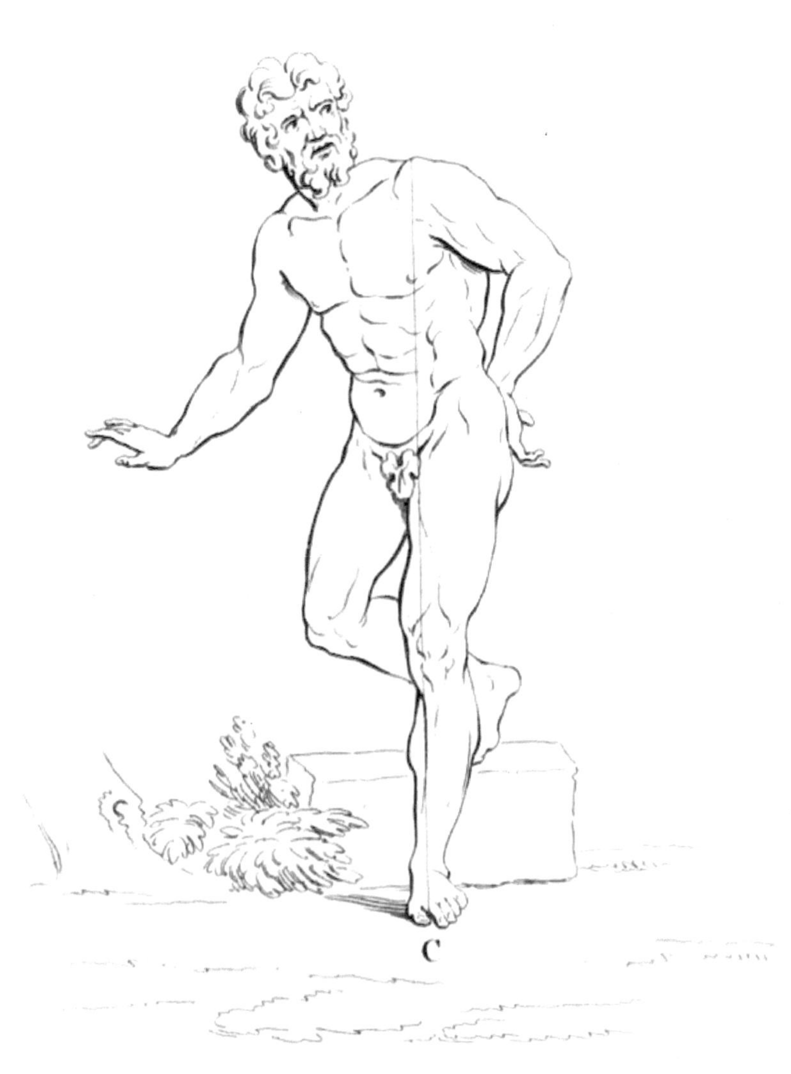

Page 35.

Chap. 84.

PLATE 12.

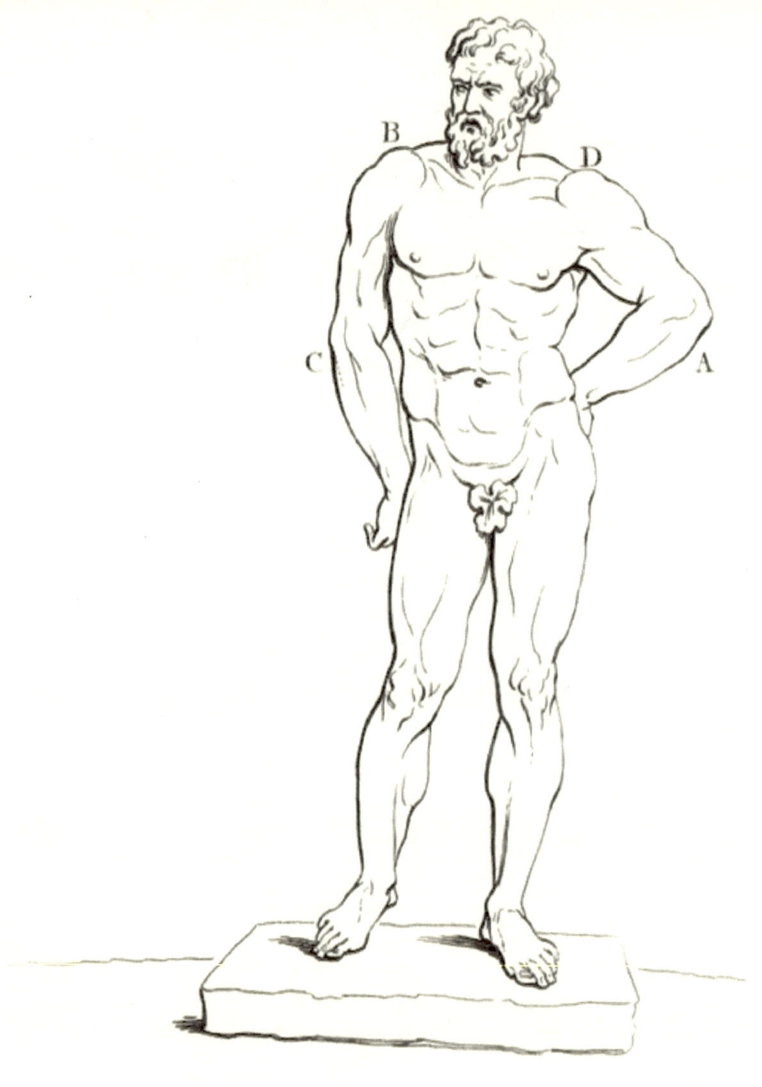

Chap. 85.

PLATE 13.

CHAP. LXXXVI.

OF THE JOINTS.

In the bending of the joints it is particularly useful to observe the difference and variety of shape they assume; how the muscles swell on one side, while they flatten on the other; and this is more apparent in the neck, because the motion of it is of three sorts, two of which are simple motions, and the other complex, participating also of the other two.

The simple motions are, first, when the neck bends towards the shoulder, either to the right or left, and when it raises or lowers the head. The second is, when it twists to the right or left, without rising or bending, but straight, with the head turned towards one of the shoulders. The third motion, which is called complex, is, when to the bending of it is added the twisting, as when the ear leans towards one of the shoulders, the head turning the same way, and the face turned upwards.

CHAP. LXXXVII.

OF THE SHOULDERS.

Of those which the shoulders can perform, simple motions are the principal, such as moving the arm upwards and downwards, backwards and forwards. Though one might almost call those motions infinite, for if the arm can trace a circle upon a wall, it will have performed all the motions belonging to the shoulders. Every continued quantity being divisible *ad infinitum*, and this circle being a continued quantity, produced by the motion of the arm going through every part of the circumference, it follows, that the motions of the shoulders may also be said to be infinite.

CHAP. LXXXVIII.

OF THE MOTIONS OF A MAN.

When you mean to represent a man removing a weight, consider that the motions are various, viz. either a simple motion, by bending himself to raise the weight from the ground upwards, or when he drags the weight after him, or pushes it before him, or pulls it down with a rope passing through a pulley. It is to be observed, that the weight of the man's body pulls the more in proportion as the centre of his gravity is removed from the centre of his support. To this must be added the strength of the effort that the legs and back make when they are bent, to return to their natural straight situation.

A man never ascends or descends, nor walks at all in any direction, without raising the heel of the back foot.

CHAP. LXXXIX.

OF THE DISPOSITION OF MEMBERS PREPARING TO ACT WITH GREAT FORCE, PLATE XIV.

WHEN a man prepares himself to strike a violent blow, he bends and twists his body as far as he can to the side contrary to that which he means to strike, and collecting all his strength, he, by a complex motion, returns and falls upon the point he has in view[231].

CHAP. XC.

OF THROWING ANY THING WITH VIOLENCE, PLATE XV.

A MAN throwing a dart, a stone, or any thing else with violence, may be represented, chiefly, two different ways; that is, he may be preparing to do it, or the act may be already performed. If you mean to place him in the act of preparation, the inside of the foot upon which he rests will be under the perpendicular line of the pit of the neck; and if it be the right foot, the left shoulder will be perpendicular over the toes of the same foot.

CHAP. XCI.

ON THE MOTION OF DRIVING ANY THING INTO OR DRAWING IT OUT OF THE GROUND.

HE who wishes to pitch a pole into the ground, or draw one out of it, will raise the leg and bend the knee opposite to the arm which acts, in order to balance himself upon the foot that rests, without which he could neither drive in, nor pull out any thing.

CHAP. XCII.

OF FORCIBLE MOTIONS, PLATE XVI.

OF the two arms, that will be most powerful in its effort, which, having been farthest removed from its natural situation, is assisted more strongly by the other parts to bring it to the place where it means to go. As the man A, who moves the arm with a club E, and brings it to the opposite side B, assisted by the motion of the whole body.

---

[231] See chapters civ. cliv.

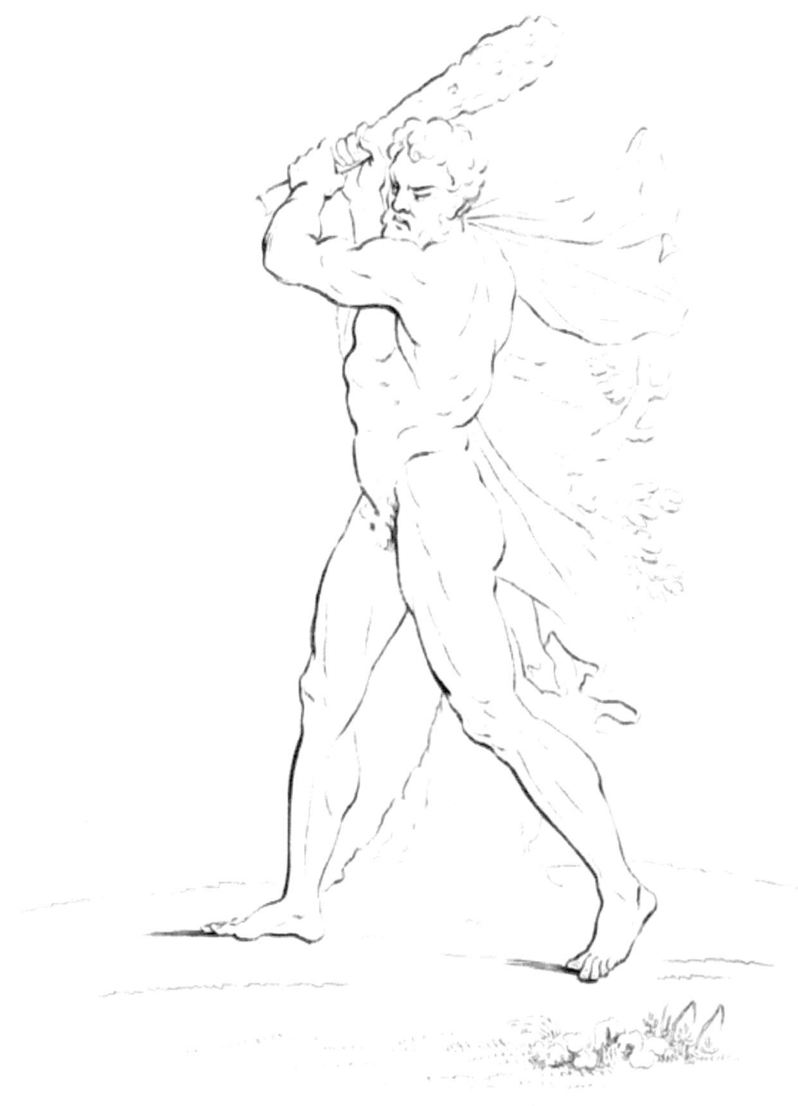

Chap. 89.

PLATE 14.

CHAP. XCIII.

THE ACTION OF JUMPING.

Nature will of itself, and without any reasoning in the mind of a man going to jump, prompt him to raise his arms and shoulders by a sudden motion, together with a great part of his body, and to lift them up high, till the power of the effort subsides. This impetuous motion is accompanied by an instantaneous extension of the body which had bent itself, like a spring or bow, along the back, the joints of the thighs, knees, and feet, and is let off obliquely, that is, upwards and forwards; so that the disposition of the body tending forwards and upwards, makes it describe a great arch when it springs up, which increases the leap.

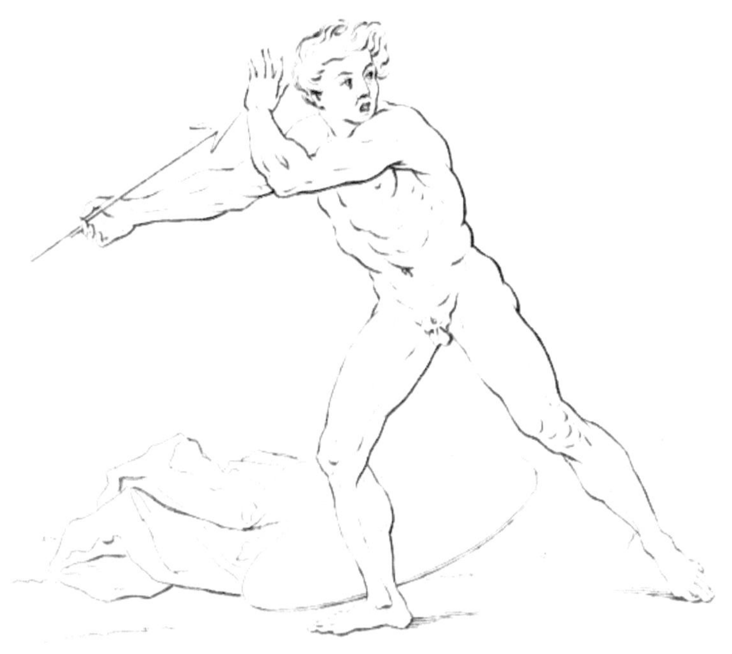

Page 40.

Chap. 90.

PLATE 15.

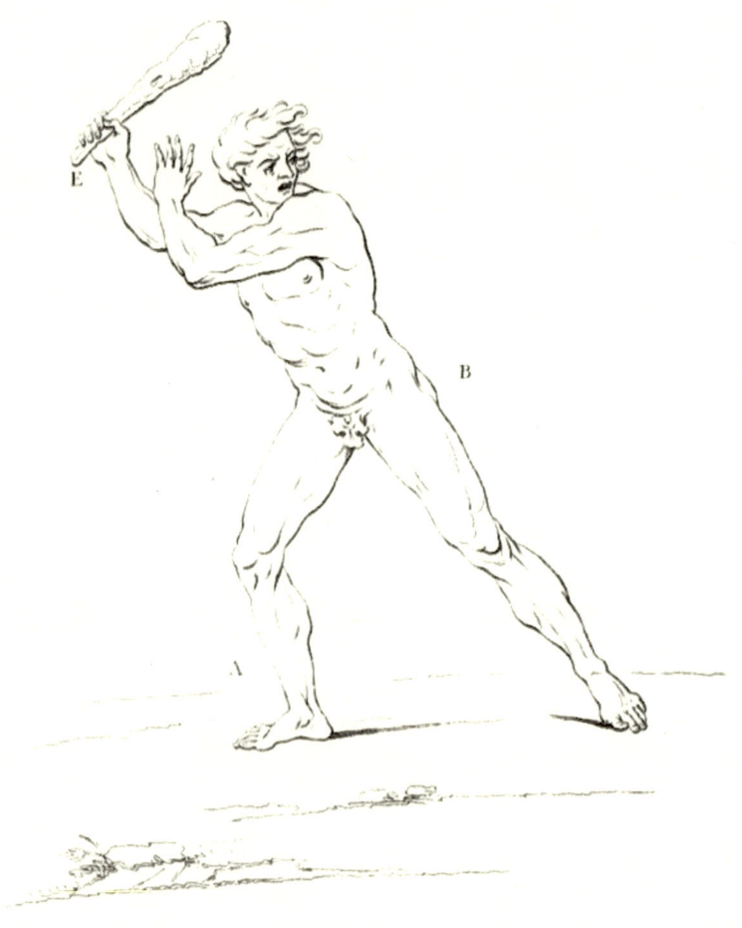

Page 40.

Chap. 92.

PLATE 16.

CHAP. XCIV.

OF THE THREE MOTIONS IN JUMPING UPWARDS.

WHEN a man jumps upwards, the motion of the head is three times quicker than that of the heel, before the extremity of the foot quits the ground, and twice as quick as that of the hips; because three angles are opened and extended at the same time: the superior one is that formed by the body at its joint with the thigh before, the second is at the joint of the thighs and legs behind, and the third is at the instep before[232].

CHAP. XCV.

OF THE EASY MOTIONS OF MEMBERS.

IN regard to the freedom and ease of motions, it is very necessary to observe, that when you mean to represent a figure which has to turn itself a little round, the feet and all the other members are not to move in the same direction as the head. But you will divide that motion among four joints, viz. the feet, the knees, the hips, and the neck. If it rests upon the right leg, the left knee should be a little bent inward, with its foot somewhat raised outward. The left shoulder should be lower than the other, and the nape of the neck turned on the same side as the outward ankle of the left foot, and the left shoulder perpendicular over the great toe of the right foot. And take it as a general maxim, that figures do not turn their heads straight with the chest, Nature having for our convenience formed the neck so as to turn with ease on every side, when the eyes want to look round; and to this the other joints are in some measure subservient. If the figure be sitting, and the arms have some employment across the body, the breast will turn over the joint of the hip.

CHAP. XCVI.

THE GREATEST TWIST WHICH A MAN CAN MAKE, IN TURNING TO LOOK AT HIMSELF BEHIND. PLATE XVII.

THE greatest twist that the body can perform is when the back of the heels and the front of the face are seen at the same time. It is not done without difficulty,

[232] The author here means to compare the different quickness of the motion of the head and the heel, when employed in the same action of jumping; and he states the proportion of the former to be three times that of the latter. The reason he gives for this is in substance, that as the head has but one motion to make, while in fact the lower part of the figure has three successive operations to perform at the places he mentions, three times the velocity, or, in other words, three times the degree of effort, is necessary in the head, the prime mover, to give the power of influencing the other parts; and the rule deducible from this axiom is, that where two different parts of the body concur in the same action, and one of them has to perform one motion only, while the other is to have several, the proportion of velocity or effort in the former must be regulated by the number of operations necessary in the latter.

and is effected by bending the leg and lowering the shoulder on that side towards which the head turns. The cause of this motion, and also which of the muscles move first and which last, I shall explain in my treatise on anatomy[233].

CHAP. XCVII.

OF TURNING THE LEG WITHOUT THE THIGH.

It is impossible to turn the leg inwards or outwards without turning the thigh by the same motion, because the setting in of the bones at the knee is such, that they have no motion but backwards and forwards, and no more than is necessary for walking or kneeling; never sideways, because the form of the bones at the joint of the knee does not allow it. If this joint had been made pliable on all sides, as that of the shoulder, or that of the thigh bone with the hip, a man would have had his legs bent on each side as often as backwards and forwards, and seldom or never straight with the thigh. Besides, this joint can bend only one way, so that in walking it can never go beyond the straight line of the leg; it bends only forwards, for if it could bend backwards, a man could never get up again upon his feet, if once he were kneeling; as when he means to get up from the kneeling posture (on both knees), he gives the whole weight of his body to one of the knees to support, unloading the other, which at that time feels no other weight than its own, and therefore is lifted up with ease, and rests his foot flat upon the ground; then returning the whole weight upon that foot, and leaning his hand upon his knee, he at once extends the other arm, raises his head, and straightening the thigh with the body, he springs up, and rests upon the same foot, while he brings up the other.

CHAP. XCVIII.

POSTURES OF FIGURES.

Figures that are set in a fixed attitude, are nevertheless to have some contrast of parts. If one arm come before, the other remains still or goes behind. If the figure rest upon one leg, the shoulder on that side will be lower than the other. This is observed by artists of judgment, who always take care to balance the figure well upon its feet, for fear it should appear to fall. Because by resting upon one foot, the other leg, being a little bent, does not support the body any more than if it were dead; therefore it is necessary that the parts above that leg should transfer the centre of their weight upon the leg which supports the body.

---

[233] It is explained in this work, or at least there is something respecting it in the preceding chapter, and in chap. cli.

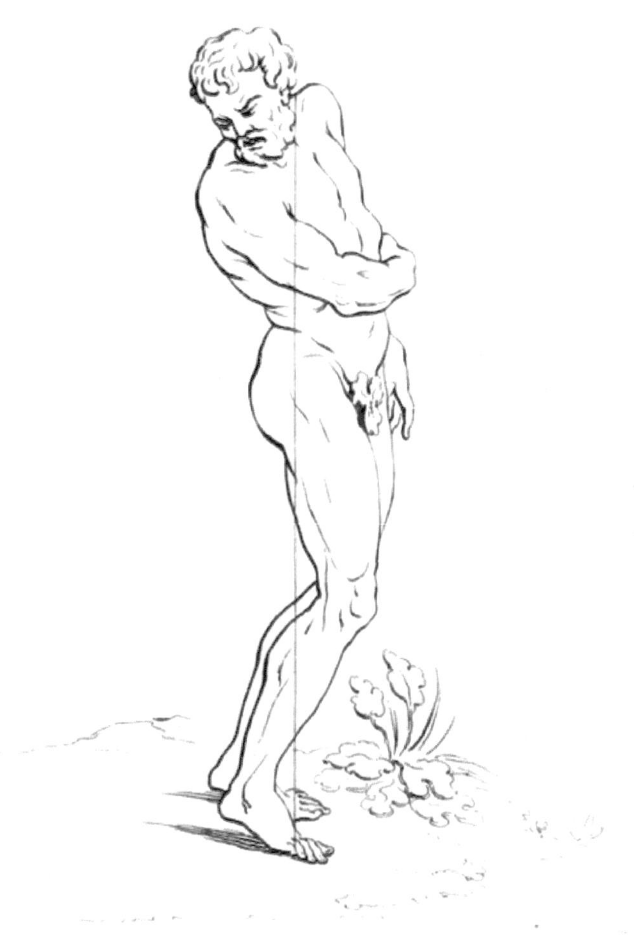

Chap. 96.

PLATE 17.

CHAP. XCIX.

OF THE GRACEFULNESS OF THE MEMBERS.

THE members are to be suited to the body in graceful motions, expressive of the meaning which the figure is intended to convey. If it had to give the idea of genteel and agreeable carriage, the members must be slender and well turned, but not lean; the muscles very slightly marked, indicating in a soft manner such as must necessarily appear; the arms, particularly, pliant, and no member in a straight line with any other adjoining member. If it happen, on account of the motion of the figure, that the right hip be higher than the left, make the joint of the shoulder fall perpendicularly on the highest part of that hip; and let that right shoulder be lower than the left. The pit of the neck will always be perpendicular over the middle of the instep of the foot that supports the body. The leg that does not bear will have its knee a little lower than the other, and near the other leg.

In regard to the positions of the head and arms, they are infinite, and for that reason I shall not enter into any detailed rule concerning them; suffice it to say, that they are to be easy and free, graceful, and varied in their bendings, so that they may not appear stiff like pieces of wood.

CHAP. C.

THAT IT IS IMPOSSIBLE FOR ANY MEMORY TO RETAIN THE ASPECTS AND CHANGES OF THE MEMBERS.

IT is impossible that any memory can be able to retain all the aspects or motions of any member of any animal whatever. This case we shall exemplify by the appearance of the hand. And because any continued quantity is divisible *ad infinitum*, the motion of the eye which looks at the hand, and moves from A to B, moves by a space A B, which is also a continued quantity, and consequently divisible *ad infinitum*, and in every part of the motion varies to its view the aspect and figure of the hand; and so it will do if it move round the whole circle. The same will the hand do which is raised in its motion, that is, it will pass over a space, which is a continued quantity[234].

---

[234] The eyeball moving up and down to look at the hand, describes a part of a circle, from every point of which it sees it in an infinite variety of aspects. The hand also is moveable *ad infinitum* (for it can go round the whole circle—see chap. lxxxvii.), and consequently shew itself in an infinite variety of aspects, which it is impossible for any memory to retain.

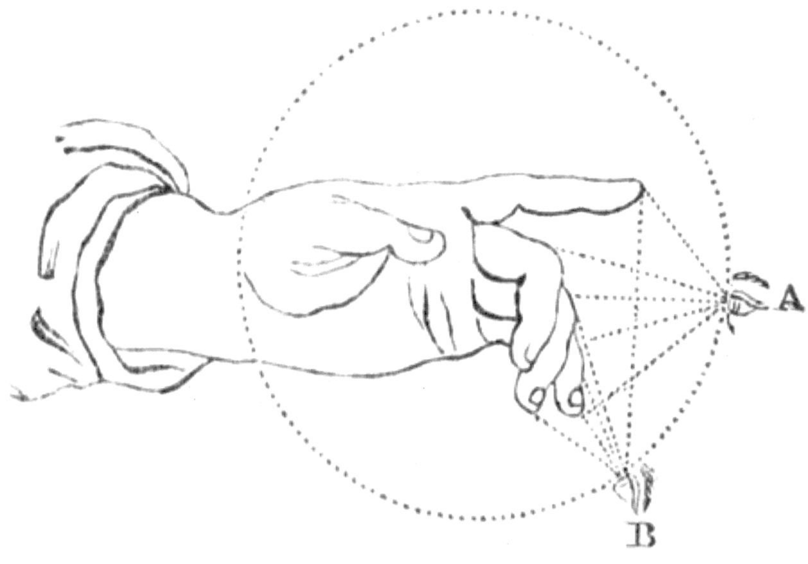

CHAP. CI.

THE MOTIONS OF FIGURES.

NEVER put the head straight upon the shoulders, but a little turned sideways to the right or left, even though the figures should be looking up or down, or straight, because it is necessary to give them some motion of life and spirit. Nor ever compose a figure in such a manner, either in a front or back view, as that every part falls straight upon another from the top to the bottom. But if you wish to introduce such a figure, use it for old age. Never repeat the same motion of arms, or of legs, not only not in the same figure, but in those which are standing by, or near; if the necessity of the case, or the expression of the subject you represent, do not oblige you to it[235].

CHAP. CII.

OF COMMON MOTIONS.

THE variety of motions in man are equal to the variety of accidents or thoughts affecting the mind, and each of these thoughts, or accidents, will operate more or less, according to the temper and age of the subject; for the same cause will in the actions of youth, or of old age, produce very different effects.

---

[235] See chap. xx. clv.

CHAP. CIII.

OF SIMPLE MOTIONS.

SIMPLE motion is that which a man performs in merely bending backwards or forwards.

CHAP. CIV.

COMPLEX MOTION.

COMPLEX motion is that which, to produce some particular action, requires the body to bend downwards and sideways at the same time. The painter must be careful in his compositions to apply these complex motions according to the nature of the subject, and not to weaken or destroy the effect of it by introducing figures with simple motions, without any connexion with the subject.

CHAP. CV.

MOTIONS APPROPRIATED TO THE SUBJECT.

THE motions of your figures are to be expressive of the quantity of strength requisite to the force of the action. Let not the same effort be used to take up a stick as would easily raise a piece of timber. Therefore shew great variety in the expression of strength, according to the quality of the load to be managed.

CHAP. CVI.

APPROPRIATE MOTIONS.

THERE are some emotions of the mind which are not expressed by any particular motion of the body, while in others, the expression cannot be shewn without it. In the first, the arms fall down, the hands and all the other parts, which in general are the most active, remain at rest. But such emotions of the soul as produce bodily action, must put the members into such motions as are appropriated to the intention of the mind. This, however, is an ample subject, and we have a great deal to say upon it. There is a third kind of motion, which participates of the two already described; and a fourth, which depends neither on the one nor the other. This last belongs to insensibility, or fury, and should be ranked with madness or stupidity; and so adapted only to grotesque or Moresco work.

CHAP. CVII.

OF THE POSTURES OF WOMEN AND YOUNG PEOPLE.

IT is not becoming in women and young people to have their legs too much asunder, because it denotes boldness; while the legs close together shew modesty.

CHAP. CVIII.

OF THE POSTURES OF CHILDREN.

CHILDREN and old people are not to express quick motions, in what concerns their legs.

CHAP. CIX.

OF THE MOTION OF THE MEMBERS.

LET every member be employed in performing its proper functions. For instance, in a dead body, or one asleep, no member should appear alive or awake. A foot bearing the weight of the whole body, should not be playing its toes up and down, but flat upon the ground; except when it rests entirely upon the heel.

CHAP. CX.

OF MENTAL MOTIONS.

A MERE thought, or operation of the mind, excites only simple and easy motions of the body; not this way, and that way, because its object is in the mind, which does not affect the senses when it is collected within itself.

CHAP. CXI.

EFFECT OF THE MIND UPON THE MOTIONS OF THE BODY, OCCASIONED BY SOME OUTWARD OBJECT.

WHEN the motion is produced by the presence of some object, either the cause is immediate or not. If it be immediate, the figure will first turn towards it the organs most necessary, the eyes; leaving its feet in the same place; and will only move the thighs, hips, and knees a little towards the same side, to which the eyes are directed.

LINEAR PERSPECTIVE.

CHAP. CXII.

OF THOSE WHO APPLY THEMSELVES TO THE PRACTICE, WITHOUT HAVING LEARNT THE THEORY OF THE ART.

THOSE who become enamoured of the practice of the art, without having previously applied to the diligent study of the scientific part of it, may be compared to mariners, who put to sea in a ship without rudder or compass, and therefore cannot be certain of arriving at the wished-for port.

Practice must always be founded on good theory; to this, Perspective is the guide and entrance, without which nothing can be well done.

CHAP. CXIII.

PRECEPTS IN PAINTING.

PERSPECTIVE is to Painting what the bridle is to a horse, and the rudder to a ship.

The size of a figure should denote the distance at which it is situated.

If a figure be seen of the natural size, remember that it denotes its being near to the eye.

CHAP. CXIV.

OF THE BOUNDARIES OF OBJECTS CALLED OUTLINES OR CONTOURS.

THE outlines or contours of bodies are so little perceivable, that at any small distance between that and the object, the eye will not be able to recognise the features of a friend or relation, if it were not for their clothes and general appearance. So that by the knowledge of the whole it comes to know the parts.

CHAP. CXV.

OF LINEAR PERSPECTIVE.

LINEAR Perspective consists in giving, by established rules, the true dimensions of objects, according to their respective distances; so that the second object be less than the first, the third than the second, and by degrees at last they become invisible. I find by experience, that, if the second object be at the same distance from the first, as the first is from the eye, though they be of the same size, the second will appear half the size of the first; and, if the third be at the same distance behind the second, it will diminish two thirds; and so on, by degrees, they will, at equal distances, diminish in proportion; provided that the interval be not more than twenty cubits[236]; at which distance it will lose two fourths of its size: at forty it will diminish three fourths; and at sixty it will lose five sixths, and so on progressively. But you must be distant from your picture twice the size of it; for, if you be only once the size, it will make a great difference in the measure from the first to the second.

CHAP. CXVI.

WHAT PARTS OF OBJECTS DISAPPEAR FIRST BY DISTANCE.

THOSE parts which are of less magnitude will first vanish from the sight[237]. This happens, because the shape of small objects, at an equal distance, comes to the eye under a more acute angle than the large ones, and the perception of them is less, in proportion as they are less in magnitude. It follows then, that if the large objects, by being removed to a great distance, and consequently coming to the eye by a small angle, are almost lost to the sight, the small objects will entirely disappear.

CHAP. CXVII.

OF REMOTE OBJECTS.

THE outlines of objects will be less seen, in proportion as they are more distant from the eye.

CHAP. CXVIII.

OF THE POINT OF SIGHT.

THE point of sight must be on a level with the eyes of a common-sized man, and placed upon the horizon, which is the line formed by a flat country terminating with the sky. An exception must be made as to mountains, which are above

[236] About thirteen yards of our measure, the Florentine braccia, or cubit, by which the author measures, being 1 foot 10 inches 7-8ths English measure.

[237] See chap. cxxi. and cccv.

that line.

CHAP. CXIX.

A PICTURE IS TO BE VIEWED FROM ONE POINT ONLY.

This will be proved by one single example. If you mean to represent a round ball very high up, on a flat and perpendicular wall, it will be necessary to make it oblong, like the shape of an egg, and to place yourself (that is, the eye, or point of view) so far back, as that its outline or circumference may appear round.

CHAP. CXX.

OF THE DIMENSIONS OF THE FIRST FIGURE IN AN HISTORICAL PAINTING.

The first figure in your picture will be less than Nature, in proportion as it recedes from the front of the picture, or the bottom line; and by the same rule the others behind it will go on lessening in an equal degree[238].

CHAP. CXXI.

OF OBJECTS THAT ARE LOST TO THE SIGHT IN PROPORTION TO THEIR DISTANCE.

The first things that disappear, by being removed to some distance, are the outlines or boundaries of objects. The second, as they remove farther, are the shadows which divide contiguous bodies. The third are the thickness of legs and feet; and so in succession the small parts are lost to the sight, till nothing remains but a confused mass, without any distinct parts.

CHAP. CXXII.

ERRORS NOT SO EASILY SEEN IN SMALL OBJECTS AS IN LARGE ONES.

Supposing this small object to represent a man, or any other animal, although the parts, by being so much diminished or reduced, cannot be executed with the same exactness of proportion, nor finished with the same accuracy, as if on a larger scale, yet on that very account the faults will be less conspicuous. For example, if you look at a man at the distance of two hundred yards, and with all due attention

[238] It is supposed that the figures are to appear of the natural size, and not bigger. In that case, the measure of the first, to be of the exact dimension, should have its feet resting upon the bottom line; but as you remove it from that, it should diminish.

No allusion is here intended to the distance at which a picture is to be placed from the eye.

mean to form a judgment, whether he be handsome or ugly, deformed or well made, you will find that, with all your endeavours, you can hardly venture to decide. The reason is, that the man diminishes so much by the distance, that it is impossible to distinguish the parts minutely. If you wish to know by demonstration the diminution of the above figure, hold your finger up before your eye at about nine inches distance, so that the top of your finger corresponds with the top of the head of the distant figure: you will perceive that your finger covers, not only its head, but part of its body; which is an evident proof of the apparent diminution of that object. Hence it often happens, that we are doubtful, and can scarcely, at some distance, distinguish the form of even a friend.

CHAP. CXXIII.

HISTORICAL SUBJECTS ONE ABOVE ANOTHER ON THE SAME WALL TO BE AVOIDED.

This custom, which has been generally adopted by painters, on the front and sides of chapels, is much to be condemned. They begin with an historical picture, its landscape and buildings, in one compartment. After which, they raise another compartment, and execute another history with other buildings upon another level; and from thence they proceed to a third and fourth, varying the point of sight, as if the beholder was going up steps, while, in fact, he must look at them all from below, which is very ill judged in those matters.

We know that the point of sight is the eye of the spectator; and if you ask, how is a series of subjects, such as the life of a saint, to be represented, in different compartments on the same wall? I answer, that you are to place the principal event in the largest compartment, and make the point of sight as high as the eye of the spectator. Begin that subject with large figures; and as you go up, lessen the objects, as well the figures, as buildings, varying the plans according to the effect of perspective; but never varying the point of sight: and so complete the series of subjects, till you come to a certain height, where terrestrial objects can be seen no more, except the tops of trees, or clouds and birds; or if you introduce figures, they must be aerial, such as angels, or saints in glory, or the like, if they suit the purpose of your history. If not, do not undertake this kind of painting, for your work will be faulty, and justly reprehensible[239].

---

[239] The author does not mean here to say, that one historical picture cannot be hung over another. It certainly may, because, in viewing each, the spectator is at liberty (especially if they are subjects independent of each other) to shift his place so as to stand at the true point of sight for viewing every one of them; but in covering a wall with a succession of subjects from the same history, the author considers the whole as, in fact, but one picture, divided into compartments, and to be seen at one view, and which cannot therefore admit more than one point of sight. In the former case, the pictures are in fact so many distinct subjects unconnected with each other.

CHAP. CXXIV.

WHY OBJECTS IN PAINTING CAN NEVER DETACH, AS NATURAL OBJECTS DO.

PAINTERS often despair of being able to imitate Nature, from observing, that their pictures have not the same relief, nor the same life, as natural objects have in a looking-glass, though they both appear upon a plain surface. They say, they have colours which surpass in brightness the quality of the lights, and in darkness the quality of the shades of the objects seen in the looking-glass; but attribute this circumstance to their own ignorance, and not to the true cause, because they do not know it. It is impossible that objects in painting should appear with the same relief as those in the looking-glass, unless we look at them with only one eye.

The reason is this. The two eyes A B looking at objects one behind another, as M and N, see them both; because M cannot entirely occupy the space of N, by reason that the base of the visual rays is so broad, that the second object is seen behind the first. But if one eye be shut, and you look with the other S, the body F will entirely cover the body R, because the visual rays beginning at one point, form a triangle, of which the body F is the base, and being prolonged, they form two diverging tangents at the two extremities of F, which cannot touch the body R behind it, therefore can never see it[240].

[240] See chap. cccxlviii.

This chapter is obscure, and may probably be made clear by merely stating it in other words. Leonardo objects to the use of both eyes, because, in viewing in that manner the objects here mentioned, two balls, one behind the other, the second is seen, which would not be the case, if the angle of the visual rays were not too big for the first object. Whoever is at all acquainted with optics, need not be told, that the visual rays commence in a single point in the centre, or nearly the centre of each eye, and continue diverging. But, in using both eyes, the visual rays proceed not from one and the same centre, but from a different centre in each eye, and intersecting each other, as they do a little before passing the first object, they become together broader than the extent of the first object, and consequently give a view of part of the second. On the contrary, in using but one eye, the visual rays proceed but from one centre; and as, therefore, there cannot be any intersection, the visual rays, when they reach the first object, are not broader than the first object, and the second is completely hidden. Properly speaking, therefore, in using both eyes we introduce more than one point of sight, which renders the perspective false in the painting; but in using one eye only, there can be, as there ought, but one point of sight. There is, however, this difference between viewing real objects and those represented in painting, that in looking at the former, whether we use one or both eyes, the objects, by being actually detached from the back ground, admit the visual rays to strike on them, so as to form a correct perspective, from whatever point they are viewed, and the eye accordingly forms a perspective of its own; but in viewing the latter, there is no possibility of varying the perspective; and, unless the picture is seen precisely under the same angle as it was painted under, the perspective in all other views must be false. This is observable in the perspective views painted for scenes at the playhouse. If the beholder is seated in the central line of the house, whether in the boxes or pit, the perspective is correct; but, in proportion as he is placed at a greater or less distance to the right or left of that line, the perspective appears to him more or less faulty. And hence arises the necessity of using but one eye in viewing a painting, in order thereby to reduce it to one point of sight.

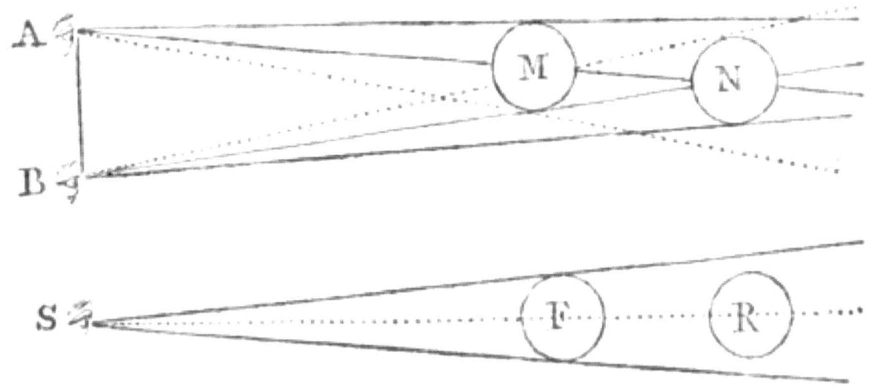

CHAP. CXXV.

HOW TO GIVE THE PROPER DIMENSION TO OBJECTS IN PAINTING.

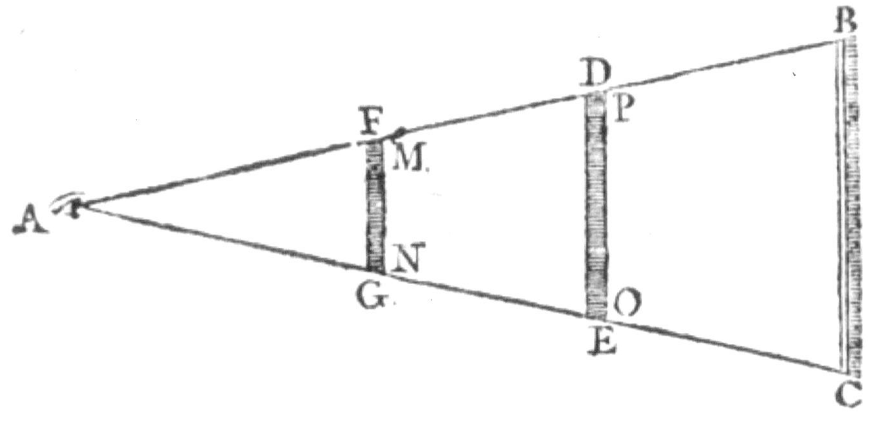

IN order to give the appearance of the natural size, if the piece be small (as miniatures), the figures on the fore-ground are to be finished with as much precision as those of any large painting, because being small they are to be brought up close to the eye. But large paintings are seen at some distance; whence it happens, that though the figures in each are so different in size, in appearance they will be the same. This proceeds from the eye receiving those objects under the same angle; and it is proved thus. Let the large painting be B C, the eye A, and D E a pane of glass, through which are seen the figures situated at B C. I say that the eye being fixed, the figures in the copy of the paintings B C are to be smaller, in proportion as the glass D E is nearer the eye A, and are to be as precise and finished. But if you will execute the picture B C upon the glass D E, this ought to be less finished than the picture B C, and more so than the figure M N transferred upon the glass F G; because, supposing the figure P O to be as much finished as the natural one in B C, the perspective of O P would be false, since, though in regard to the diminution of the figure it would be right, B C being diminished in P O, the finishing would not agree with the distance, because in giving it the perfection of the natural B C, B C would appear as near as O P; but, if you search for the diminution of O P, O P will be found at the distance B C, and the diminution of the finishing as at F G.

CHAP. CXXVI.

HOW TO DRAW ACCURATELY ANY PARTICULAR SPOT.

Take a glass as large as your paper, fasten it well between your eye and the object you mean to draw, and fixing your head in a frame (in such a manner as not to be able to move it) at the distance of two feet from the glass; shut one eye, and draw with a pencil accurately upon the glass all that you see through it. After that, trace upon paper what you have drawn on the glass, which tracing you may paint at pleasure, observing the aerial perspective.

CHAP. CXXVII.

DISPROPORTION TO BE AVOIDED, EVEN IN THE ACCESSORY PARTS.

A great fault is committed by many painters, which is highly to be blamed, that is, to represent the habitations of men, and other parts of their compositions, so low, that the doors do not reach as high as the knees of their inhabitants, though, according to their situation, they are nearer to the eye of the spectator, than the men who seem willing to enter them. I have seen some pictures with porticos, supported by columns loaded with figures; one grasping a column against which it leans, as if it were a walking-stick, and other similar errors, which are to be avoided with the greatest care.

INVENTION, OR COMPOSITION.

INVENTION, OR COMPOSITION.

CHAP. CXXVIII.

PRECEPT FOR AVOIDING A BAD CHOICE IN THE STYLE OR PROPORTION OF FIGURES.

The painter ought to form his style upon the most proportionate model in Nature; and after having measured that, he ought to measure himself also, and be perfectly acquainted with his own defects or deficiencies; and having acquired this knowledge, his constant care should be to avoid conveying into his work those defects which he has found in his own person; for these defects, becoming habitual to his observation, mislead his judgment, and he perceives them no longer. We ought, therefore, to struggle against such a prejudice, which grows up with us; for the mind, being fond of its own habitation, is apt to represent it to our imagination as beautiful. From the same motive it may be, that there is not a woman, however plain in her person, who may not find her admirer, if she be not a monster. Against this bent of the mind you ought very cautiously to be on your guard.

CHAP. CXXIX.

VARIETY IN FIGURES.

A painter ought to aim at universal excellence; for he will be greatly wanting in dignity, if he do one thing well and another badly, as many do, who study only the naked figure, measured and proportioned by a pair of compasses in their hands, and do not seek for variety. A man may be well proportioned, and yet be tall or short, large or lean, or of a middle size; and whoever does not make great use of these varieties, which are all existing in Nature in its most perfect state, will produce figures as if cast in one and the same mould, which is highly reprehensible.

CHAP. CXXX.

HOW A PAINTER OUGHT TO PROCEED IN HIS STUDIES.

The painter ought always to form in his mind a kind of system of reasoning or discussion within himself on any remarkable object before him. He should stop, take notes, and form some rule upon it; considering the place, the circumstances, the lights and shadows.

CHAP. CXXXI.
OF SKETCHING HISTORIES AND FIGURES.

SKETCHES of historical subjects must be slight, attending only to the situation of the figures, without regard to the finishing of particular members, which may be done afterwards at leisure, when the mind is so disposed.

CHAP. CXXXII.
HOW TO STUDY COMPOSITION.

THE young student should begin by sketching slightly some single figure, and turn that on all sides, knowing already how to contract, and how to extend the members; after which, he may put two together in various attitudes, we will suppose in the act of fighting boldly. This composition also he must try on all sides, and in a variety of ways, tending to the same expression. Then he may imagine one of them very courageous, while the other is a coward. Let these attitudes, and many other accidental affections of the mind, be with great care studied, examined, and dwelt upon.

CHAP. CXXXIII.
OF THE ATTITUDES OF MEN.

THE attitudes and all the members are to be disposed in such a manner, that by them the intentions of the mind may be easily discovered.

CHAP. CXXXIV.
VARIETY OF POSITIONS.

THE positions of the human figure are to be adapted to the age and rank; and to be varied according to the difference of the sexes, men or women.

CHAP. CXXXV.
OF STUDIES FROM NATURE FOR HISTORY.

IT is necessary to consider well the situation for which the history is to be painted, particularly the height; and let the painter place accordingly the model, from which he means to make his studies for that historical picture; and set himself as much below the object, as the picture is to be above the eye of the spectator, otherwise the work will be faulty.

CHAP. CXXXVI.

OF THE VARIETY OF FIGURES IN HISTORY PAINTING.

History painting must exhibit variety in its fullest extent. In temper, size, complexion, actions, plumpness, leanness, thick, thin, large, small, rough, smooth, old age and youth, strong and muscular, weak, with little appearance of muscles, cheerfulness and melancholy. Some should be with curled hair, and some with straight; some short, some long, some quick in their motions, and some slow, with a variety of dresses and colours, according as the subject may require.

CHAP. CXXXVII.

OF VARIETY IN HISTORY.

A painter should delight in introducing great variety into his compositions, avoiding repetition, that by this fertility of invention he may attract and charm the eye of the beholder. If it be requisite according to the subject meant to be represented, that there should be a mixture of men differing in their faces, ages, and dress, grouped with women, children, dogs, and horses, buildings, hills and flat country; observe dignity and decorum in the principal figure; such as a king, magistrate, or philosopher, separating them from the low classes of the people. Mix not afflicted or weeping figures with joyful and laughing ones; for Nature dictates that the cheerful be attended by others of the same disposition of mind. Laughter is productive of laughter, and *vice versâ*.

CHAP. CXXXVIII.

OF THE AGE OF FIGURES.

Do not bring together a number of boys with as many old men, nor young men with infants, nor women with men; if the subject you mean to represent does not oblige you to it.

CHAP. CXXXIX.

OF VARIETY OF FACES.

The Italian painters have been accused of a common fault, that is, of introducing into their compositions the faces, and even the whole figures, of Roman emperors, which they take from the antique. To avoid such an error, let no repetition take place, either in parts, or the whole of a figure; nor let there be even the same face in another composition: and the more the figures are contrasted, viz. the deformed opposed to the beautiful, the old to the young, the strong to the feeble, the more the picture will please and be admired. These different characters, contrasted with each other, will increase the beauty of the whole.

It frequently happens that a painter, while he is composing, will use any little sketch or scrap of drawing he has by him, and endeavour to make it serve his purpose; but this is extremely injudicious, because he may very often find that the members he has drawn have not the motion suited to what he means to express; and after he has adopted, accurately drawn, and even well finished them, he will be loth to rub out and change them for others.

CHAP. CXL.

A FAULT IN PAINTERS.

It is a very great fault in a painter to repeat the same motions in figures, and the same folds in draperies in the same composition, as also to make all the faces alike.

CHAP. CXLI.

HOW YOU MAY LEARN TO COMPOSE GROUPS FOR HISTO-RY PAINTING.

When you are well instructed in perspective, and know perfectly how to draw the anatomy and forms of different bodies or objects, it should be your delight to observe and consider in your walks the different actions of men, when they are talking, or quarrelling; when they laugh, and when they fight. Attend to their positions, and to those of the spectators; whether they are attempting to separate those who fight, or merely lookers-on. Be quick in sketching these with slight strokes in your pocket-book, which should always be about you, and made of stained paper, as you ought not to rub out. When it is full, take another, for these are not things to be rubbed out, but kept with the greatest care; because forms and motions of bodies are so infinitely various, that the memory is not able to retain them; therefore preserve these sketches as your assistants and masters.

CHAP. CXLII.

HOW TO STUDY THE MOTIONS OF THE HUMAN BODY.

The first requisite towards a perfect acquaintance with the various motions of the human body, is the knowledge of all the parts, particularly the joints, in all the attitudes in which it may be placed. Then make slight sketches in your pocket-book, as opportunities occur, of the actions of men, as they happen to meet your eye, without being perceived by them; because, if they were to observe you, they would be disturbed from that freedom of action, which is prompted by inward feeling; as when two men are quarrelling and angry, each of them seeming to be in the right, and with great vehemence move their eyebrows, arms, and all the other members, using motions appropriated to their words and feelings. This they could not do, if you wanted them to imitate anger, or any other accidental emotion; such as laughter, weeping, pain, admiration, fear, and the like. For that reason, take care never to be without a little book, for the purpose of sketching those various motions, and also groups of people standing by. This will teach you how to compose history. Two things demand the principal attention of a good painter. One is the exact outline and shape of the figure; the other, the true expression of what passes in the mind of that figure, which he must feel, and that is very important.

CHAP. CXLIII.

OF DRESSES, AND OF DRAPERIES AND FOLDS.

THE draperies with which you dress figures ought to have their folds so accommodated as to surround the parts they are intended to cover; that in the mass of light there be not any dark fold, and in the mass of shadows none receiving too great a light. They must go gently over, describing the parts; but not with lines across, cutting the members with hard notches, deeper than the part can possibly be; at the same time, it must fit the body, and not appear like an empty bundle of cloth; a fault of many painters, who, enamoured of the quantity and variety of folds, have encumbered their figures, forgetting the intention of clothes, which is to dress and surround the parts gracefully wherever they touch; and not to be filled with wind, like bladders, puffed up where the parts project. I do not deny that we ought not to neglect introducing some handsome folds among these draperies, but it must be done with great judgment, and suited to the parts, where, by the actions of the limbs and position of the whole body, they gather together. Above all, be careful to vary the quality and quantity of your folds in compositions of many figures; so that, if some have large folds, produced by thick woollen cloth; others, being dressed in thinner stuff, may have them narrower; some sharp and straight, others soft and undulating.

CHAP. CXLIV.

OF THE NATURE OF FOLDS IN DRAPERIES.

MANY painters prefer making the folds of their draperies with acute angles, deep and precise; others with angles hardly perceptible; and some with none at all; but instead of them, certain curved lines.

CHAP. CXLV.

HOW THE FOLDS OF DRAPERIES OUGHT TO BE REPRESENTED, PLATE XVIII.

THAT part of the drapery, which is the farthest from the place where it is gathered, will appear more approaching its natural state. Every thing naturally inclines to preserve its primitive form. Therefore a stuff or cloth, which is of equal thickness on both sides, will always incline to remain flat. For that reason, when it is constrained by some fold to relinquish its flat situation, it is observed that, at the part of its greatest restraint, it is continually making efforts to return to its natural shape; and the parts most distant from it reassume more of their primitive state by ample and distended folds. For example, let A B C be the drapery mentioned above; A B the place where it is folded or restrained. I have said that the part, which is farthest from the place of its restraint, would return more towards its primitive shape. Therefore C being the farthest, will be broader and more extended than any other part.

CHAP. CXLVI.

HOW THE FOLDS IN DRAPERIES OUGHT TO BE MADE.

DRAPERIES are not to be encumbered with many folds: on the contrary, there ought to be some only where they are held up with the hands or arms of the figures, and the rest left to fall with natural simplicity. They ought to be studied from Nature; that is to say, if a woollen cloth be intended, the folds ought to be drawn after such cloth; if it be of silk, or thin stuff, or else very thick for labourers, let it be distinguished by the nature of the folds. But never copy them, as some do, after models dressed in paper, or thin leather, for it greatly misleads.

CHAP. CXLVII.

FORE-SHORTENING OF FOLDS, PLATE XIX.

WHERE the figure is fore-shortened, there ought to appear a greater number of folds, than on the other parts, all surrounding it in a circular manner. Let E be the situation of the eye. M N will have the middle of every circular fold successively removed farther from its outline, in proportion as it is more distant from the eye. In M O of the other figure the outlines of these circular folds will appear almost straight, because it is situated opposite the eye; but in P and Q quite the contrary, as in N and M.

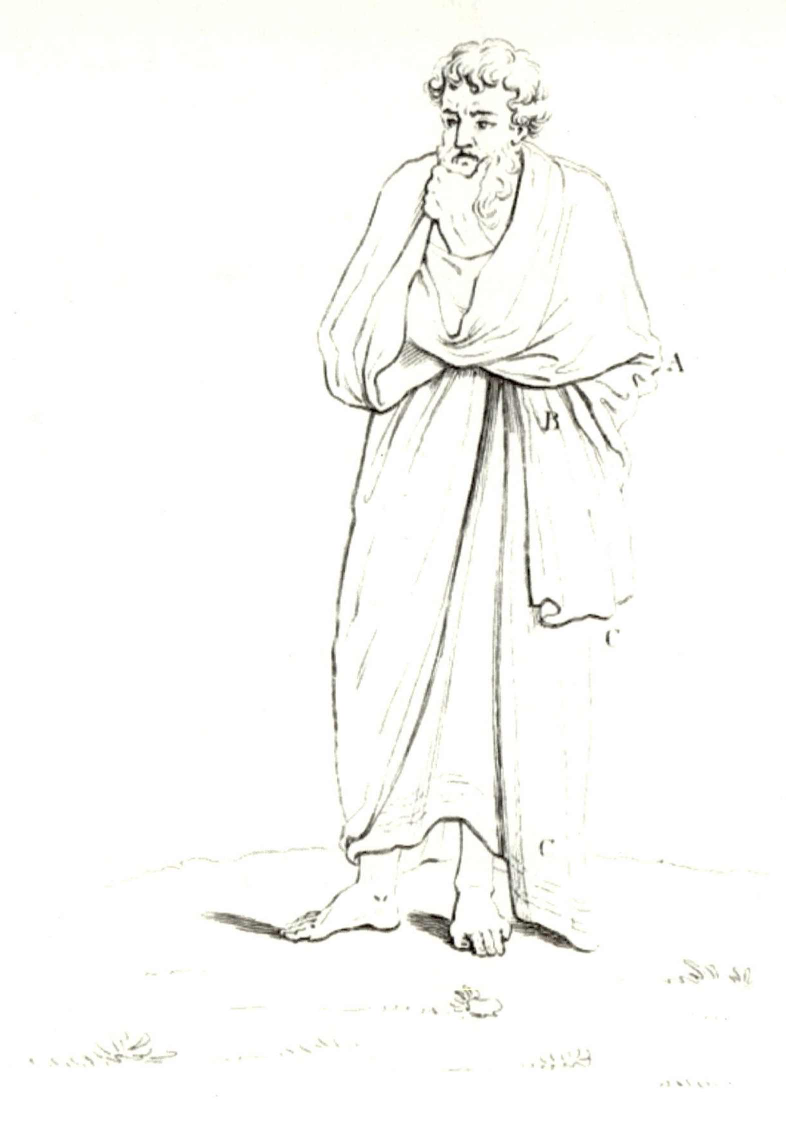

Chap. 145.

PLATE 18.

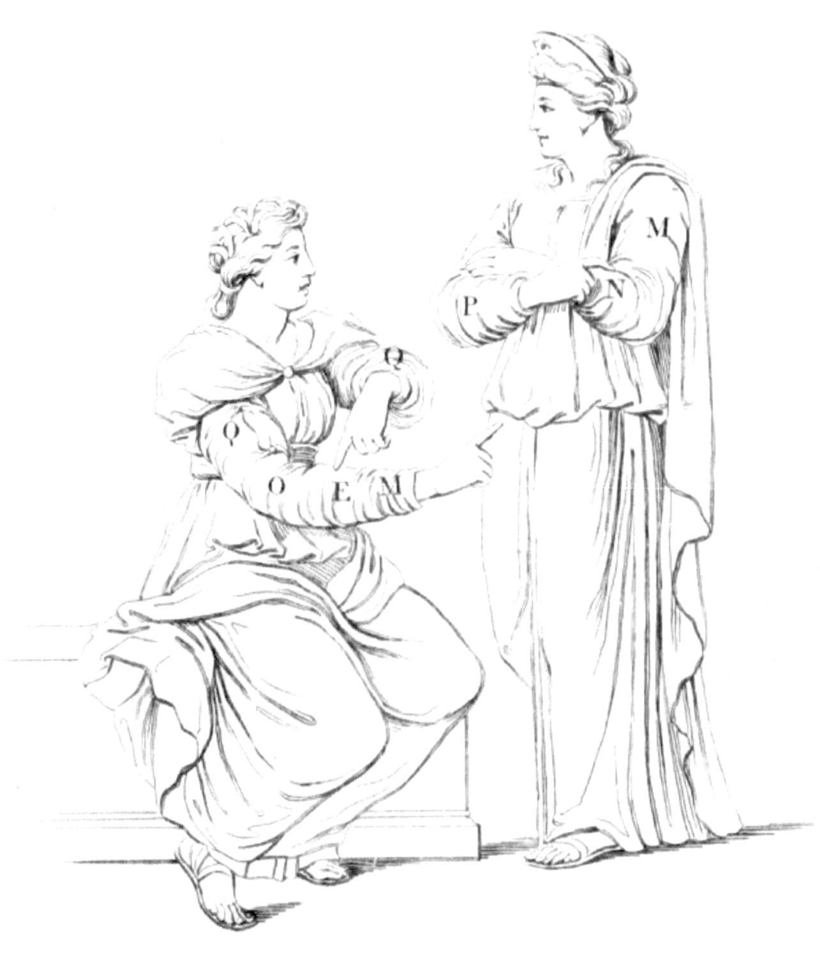

Page 65.

Chap. 147.

PLATE 19.

CHAP. CXLVIII.

OF FOLDS.

THE folds of draperies, whatever be the motion of the figure, ought always to shew, by the form of their outlines, the attitude of such figure; so as to leave, in the mind of the beholder, no doubt or confusion in regard to the true position of the body; and let there be no fold, which, by its shadow, breaks through any of the members; that is to say, appearing to go in deeper than the surface of the part it covers. And if you represent the figure clothed with several garments, one over the other, let it not appear as if the upper one covered only a mere skeleton; but let it express that it is also well furnished with flesh, and a thickness of folds, suitable to the number of its under garments.

The folds surrounding the members ought to diminish in thickness near the extremities of the part they surround.

The length of the folds, which are close to the members, ought to produce other folds on that side where the member is diminished by fore-shortening, and be more extended on the opposite side.

CHAP. CXLIX.

OF DECORUM.

OBSERVE decorum in every thing you represent, that is, fitness of action, dress, and situation, according to the dignity or meanness of the subject to be represented. Be careful that a king, for instance, be grave and majestic in his countenance and dress; that the place be well decorated; and that his attendants, or the by-standers, express reverence and admiration, and appear as noble, in dresses suitable to a royal court.

On the contrary, in the representation of a mean subject, let the figures appear low and despicable; those about them with similar countenances, and actions, denoting base and presumptuous minds, and meanly clad. In short, in both cases, the parts must correspond with the general sentiment of the composition.

The motions of old age should not be similar to those of youth; those of a woman to those of a man; nor should the latter be the same as those of a boy.

CHAP. CL.

THE CHARACTER OF FIGURES IN COMPOSITION.

IN general, the painter ought to introduce very few old men, in the ordinary course of historical subjects, and those few separated from young people; because old people are few, and their habits do not agree with those of youth. Where there is no conformity of custom, there can be no intimacy, and, without it, a company is soon separated. But if the subject require an appearance of gravity, a meeting on important business, as a council, for instance, let there be few young men introduced, for youth willingly avoids such meetings.

CHAP. CLI.

THE MOTION OF THE MUSCLES, WHEN THE FIGURES ARE IN NATURAL POSITIONS.

A FIGURE, which does not express by its position the sentiments and passions, by which we suppose it animated, will appear to indicate that its muscles are not obedient to its will, and the painter very deficient in judgment. For that reason, a figure is to shew great eagerness and meaning; and its position is to be so well appropriated to that meaning, that it cannot be mistaken, nor made use of for any other.

CHAP. CLII.

A PRECEPT IN PAINTING.

THE painter ought to notice those quick motions, which men are apt to make without thinking, when impelled by strong and powerful affections of the mind. He ought to take memorandums of them, and sketch them in his pocket-book, in order to make use of them when they may answer his purpose; and then to put a living model in the same position, to see the quality and aspect of the muscles which are in action.

CHAP. CLIII.

OF THE MOTION OF MAN, PLATES XX. AND XXI.

THE first and principal part of the art is composition of any sort, or putting things together. The second relates to the expression and motion of the figures, and requires that they be well appropriated, and seeming attentive to what they are about; appearing to move with alacrity and spirit, according to the degree of expression suitable to the occasion; expressing slow and tardy motions, as well as those of eagerness in pursuit: and that quickness and ferocity be expressed with such force as to give an idea of the sensations of the actors. When a figure is to throw a dart, stones, or the like, let it be seen evidently by the attitude and disposition of all the members, that such is its intention; of which there are two examples in the opposite plates, varied both in action and power. The first in point of vigour is A. The second is B. But A will throw his weapon farther than B, because, though they seem desirous of throwing it to the same point, A having turned his feet towards the object, while his body is twisted and bent back the contrary way, to increase his power, returns with more velocity and force to the point to which he means to throw. But the figure B having turned his feet the same way as his body, it returns to its place with great inconvenience, and consequently with weakened powers. For in the expression of great efforts, the preparatory motions of the body must be strong and violent, twisting and bending, so that it may return with convenient ease, and by that means have a great effect. In the same manner, if a crossbow be not strung with force, the motion of whatever it shoots will be short and without effect; because, where there is no impulse, there can be no motion; and if the impulse be not violent, the motion is but tardy and feeble. So a bow, which is not strong, has no motion; and, if it be strung, it will remain in that state till the impulse be given by another power which puts it in motion, and it will shoot with a violence equal to that which was employed in bending it. In the same manner, the man who does not twist and bend his body will have acquired no power. Therefore, after A has thrown his dart, he will find himself twisted the contrary way, viz. on the side where he has thrown; and he will have acquired only power sufficient to serve him to return to where he was at first.

CHAP. CLIV.

OF ATTITUDES, AND THE MOTIONS OF THE MEMBERS.

The same attitude is not to be repeated in the same picture, nor the same motion of members in the same figure, nay, not even in the hands or fingers. And if the history requires a great number of figures, such as a battle, or a massacre of soldiers, in which there are but three ways of striking, viz. thrusting, cutting, or back-handed; in that case you must take care, that all those who are cutting be expressed in different views; some turning their backs, some their sides, and others be seen in front; varying in the same manner the three different ways of fighting, so that all the actions may have a relation to those three principles. In battles, complex motions display great art, giving spirit and animation to the whole. By complex motion is meant, for instance, that of a single figure shewing the front of the legs, and at the same time the profile of the shoulder. But of this I shall treat in another place[241].

CHAP. CLV.

OF A SINGLE FIGURE SEPARATE FROM AN HISTORICAL GROUP.

The same motion of members should not be repeated in a figure which you mean to be alone; for instance, if the figure be represented running, it must not throw both hands forward; but one forward and the other backward, or else it cannot run. If the right foot come forward, the right arm must go backward and the left forward, because, without such disposition and contraste of parts, it is impossible to run well. If another figure be supposed to follow this, one of its legs should be brought somewhat forward, and the other be perpendicular under the head; the arm on the same side should pass forward. But of this we shall treat more fully in the book on motion[242].

[241] Chap. xcvi. and civ.

[242] See the Life of the Author prefixed, and chap. xx. and ci. of the present work.

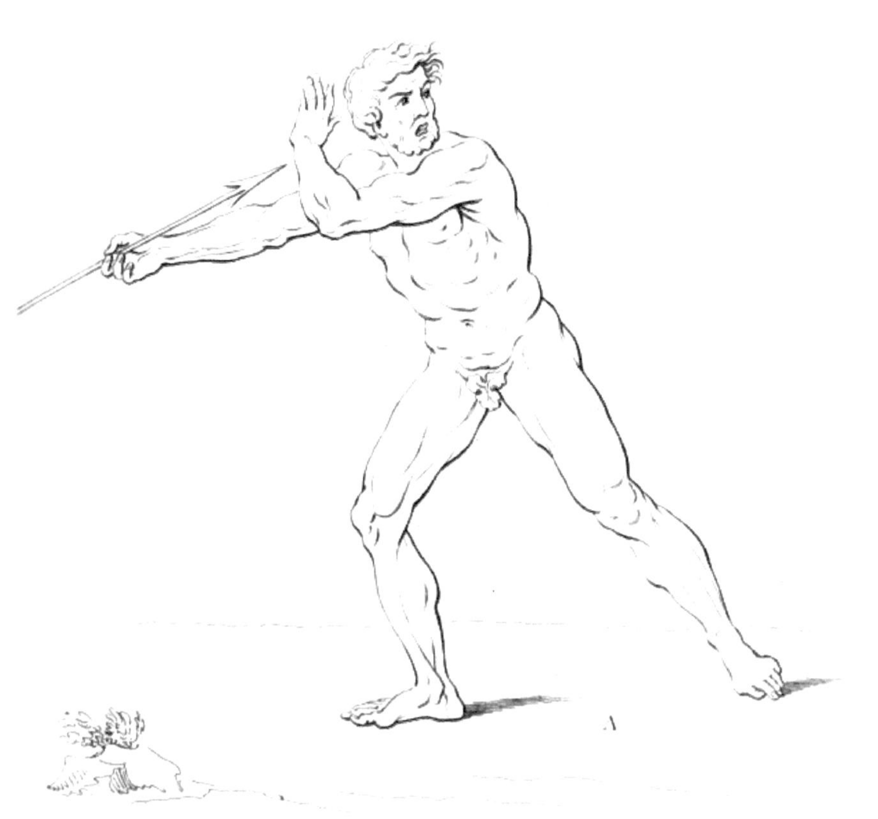

Page 69.

Chap. 153.
PLATE 20.

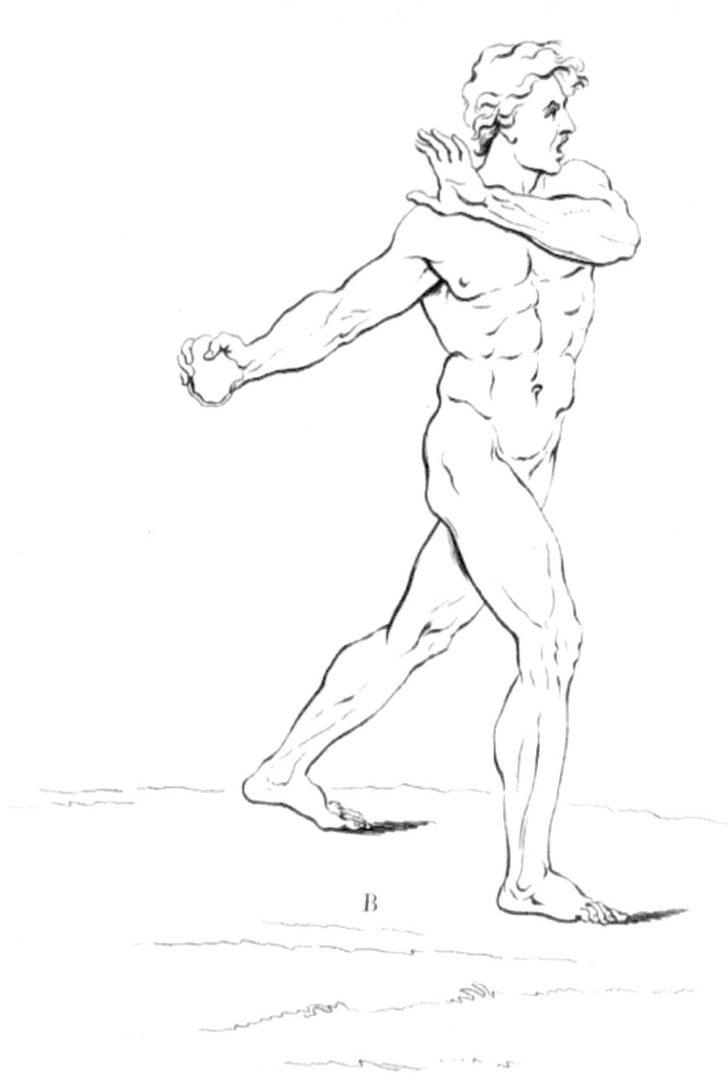

Page 69.

Chap. 153.

PLATE 21.

CHAP. CLVI.

ON THE ATTITUDES OF THE HUMAN FIGURE.

A PAINTER is to be attentive to the motions and actions of men, occasioned by some sudden accident. He must observe them on the spot, take sketches, and not wait till he wants such expression, and then have it counterfeited for him; for instance, setting a model to weep when there is no cause; such an expression without a cause will be neither quick nor natural. But it will be of great use to have observed every action from nature, as it occurs, and then to have a model set in the same attitude to help the recollection, and find out something to the purpose, according to the subject in hand.

CHAP. CLVII.

HOW TO REPRESENT A STORM.

To form a just idea of a storm, you must consider it attentively in its effects. When the wind blows violently over the sea or land, it removes and carries off with it every thing that is not firmly fixed to the general mass. The clouds must appear straggling and broken, carried according to the direction and the force of the wind, and blended with clouds of dust raised from the sandy shore. Branches and leaves of trees must be represented as carried along by the violence of the storm, and, together with numberless other light substances, scattered in the air. Trees and grass must be bent to the ground, as if yielding to the course of the wind. Boughs must be twisted out of their natural form, with their leaves reversed and entangled. Of the figures dispersed in the picture, some should appear thrown on the ground, so wrapped up in their cloaks and covered with dust, as to be scarcely distinguishable. Of those who remain on their feet, some should be sheltered by and holding fast behind some great trees, to avoid the same fate: others bending to the ground, their hands over their faces to ward off the dust; their hair and their clothes flying straight up at the mercy of the wind.

The high tremendous waves of the stormy sea will be covered with foaming froth; the most subtle parts of which, being raised by the wind, like a thick mist, mix with the air. What vessels are seen should appear with broken cordage, and torn sails, fluttering in the wind; some with broken masts fallen across the hulk, already on its side amidst the tempestuous waves. Some of the crew should be represented as if crying aloud for help, and clinging to the remains of the shattered vessel. Let the clouds appear as driven by tempestuous winds against the summits of lofty mountains, enveloping those mountains, and breaking and recoiling with redoubled force, like waves against a rocky shore. The air should be rendered awfully dark, by the mist, dust, and thick clouds.

CHAP. CLVIII.

HOW TO COMPOSE A BATTLE.

First, let the air exhibit a confused mixture of smoke, arising from the discharge of artillery and musquetry, and the dust raised by the horses of the combatants; and observe, that dust being of an earthy nature, is heavy; but yet, by reason of its minute particles, it is easily impelled upwards, and mixes with the air; nevertheless, it naturally falls downwards again, the most subtle parts of it alone gaining any considerable degree of elevation, and at its utmost height it is so thin and transparent, as to appear nearly of the colour of the air. The smoke, thus mixing with the dusty air, forms a kind of dark cloud, at the top of which it is distinguished from the dust by a blueish cast, the dust retaining more of its natural colour. On that part from which the light proceeds, this mixture of air, smoke, and dust, will appear much brighter than on the opposite side. The more the combatants are involved in this turbulent mist, the less distinctly they will be seen, and the more confused will they be in their lights and shades. Let the faces of the musketeers, their bodies, and every object near them, be tinged with a reddish hue, even the air or cloud of dust; in short, all that surrounds them. This red tinge you will diminish, in proportion to their distance, from the primary cause. The groups of figures, which appear at a distance between the spectator and the light, will form a dark mass upon a light ground; and their legs will be more undetermined and lost as they approach nearer to the ground; because there the dust is heavier and thicker.

If you mean to represent some straggling horses, running out of the main body, introduce also some small clouds of dust, as far distant from each other as the leap of the horse, and these little clouds will become fainter, more scanty, and diffused, in proportion to their distance from the horse. That nearest to his feet will consequently be the most determined, smallest, and the thickest of all.

Let the air be full of arrows, in all directions; some ascending, some falling down, and some darting straight forwards. The bullets of the musketry, though not seen, will be marked in their course by a train of smoke, which breaks through the general confusion. The figures in the fore-ground should have their hair covered with dust, as also their eyebrows, and all parts liable to receive it.

The victorious party will be running forwards, their hair and other light parts flying in the wind, their eyebrows lowered, and the motion of every member properly contrasted; for instance, in moving the right foot forwards, the left arm must be brought forwards also. If you make any of them fallen down, mark the trace of his fall on the slippery, gore-stained dust; and where the ground is less impregnated with blood, let the print of men's feet and of horses, that have passed that way, be marked. Let there be some horses dragging the bodies of their riders, and leaving behind them a furrow, made by the body thus trailed along.

The countenances of the vanquished will appear pale and dejected. Their eyebrows raised, and much wrinkled about the forehead and cheeks. The tip of their noses somewhat divided from the nostrils by arched wrinkles terminating at the corner of the eyes, those wrinkles being occasioned by the opening and raising of the nostrils; the upper lips turned up, discovering the teeth. Their mouths wide open, and expressive of violent lamentation. One may be seen fallen wounded on the ground, endeavouring with one hand to support his body, and covering his eyes with the other, the palm of which is turned towards the enemy. Others running away, and with open mouths seeming to cry aloud. Between the legs of the combatants let the ground be strewed with all sorts of arms; as broken shields, spears, swords, and the like. Many dead bodies should be introduced, some entirely covered with dust, others in part only; let the blood, which seems to issue immediately from the wound, appear of its natural colour, and running in a winding course, till, mixing with the dust, it forms a reddish kind of mud. Some should be in the agonies of death; their teeth shut, their eyes wildly staring, their fists clenched, and their legs in a distorted position. Some may appear disarmed, and beaten down by the enemy, still fighting with their fists and teeth, and endeavouring to take a passionate, though unavailing revenge. There may be also a straggling horse without a rider, running in wild disorder; his mane flying in the wind, beating down with his feet all before him, and doing a deal of damage. A wounded soldier may also be seen falling to the ground, and attempting to cover himself with his shield, while an enemy bending over him endeavours to give him the finishing stroke. Several dead bodies should be heaped together under a dead horse. Some of the conquerors, as having ceased fighting, may be wiping their faces from the dirt, collected on them by the mixture of dust with the water from their eyes.

The *corps de reserve* will be seen advancing gaily, but cautiously, their eyebrows directed forwards, shading their eyes with their hands to observe the motions of the enemy, amidst clouds of dust and smoke, and seeming attentive to the orders of their chief. You may also make their commander holding up his staff, pushing forwards, and pointing towards the place where they are wanted. A river may likewise be introduced, with horses fording it, dashing the water about between their legs, and in the air, covering all the adjacent ground with water and foam. Not a spot is to be left without some marks of blood and carnage.

CHAP. CLIX.

THE REPRESENTATION OF AN ORATOR AND HIS AUDIENCE.

IF you have to represent a man who is speaking to a large assembly of people, you are to consider the subject matter of his discourse, and to adapt his attitude to such subject. If he means to persuade, let it be known by his gesture. If he is giving an explanation, deduced from several reasons, let him put two fingers of the right hand within one of the left, having the other two bent close, his face turned towards the audience, with the mouth half open, seeming to speak. If he is sitting, let him appear as going to raise himself up a little, and his head be forward. But if he is represented standing, let him bend his chest and his head forward towards the people.

The auditory are to appear silent and attentive, with their eyes upon the speaker, in the act of admiration. There should be some old men, with their mouths close shut, in token of approbation, and their lips pressed together, so as to form wrinkles at the corners of the mouth, and about the cheeks, and forming others about the forehead, by raising the eyebrows, as if struck with astonishment. Some others of those sitting by, should be seated with their hands within each other, round one of their knees; some with one knee upon the other, and upon that, one hand receiving the elbow, the other supporting the chin, covered with a venerable beard.

CHAP. CLX.

OF DEMONSTRATIVE GESTURES.

The action by which a figure points at any thing near, either in regard to time or situation, is to be expressed by the hand very little removed from the body. But if the same thing is far distant, the hand must also be far removed from the body, and the face of the figure pointing, must be turned towards those to whom he is pointing it out.

CHAP. CLXI.

OF THE ATTITUDES OF THE BY-STANDERS AT SOME RE-MARKABLE EVENT.

All those who are present at some event deserving notice, express their admiration, but in various manners. As when the hand of justice punishes some malefactor. If the subject be an act of devotion, the eyes of all present should be directed towards the object of their adoration, aided by a variety of pious actions with the other members; as at the elevation of the host at mass, and other similar ceremonies. If it be a laughable subject, or one exciting compassion and moving to tears, in those cases it will not be necessary for all to have their eyes turned towards the object, but they will express their feelings by different actions; and let there be several assembled in groups, to rejoice or lament together. If the event be terrific, let the faces of those who run away from the fight, be strongly expressive of fright, with various motions; as shall be described in the tract on Motion.

CHAP. CLXII.

HOW TO REPRESENT NIGHT.

Those objects which are entirely deprived of light, are lost to the sight, as in the night; therefore if you mean to paint a history under those circumstances, you must suppose a large fire, and those objects that are near it to be tinged with its colour, and the nearer they are the more they will partake of it. The fire being red, all those objects which receive light from it will appear of a reddish colour, and those that are most distant from it will partake of the darkness that surrounds them. The figures which are represented before the fire will appear dark in proportion to the brightness of the fire, because those parts of them which we see, are tinged by that darkness of the night, and not by the light of the fire, which they intercept. Those that are on either side of the fire, will be half in the shade of night, and half in the red light. Those seen beyond the extent of the flames, will be all of a reddish light upon a black ground. In regard to their attitudes, let those who are nearest the fire, make screens of their hands and cloaks, against the scorching heat, with their faces turned on the contrary side, as if ready to run away from it. The most remote will only be shading their eyes with their hands, as if hurt by the too great glare.

CHAP. CLXIII.

THE METHOD OF AWAKENING THE MIND TO A VARIETY OF INVENTIONS.

I WILL not omit to introduce among these precepts a new kind of speculative invention, which though apparently trifling, and almost laughable, is nevertheless of great utility in assisting the genius to find variety for composition.

By looking attentively at old and smeared walls, or stones and veined marble of various colours, you may fancy that you see in them several compositions, landscapes, battles, figures in quick motion, strange countenances, and dresses, with an infinity of other objects. By these confused lines the inventive genius is excited to new exertions.

CHAP. CLXIV.

OF COMPOSITION IN HISTORY.

WHEN the painter has only a single figure to represent, he must avoid any shortening whatever, as well of any particular member, as of the whole figure, because he would have to contend with the prejudices of those who have no knowledge in that branch of the art. But in subjects of history, composed of many figures, shortenings may be introduced with great propriety, nay, they are indispensable, and ought to be used without reserve, as the subject may require; particularly in battles, where of course many shortenings and contortions of figures happen, amongst such an enraged multitude of actors, possessed, as it were, of a brutal madness.

EXPRESSION AND CHARACTER.

CHAP. CLXV.
OF EXPRESSIVE MOTIONS.

LET your figures have actions appropriated to what they are intended to think or say, and these will be well learnt by imitating the deaf, who by the motion of their hands, eyes, eyebrows, and the whole body, endeavour to express the sentiments of their mind. Do not ridicule the thought of a master without a tongue teaching you an art he does not understand; he will do it better by his expressive motions, than all the rest by their words and examples. Let then the painter, of whatever school, attend well to this maxim, and apply it to the different qualities of the figures he represents, and to the nature of the subject in which they are actors.

CHAP. CLXVI.
HOW TO PAINT CHILDREN.

CHILDREN are to be represented with quick and contorted motions, when they are sitting; but when standing, with fearful and timid motions.

CHAP. CLXVII.
HOW TO REPRESENT OLD MEN.

OLD men must have slow and heavy motions; their legs and knees must be bent when they are standing, and their feet placed parallel and wide asunder. Let them be bowed downwards, the head leaning much forward, and their arms very little extended.

CHAP. CLXVIII.
HOW TO PAINT OLD WOMEN.

OLD women, on the contrary, are to be represented bold and quick, with passionate motions, like furies[243]. But the motions are to appear a great deal quicker

[243] The author here speaks of unpolished Nature; and indeed it is from such subjects only, that the genuine and characteristic operations of Nature are to be learnt. It is the effect

in their arms than in their legs.

CHAP. CLXIX.
HOW TO PAINT WOMEN.

WOMEN are to be represented in modest and reserved attitudes, with their knees rather close, their arms drawing near each other, or folded about the body; their heads looking downwards, and leaning a little on one side.

CHAP. CLXX.
OF THE VARIETY OF FACES.

THE countenances of your figures should be expressive of their different situations: men at work, at rest, weeping, laughing, crying out, in fear, or joy, and the like. The attitudes also, and all the members, ought to correspond with the sentiment expressed in the faces.

CHAP. CLXXI.
THE PARTS OF THE FACE, AND THEIR MOTIONS.

THE motions of the different parts of the face, occasioned by sudden agitations of the mind, are many. The principal of these are, Laughter, Weeping, Calling out, Singing, either in a high or low pitch, Admiration, Anger, Joy, Sadness, Fear, Pain, and others, of which I propose to treat. First, of Laughing and Weeping, which are very similar in the motion of the mouth, the cheeks, the shutting of the eyebrows, and the space between them; as we shall explain in its place, in treating of the changes which happen in the face, hands, fingers, and all the other parts of the body, as they are affected by the different emotions of the soul; the knowledge of which is absolutely necessary to a painter, or else his figures may be said to be twice dead. But it is very necessary also that he be careful not to fall into the contrary extreme; giving extraordinary motions to his figures, so that in a quiet and peaceable subject, he does not seem to represent a battle, or the revellings of drunken men: but, above all, the actors in any point of history must be attentive to what they are about, or to what is going forward; with actions that denote admiration, respect, pain, suspicion, fear, and joy, according as the occasion, for which they are brought together, may require. Endeavour that different points of history be not placed one above the other on the same canvass, nor walls with different horizons[244], as if it were a jeweller's shop, shewing the goods in different square caskets.

---

of education to correct the natural peculiarities and defects, and, by so doing, to assimilate one person to the rest of the world.

[244] See chap. cxxiii.

CHAP. CLXXII.

LAUGHING AND WEEPING.

Between the expression of laughter and that of weeping there is no difference in the motion of the features either in the eyes, mouth, or cheeks; only in the ruffling of the brows, which is added when weeping, but more elevated and extended in laughing. One may represent the figure weeping as tearing his clothes, or some other expression, as various as the cause of his feeling may be; because some weep for anger, some through fear, others for tenderness and joy, or for suspicion; some for real pain and torment; whilst others weep through compassion, or regret at the loss of some friend and near relation. These different feelings will be expressed by some with marks of despair, by others with moderation; some only shed tears, others cry aloud, while another has his face turned towards heaven, with his hand depressed, and his fingers twisted. Some again will be full of apprehension, with their shoulders raised up to their ears, and so on, according to the above causes.

Those who weep, raise the brows, and bring them close together above the nose, forming many wrinkles on the forehead, and the corners of the mouth are turned downwards. Those who laugh have them turned upwards, and the brows open and extended.

CHAP. CLXXIII.

OF ANGER.

If you represent a man in a violent fit of anger, make him seize another by the hair, holding his head writhed down against the ground, with his knee fixed upon the ribs of his antagonist; his right arm up, and his fist ready to strike; his hair standing on end, his eyebrows low and straight; his teeth close, and seen at the corner of the mouth; his neck swelled, and his body covered in the Abdomen with creases, occasioned by his bending over his enemy, and the excess of his passion.

CHAP. CLXXIV.

DESPAIR.

The last act of despondency is, when a man is in the act of putting a period to his own existence. He should be represented with a knife in one hand, with which he has already inflicted the wound, and tearing it open with the other. His garments and hair should be already torn. He will be standing with his feet asunder, his knees a little bent, and his body leaning forward, as if ready to fall to the ground.

LIGHT AND SHADOW.

LIGHT AND SHADOW.

CHAP. CLXXV.
THE COURSE OF STUDY TO BE PURSUED.

The student who is desirous of making great proficiency in the art of imitating the works of Nature, should not only learn the shape of figures or other objects, and be able to delineate them with truth and precision, but he must also accompany them with their proper lights and shadows, according to the situation in which those objects appear.

CHAP. CLXXVI.
WHICH OF THE TWO IS THE MOST USEFUL KNOWLEDGE, THE OUTLINES OF FIGURES, OR THAT OF LIGHT AND SHADOW.

The knowledge of the outline is of most consequence, and yet may be acquired to great certainty by dint of study; as the outlines of the different parts of the human figure, particularly those which do not bend, are invariably the same. But the knowledge of the situation, quality, and quantity of shadows, being infinite, requires the most extensive study.

CHAP. CLXXVII.
WHICH IS THE MOST IMPORTANT, THE SHADOWS OR OUTLINES IN PAINTING.

It requires much more observation and study to arrive at perfection in the shadowing of a picture, than in merely drawing the lines of it. The proof of this is, that the lines may be traced upon a veil or a flat glass placed between the eye and the object to be imitated. But that cannot be of any use in shadowing, on account of the infinite gradation of shades, and the blending of them, which does not allow of any precise termination; and most frequently they are confused, as will be demonstrated in another place[245].

---

[245] See chap. cclxiv.

CHAP. CLXXVIII.

WHAT IS A PAINTER'S FIRST AIM, AND OBJECT.

THE first object of a painter is to make a simple flat surface appear like a relievo, and some of its parts detached from the ground; he who excels all others in that part of the art, deserves the greatest praise. This perfection of the art depends on the correct distribution of lights and shades, called *Chiaro-scuro*. If the painter then avoids shadows, he may be said to avoid the glory of the art, and to render his work despicable to real connoisseurs, for the sake of acquiring the esteem of vulgar and ignorant admirers of fine colours, who never have any knowledge of relievo.

CHAP. CLXXIX.

THE DIFFERENCE OF SUPERFICIES, IN REGARD TO PAINTING.

SOLID bodies are of two sorts: the one has the surface curvilinear, oval, or spherical; the other has several surfaces, or sides producing angles, either regular or irregular. Spherical, or oval bodies, will always appear detached from their ground, though they are exactly of the same colour. Bodies also of different sides and angles will always detach, because they are always disposed so as to produce shades on some of their sides, which cannot happen to a plain superficies[246].

CHAP. CLXXX.

HOW A PAINTER MAY BECOME UNIVERSAL.

THE painter who wishes to be universal, and please a variety of judges, must unite in the same composition, objects susceptible of great force in the shadows, and great sweetness in the management of them; accounting, however, in every instance, for such boldness and softenings.

CHAP. CLXXXI.

ACCURACY OUGHT TO BE LEARNT BEFORE DISPATCH IN THE EXECUTION.

IF you wish to make good and useful studies, use great deliberation in your drawings, observe well among the lights which, and how many, hold the first rank in point of brightness; and so among the shadows, which are darker than others, and in what manner they blend together; compare the quality and quantity of one with the other, and observe to what part they are directed. Be careful also in your outlines, or divisions of the members. Remark well what quantity of parts are to be on one side, and what on the other; and where they are more or less apparent,

[246] See chapter cclxvii.

or broad, or slender. Lastly, take care that the shadows and lights be united, or lost in each other; without any hard strokes, or lines: as smoke loses itself in the air, so are your lights and shadows to pass from the one to the other, without any apparent separation.

When you have acquired the habit, and formed your hand to accuracy, quickness of execution will come of itself[247].

CHAP. CLXXXII.

HOW THE PAINTER IS TO PLACE HIMSELF IN REGARD TO THE LIGHT, AND HIS MODEL.

Let A B be the window, M the centre of it, C the model. The best situation for the painter will be a little sideways, between the window and his model, as D, so that he may see his object partly in the light and partly in the shadow.

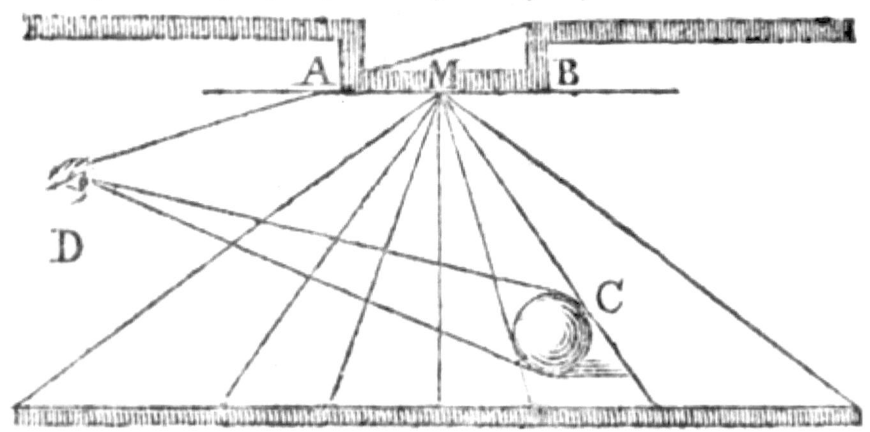

CHAP. CLXXXIII.

OF THE BEST LIGHT.

The light from on high, and not too powerful, will be found the best calculated to shew the parts to advantage.

CHAP. CLXXXIV.

OF DRAWING BY CANDLE-LIGHT.

To this artificial light apply a paper blind, and you will see the shadows undetermined and soft.

---

[247] Sir Joshua Reynolds frequently inculcated these precepts in his lectures, and indeed they cannot be too often enforced.

CHAP. CLXXXV.

OF THOSE PAINTERS WHO DRAW AT HOME FROM ONE LIGHT, AND AFTERWARDS ADAPT THEIR STUDIES TO AN-OTHER SITUATION IN THE COUNTRY, AND A DIFFERENT LIGHT.

It is a great error in some painters who draw a figure from Nature at home, by any particular light, and afterwards make use of that drawing in a picture representing an open country, which receives the general light of the sky, where the surrounding air gives light on all sides. This painter would put dark shadows, where Nature would either produce none, or, if any, so very faint as to be almost imperceptible; and he would throw reflected lights where it is impossible there should be any.

CHAP. CLXXXVI.

HOW HIGH THE LIGHT SHOULD BE IN DRAWING FROM NATURE.

To paint well from Nature, your window should be to the North, that the lights may not vary. If it be to the South, you must have paper blinds, that the sun, in going round, may not alter the shadows. The situation of the light should be such as to produce upon the ground a shadow from your model as long as that is high.

CHAP. CLXXXVII.

WHAT LIGHT THE PAINTER MUST MAKE USE OF TO GIVE MOST RELIEF TO HIS FIGURES.

The figures which receive a particular light shew more relief than those which receive an universal one; because the particular light occasions some reflexes, which proceed from the light of one object upon the shadows of another, and helps to detach it from the dark ground. But a figure placed in front of a dark and large space, and receiving a particular light, can receive no reflexion from any other objects, and nothing is seen of the figure but what the light strikes on, the rest being blended and lost in the darkness of the back ground. This is to be applied only to the imitation of night subjects with very little light.

CHAP. CLXXXVIII.

ADVICE TO PAINTERS.

Be very careful, in painting, to observe, that between the shadows there are other shadows, almost imperceptible, both for darkness and shape; and this is proved by the third proposition[248], which says, that the surfaces of globular or convex bodies have as great a variety of lights and shadows as the bodies that surround them have.

CHAP. CLXXXIX.

OF SHADOWS.

THOSE shadows which in Nature are undetermined, and the extremities of which can hardly be perceived, are to be copied in your painting in the same manner, never to be precisely finished, but left confused and blended. This apparent neglect will shew great judgment, and be the ingenious result of your observation of Nature.

CHAP. CXC.

OF THE KIND OF LIGHT PROPER FOR DRAWING FROM RELIEVOS, OR FROM NATURE.

LIGHTS separated from the shadows with too much precision, have a very bad effect. In order, therefore, to avoid this inconvenience, if the object be in the open country, you need not let your figures be illumined by the sun; but may suppose some transparent clouds interposed, so that the sun not being visible, the termination of the shadows will be also imperceptible and soft.

CHAP. CXCI.

WHETHER THE LIGHT SHOULD BE ADMITTED IN FRONT OR SIDEWAYS; AND WHICH IS MOST PLEASING AND GRACEFUL.

THE light admitted in front of heads situated opposite to side walls that are dark, will cause them to have great relievo, particularly if the light be placed high; and the reason is, that the most prominent parts of those faces are illumined by the general light striking them in front, which light produces very faint shadows on the part where it strikes; but as it turns towards the sides, it begins to participate of the dark shadows of the room, which grow darker in proportion as it sinks into them. Besides, when the light comes from on high, it does not strike on every part of the face alike, but one part produces great shadows upon another; as the eyebrows, which deprive the whole sockets of the eyes of light. The nose keeps it off from great part of the mouth, and the chin from the neck, and such other parts. This, by concentrating the light upon the most projecting parts, produces a very great relief.

---

[248] Probably this would have formed a part of his intended Treatise on Light and Shadow, but no such proposition occurs in the present work.

CHAP. CXCII.

OF THE DIFFERENCE OF LIGHTS ACCORDING TO THE SITUATION.

A SMALL light will cast large and determined shadows upon the surrounding bodies. A large light, on the contrary, will cast small shadows on them, and they will be much confused in their termination. When a small but strong light is surrounded by a broad but weaker light, the latter will appear like a demi-tint to the other, as the sky round the sun. And the bodies which receive the light from the one, will serve as demi-tints to those which receive the light from the other.

CHAP. CXCIII.

HOW TO DISTRIBUTE THE LIGHT ON FIGURES.

THE lights are to be distributed according to the natural situation you mean your figures should occupy. If you suppose them in sunshine, the shades must be dark, the lights broad and extended, and the shadows of all the surrounding objects distinctly marked upon the ground. If seen in a gloomy day, there will be very little difference between the lights and shades, and no shadows at the feet. If the figures be represented within doors, the lights and shadows will again be distinctly divided, and produce shadows on the ground. But if you suppose a paper blind at the window, and the walls painted white, the effect will be the same as in a gloomy day, when the lights and shadows have little difference. If the figures are enlightened by the fire, the lights must be red and powerful, the shadows dark, and the shadows upon the ground and upon the walls must be precise; observing that they spread wider as they go off from the body. If the figures be enlightened, partly by the sky and partly by the fire, that side which receives the light from the sky will be the brightest, and on the other side it will be reddish, somewhat of the colour of the fire. Above all, contrive, that your figures receive a broad light, and that from above; particularly in portraits, because the people we see in the street receive all the light from above; and it is curious to observe, that there is not a face ever so well known amongst your acquaintance, but would be recognised with difficulty, if it were enlightened from beneath.

CHAP. CXCIV.

OF THE BEAUTY OF FACES.

YOU must not mark any muscles with hardness of line, but let the soft light glide upon them, and terminate imperceptibly in delightful shadows: from this will arise grace and beauty to the face.

CHAP. CXCV.

HOW, IN DRAWING A FACE, TO GIVE IT GRACE, BY THE MANAGEMENT OF LIGHT AND SHADE.

A FACE placed in the dark part of a room, acquires great additional grace by means of light and shadow. The shadowed part of the face blends with the darkness of the ground, and the light part receives an increase of brightness from the open air, the shadows on this side becoming almost insensible; and from this augmentation of light and shadow, the face has much relief, and acquires great beauty.

CHAP. CXCVI.

HOW TO GIVE GRACE AND RELIEF TO FACES.

IN streets running towards the west, when the sun is in the meridian, and the walls on each side so high that they cast no reflexions on that side of the bodies which is in shade, and the sky is not too bright, we find the most advantageous situation for giving relief and grace to figures, particularly to faces; because both sides of the face will participate of the shadows of the walls. The sides of the nose and the face towards the west, will be light, and the man whom we suppose placed at the entrance, and in the middle of the street, will see all the parts of that face, which are before him, perfectly illumined, while both sides of it, towards the walls, will be in shadow. What gives additional grace is, that these shades do not appear cutting, hard, or dry, but softly blended and lost in each other. The reason of it is, that the light which is spread all over in the air, strikes also the pavement of the street, and reflecting upon the shady part of the face, it tinges that slightly with the same hue: while the great light which comes from above being confined by the tops of houses, strikes on the face from different points, almost to the very beginning of the shadows under the projecting parts of the face. It diminishes by degrees the strength of them, increasing the light till it comes upon the chin, where it terminates, and loses itself, blending softly into the shades on all sides. For instance, if such light were A E, the line F E would give light even to the bottom of the nose. The line C F will give light only to the under lip; but the line A H would extend the shadow to all the under parts of the face, and under the chin.

In this situation the nose receives a very strong light from all the points A B C D E.

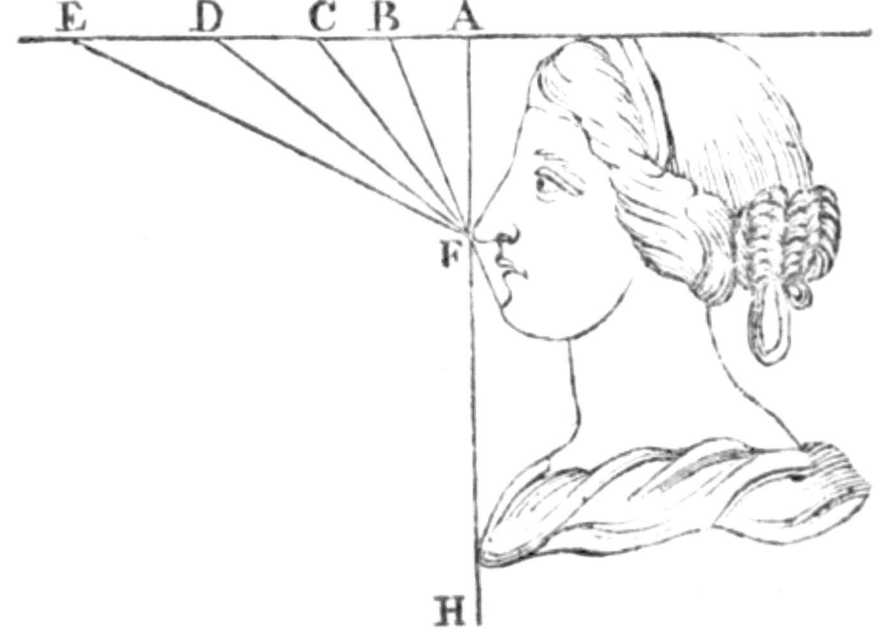

CHAP. CXCVII.

OF THE TERMINATION OF BODIES UPON EACH OTHER.

When a body, of a cylindrical or convex surface, terminates upon another body of the same colour, it will appear darker on the edge, than the body upon which it terminates. And any flat body, adjacent to a white surface, will appear very dark; but upon a dark ground it will appear lighter than any other part, though the lights be equal.

CHAP. CXCVIII.

OF THE BACK-GROUNDS OF PAINTED OBJECTS.

The ground which surrounds the figures in any painting, ought to be darker than the light part of those figures, and lighter than the shadowed part.

CHAP. CXCIX.

HOW TO DETACH AND BRING FORWARD FIGURES OUT OF THEIR BACK-GROUND.

If your figure be dark, place it on a light ground; if it be light, upon a dark ground; and if it be partly light and partly dark, as is generally the case, contrive that the dark part of the figure be upon the light part of the ground, and the light side of it against the dark[249].

CHAP. CC.

OF PROPER BACK-GROUNDS.

Iт is of the greatest importance to consider well the nature of back-grounds, upon which any opake body is to be placed. In order to detach it properly, you should place the light part of such opake body against the dark part of the back-ground, and the dark parts on a light ground[250]; as in the cut[251].

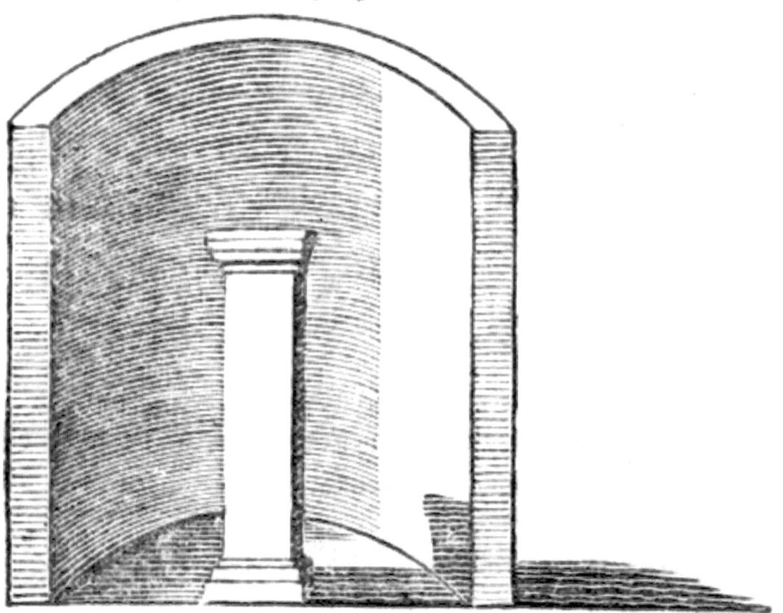

---

[249] See chapters cc. and ccix.

[250] See chap. ccix.

[251] This cannot be taken as an absolute rule; it must be left in a great measure to the judgment of the painter. For much graceful softness and grandeur is acquired, sometimes, by blending the lights of the figures with the light part of the ground; and so of the shadows; as Leonardo himself has observed in chapters cxciv. cxcv. and Sir Joshua Reynolds has often put in practice with success.

CHAP. CCI.

OF THE GENERAL LIGHT DIFFUSED OVER FIGURES.

In compositions of many figures and animals, observe, that the parts of these different objects ought to be darker in proportion as they are lower, and as they are nearer the middle of the groups, though they are all of an uniform colour. This is necessary, because a smaller portion of the sky (from which all bodies are illuminated) can give light to the lower spaces between these different figures, than to the upper parts of the spaces. It is proved thus: A B C D is that portion of the sky which gives light to all the objects beneath; M and N are the bodies which occupy the space S T R H, in which it is evidently perceived, that the point F, receiving the light only from the portion of the sky C D, has a smaller quantity of it than the point E which receives it from the whole space A B (a larger portion than C D); therefore it will be lighter in E than in F.

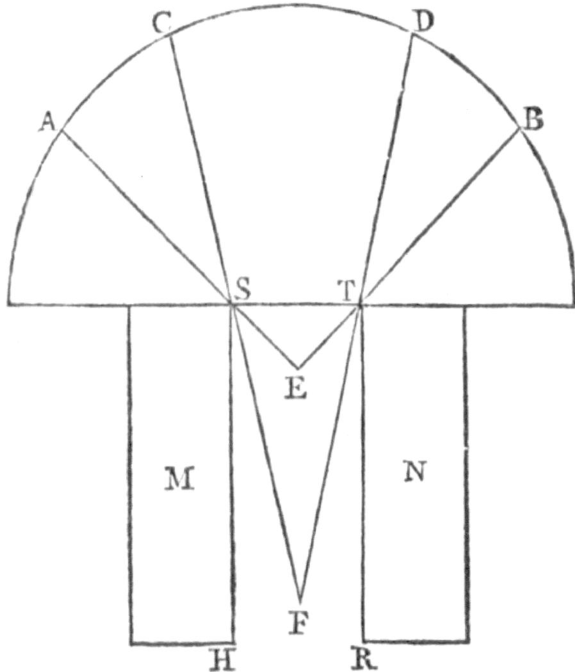

CHAP. CCII.

OF THOSE PARTS IN SHADOWS WHICH APPEAR THE DARKEST AT A DISTANCE.

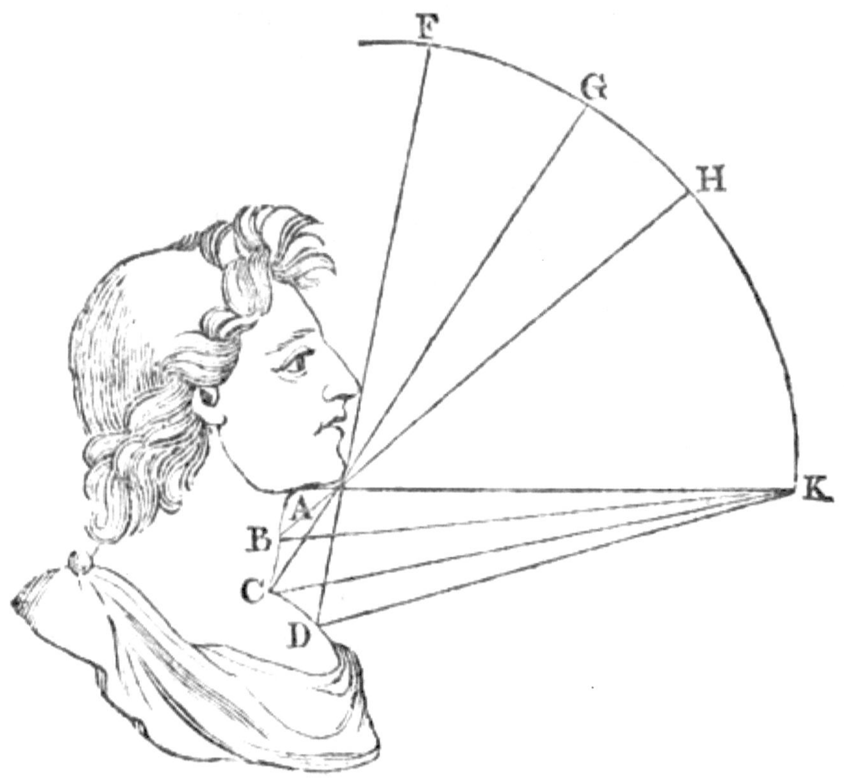

THE neck, or any other part which is raised straight upwards, and has a projection over it, will be darker than the perpendicular front of that projection; and this projecting part will be lighter, in proportion as it presents a larger surface to the light. For instance, the recess A receives no light from any part of the sky G K, but B begins to receive the light from the part of the sky H K, and C from G K; and the point D receives the whole of F K. Therefore the chest will be as light as the forehead, nose, and chin. But what I have particularly to recommend, in regard to faces, is, that you observe well those different qualities of shades which are lost at different distances (while there remain only the first and principal spots or strokes of shades, such as those of the sockets of the eyes, and other similar recesses, which are always dark), and at last the whole face becomes obscured; because the greatest lights (being small in proportion to the demi-tints) are lost. The quality, therefore, and quantity of the principal lights and shades are by means of great distance blended together into a general half-tint; and this is the reason why trees and other objects are found to be in appearance darker at some distance than they are in reality, when nearer to the eye. But then the air, which interposes between the objects and the eye, will render them light again by tinging them with azure, rather in the shades than in the lights; for the lights will preserve the truth of the different colours much longer.

CHAP. CCIII.

OF THE EYE VIEWING THE FOLDS OF DRAPERIES SURROUNDING A FIGURE.

THE shadows between the folds of a drapery surrounding the parts of the human body will be darker as the deep hollows where the shadows are generated are more directly opposite the eye. This is to be observed only when the eye is placed between the light and the shady part of the figure.

CHAP. CCIV.

OF THE RELIEF OF FIGURES REMOTE FROM THE EYE.

ANY opake body appears less relieved in proportion as it is farther distant from the eye; because the air, interposed between the eye and such body, being lighter than the shadow of it, it tarnishes and weakens that shadow, lessens its power, and consequently lessens also its relief.

CHAP. CCV.

OF OUTLINES OF OBJECTS ON THE SIDE TOWARDS THE LIGHT.

THE extremities of any object on the side which receives the light, will appear darker if upon a lighter ground, and lighter if seen upon a darker ground. But if such body be flat, and seen upon a ground equal in point of light with itself, and of the same colour, such boundaries, or outlines, will be entirely lost to the sight[252].

CHAP. CCVI.

HOW TO MAKE OBJECTS DETACH FROM THEIR GROUND, THAT IS TO SAY, FROM THE SURFACE ON WHICH THEY ARE PAINTED.

OBJECTS contrasted with a light ground will appear much more detached than those which are placed against a dark one. The reason is, that if you wish to give relief to your figures, you will make those parts which are the farthest from the light, participate the least of it; therefore they will remain the darkest, and every distinction of outline would be lost in the general mass of shadows. But to give it grace, roundness, and effect, those dark shades are always attended by reflexes, or

---

[252] See chap. cclxv.

else they would either cut too hard upon the ground, or stick to it, by the similarity of shade, and relieve the less as the ground is darker; for at some distance nothing would be seen but the light parts, therefore your figures would appear mutilated of all that remains lost in the back-ground.

CONTRASTE AND EFFECT.

CHAP. CCVII.
A PRECEPT.

Figures will have more grace, placed in the open and general light, than in any particular or small one; because the powerful and extended light will surround and embrace the objects: and works done in that kind of light appear pleasant and graceful when placed at a distance[253], while those which are drawn in a narrow light, will receive great force of shadow, but will never appear at a great distance, but as painted objects.

CHAP. CCVIII.
OF THE INTERPOSITION OF TRANSPARENT BODIES BE- TWEEN THE EYE AND THE OBJECT.

The greater the transparent interposition is between the eye and the object, the more the colour of that object will participate of, or be changed into that of the transparent medium[254].

When an opake body is situated between the eye and the luminary, so that the central line of the one passes also through the centre of the other, that object will be entirely deprived of light.

CHAP. CCIX.
OF PROPER BACK-GROUNDS FOR FIGURES.

As we find by experience, that all bodies are surrounded by lights and shad- ows, I would have the painter to accommodate that part which is enlightened, so as to terminate upon something dark; and to manage the dark parts so that they may terminate on a light ground. This will be of great assistance in detaching and bringing out his figures[255].

[253] See chap. cxcvi.

[254] He means here to say, that in proportion as the body interposed between the eye and the object is more or less transparent, the greater or less quantity of the colour of the body interposed will be communicated to the object.

[255] See the note to chap. cc.

CHAP. CCX.

OF BACK-GROUNDS.

To give a great effect to figures, you must oppose to a light one a dark ground, and to a dark figure a light ground, contrasting white with black, and black with white. In general, all contraries give a particular force and brilliancy of effect by their opposition[256].

---

[256] See the preceding chapter, and chap. cc.

REFLEXES.

CHAP. CCXI.

OF OBJECTS PLACED ON A LIGHT GROUND, AND WHY SUCH A PRACTICE IS USEFUL IN PAINTING.

When a darkish body terminates upon a light ground, it will appear detached from that ground; because all opake bodies of a curved surface are not only dark on that side which receives no light, and consequently very different from the ground; but even that side of the curved surface which is enlightened, will not carry its principal light to the extremities, but have between the ground and the principal light a certain demi-tint, darker than either the ground or that light.

CHAP. CCXII.

OF THE DIFFERENT EFFECTS OF WHITE, ACCORDING TO THE DIFFERENCE OF BACK-GROUNDS.

Any thing white will appear whiter, by being opposed to a dark ground; and, on the contrary, darker upon a light ground. This we learn from observing snow as it falls; while it is descending it appears darker against the sky, than when we see it against an open window, which (owing to the darkness of the inside of the house) makes it appear very white. Observe also, that snow appears to fall very quick and in a great quantity when near the eye; but when at some distance, it seems to come down slowly, and in a smaller quantity[257].

CHAP. CCXIII.

OF REVERBERATION.

Reverberations are produced by all bodies of a bright nature, that have a smooth and tolerably hard surface, which, repelling the light it receives, makes it rebound like a foot-ball against the first object opposed to it.

---

[257] The appearance of motion is lessened according to the distance, in the same proportion as objects diminish in size.

CHAP. CCXIV.

WHERE THERE CANNOT BE ANY REVERBERATION OF LIGHT.

THE surfaces of hard bodies are surrounded by various qualities of light and shadow. The lights are of two sorts; one is called original, the other derivative. The original light is that which comes from the sun, or the brightness of fire, or else from the air. The derivative is a reflected light. But to return to our definition, I say, there can be no reflexion on that side which is turned towards any dark body; such as roofs, either high or low, shrubs, grass, wood, either dry or green; because, though every individual part of those objects be turned towards the original light, and struck by it; yet the quantity of shadow which every one of these parts produces upon the others, is so great, that, upon the whole, the light, not forming a compact mass, loses its effect, so that those objects cannot reflect any light upon the opposite bodies.

CHAP. CCXV.

IN WHAT PART THE REFLEXES HAVE MORE OR LESS BRIGHTNESS.

THE reflected lights will be more or less apparent or bright, in proportion as they are seen against a darker or fainter ground; because if the ground be darker than the reflex, then this reflex will appear stronger on account of the great difference of colour. But, on the contrary, if this reflexion has behind it a ground lighter than itself, it will appear dark, in comparison to the brightness which is close to it, and therefore it will be hardly perceptible[258].

CHAP. CCXVI.

OF THE REFLECTED LIGHTS WHICH SURROUND THE SHADOWS.

THE reflected lights which strike upon the midst of shadows, will brighten up or lessen their obscurity in proportion to the strength of those lights, and their proximity to those shadows. Many painters neglect this observation, while others attend to and deduce their practice from it. This difference of opinion and practice divides the sentiments of artists, so that they blame each other for not thinking and acting as they themselves do. The best way is to steer a middle course, and not to admit of any reflected light, but when the cause of it is evident to every eye; and *vice versâ*, if you introduce none at all, let it appear evident that there was no reasonable cause for it. In doing so, you will neither be totally blamed nor praised by the variety of opinion, which, if not proceeding from entire ignorance, will ensure to you the approbation of both parties.

---

[258] See chap. ccxvii. and ccxix.

CHAP. CCXVII.

WHERE REFLEXES ARE TO BE MOST APPARENT.

OF all reflected lights, that is to be the most apparent, bold, and precise, which detaches from the darkest ground; and, on the contrary, that which is upon a lighter ground will be less apparent. And this proceeds from the contraste of shades, by which the faintest makes the dark ones appear still darker; so in contrasted lights, the brightest cause the others to appear less bright than they really are[259].

CHAP. CCXVIII.

WHAT PART OF A REFLEX IS TO BE THE LIGHTEST.

THAT part will be the brightest which receives the reflected light between angles the most nearly equal. For example, let N be the luminary, and A B the illuminated part of the object, reflecting the light over all the shady part of the concavity opposite to it. The light which reflects upon F will be placed between equal angles. But E at the base will not be reflected by equal angles, as it is evident that the angle E A B is more obtuse than the angle E B A. The angle A F B however, though it is between angles of less quality than the angle E, and has a common base B A, is between angles more nearly equal than E, therefore it will be lighter in F than in E; and it will also be brighter, because it is nearer to the part which gives them light. According to the 6th rule[260], which says, that part of the body is to be the lightest, which is nearest to the luminary.

---

[259] See chap. ccxv. and ccxix.

[260] This was intended to constitute a part of some book of Perspective, which we have not; but the rule here referred to will be found in chap. cccx. of the present work.

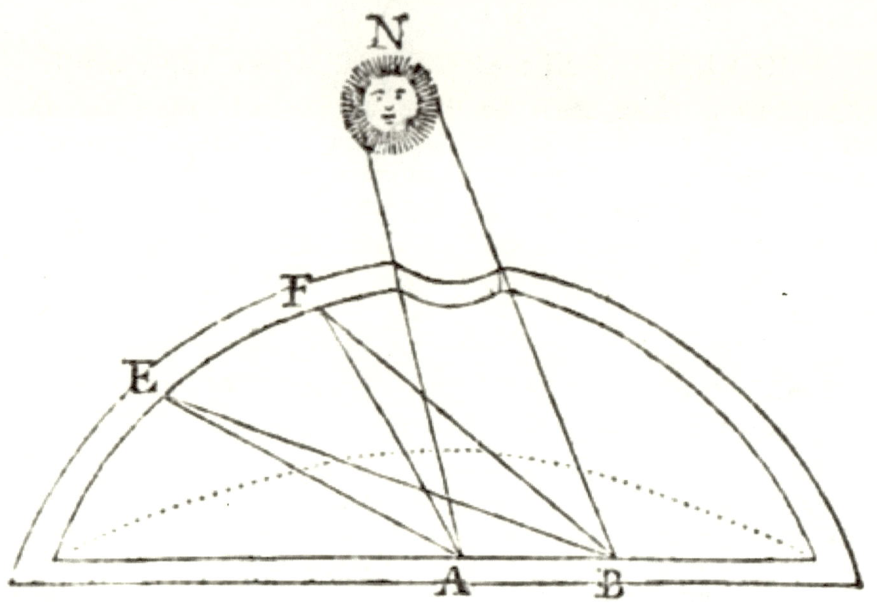

CHAP. CCXIX.

OF THE TERMINATION OF REFLEXES ON THEIR GROUNDS.

THE termination of a reflected light on a ground lighter than that reflex, will not be perceivable; but if such a reflex terminates upon a ground darker than itself, it will be plainly seen; and the more so in proportion as that ground is darker, and *vice versa*[261].

CHAP. CCXX.

OF DOUBLE AND TREBLE REFLEXIONS OF LIGHT.

DOUBLE reflexes are stronger than single ones, and the shadows which interpose between the common light and these reflexes are very faint. For instance, let A be the luminous body, A N, A S, are the direct rays, and S N the parts which receive the light from them. O and E are the places enlightened by the reflexion of that light in those parts. A N E is a single reflex, but A N O, A S O is the double reflex. The single reflex is that which proceeds from a single light, but the double reflexion is produced by two different lights. The single one E is produced by the light striking on B D, while the double one O proceeds from the enlightened bodies B D and D R co-operating together; and the shadows which are between N O and S O will be very faint.

---

[261] See chap. ccxv. and ccxvii.

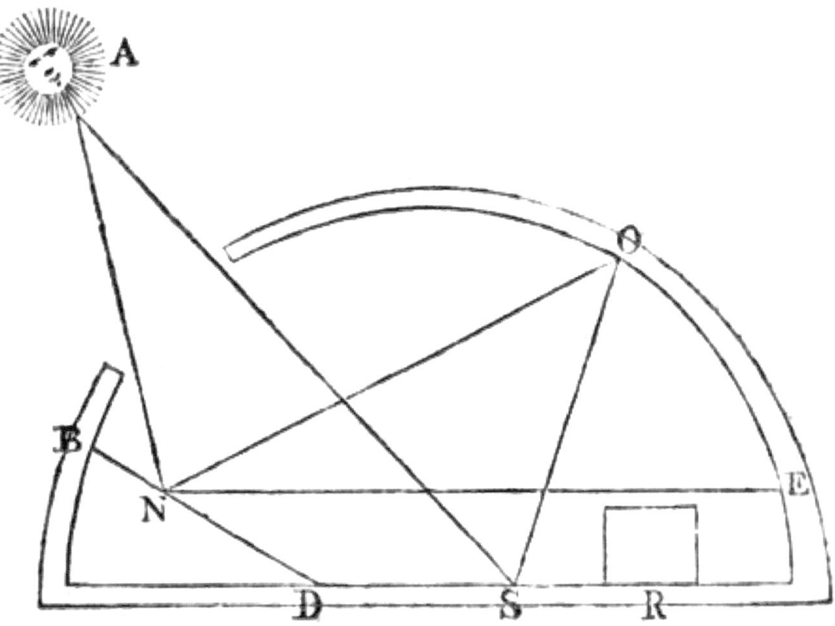

CHAP. CCXXI.

REFLEXES IN THE WATER, AND PARTICULARLY THOSE OF THE AIR.

THE only portion of air that will be seen reflected in the water, will be that which is reflected by the surface of the water to the eye between equal angles; that is to say, the angle of incidence must be equal to the angle of reflexion.

COLOURS AND COLOURING.

COLOURS.

CHAP. CCXXII.

WHAT SURFACE IS BEST CALCULATED TO RECEIVE MOST COLOURS.

White is more capable of receiving all sorts of colours, than the surface of any body whatever, that is not transparent. To prove it, we shall say, that any void space is capable of receiving what another space, not void, cannot receive. In the same manner, a white surface, like a void space, being destitute of any colour, will be fittest to receive such as are conveyed to it from any other enlightened body, and will participate more of the colour than black can do; which latter, like a broken vessel, is not able to contain any thing.

CHAP. CCXXIII.

WHAT SURFACE WILL SHEW MOST PERFECTLY ITS TRUE COLOUR.

That opake body will shew its colour more perfect and beautiful, which has near it another body of the same colour.

CHAP. CCXXIV.

ON WHAT SURFACES THE TRUE COLOUR IS LEAST APPARENT.

Polished and glossy surfaces shew least of their genuine colour. This is exemplified in the grass of the fields, and the leaves of trees, which, being smooth and glossy, will reflect the colour of the sun, and the air, where they strike, so that the parts which receive the light do not shew their natural colour.

CHAP. CCXXV.

WHAT SURFACES SHEW MOST OF THEIR TRUE AND GENUINE COLOUR.

Those objects that are the least smooth and polished shew their natural colours best; as we see in cloth, and in the leaves of such grass or trees as are of a woolly nature; which, having no lustre, are exhibited to the eye in their true natural colour; unless that colour happen to be confused by that of another body casting on them reflexions of an opposite colour, such as the redness of the setting sun, when all the clouds are tinged with its colour.

CHAP. CCXXVI.

OF THE MIXTURE OF COLOURS.

ALTHOUGH the mixture of colours may be extended to an infinite variety, almost impossible to be described, I will not omit touching slightly upon it, setting down at first a certain number of simple colours to serve as a foundation, and with each of these mixing one of the others; one with one, then two with two, and three with three, proceeding in this manner to the full mixture of all the colors together: then I would begin again, mixing two of these colours with two others, and three with three, four with four, and so on to the end. To these two colours we shall put three; to these three add three more, and then six, increasing always in the same proportion.

I call those simple colours, which are not composed, and cannot be made or supplied by any mixture of other colours. Black and White are not reckoned among colours; the one is the representative of darkness, the other of light: that is, one is a simple privation of light, the other is light itself. Yet I will not omit mentioning them, because there is nothing in painting more useful and necessary; since painting is but an effect produced by lights and shadows, viz. *chiaro-scuro*. After Black and White come Blue and Yellow, then Green, and Tawny or Umber, and then Purple and Red. These eight colours are all that Nature produces. With these I begin my mixtures, first Black and White, Black and Yellow, Black and Red; then Yellow and Red: but I shall treat more at length of these mixtures in a separate work[262], which will be of great utility, nay very necessary. I shall place this subject between theory and practice.

CHAP. CCXXVII.

OF THE COLOURS PRODUCED BY THE MIXTURE OF OTHER COLOURS, CALLED SECONDARY COLOURS.

THE first of all simple colours is White, though philosophers will not acknowledge either White or Black to be colours; because the first is the cause, or the receiver of colours, the other totally deprived of them. But as painters cannot do without either, we shall place them among the others; and according to this order of things, White will be the first, Yellow the second, Green the third, Blue the fourth, Red the fifth, and Black the sixth. We shall set down White for the representative of light, without which no colour can be seen; Yellow for the earth; Green for water; Blue for air; Red for fire; and Black for total darkness.

[262] No such work was ever published, nor, for any thing that appears, ever written.

If you wish to see by a short process the variety of all the mixed, or composed colours, take some coloured glasses, and, through them, look at all the country round: you will find that the colour of each object will be altered and mixed with the colour of the glass through which it is seen; observe which colour is made better, and which is hurt by the mixture. If the glass be yellow, the colour of the objects may either be improved, or greatly impaired by it. Black and White will be most altered, while Green and Yellow will be meliorated. In the same manner you may go through all the mixtures of colours, which are infinite. Select those which are new and agreeable to the sight; and following the same method you may go on with two glasses, or three, till you have found what will best answer your purpose.

CHAP. CCXXVIII.
OF VERDEGRIS.

This green, which is made of copper, though it be mixed with oil, will lose its beauty, if it be not varnished immediately. It not only fades, but, if washed with a sponge and pure water only, it will detach from the ground upon which it is painted, particularly in damp weather; because verdegris is produced by the strength of salts, which easily dissolve in rainy weather, but still more if washed with a wet sponge.

CHAP. CCXXIX.
HOW TO INCREASE THE BEAUTY OF VERDEGRIS.

If you mix with the Verdegris some Caballine Aloe, it will add to it a great degree of beauty. It would acquire still more from Saffron, if it did not fade. The quality and goodness of this Aloe will be proved by dissolving it in warm Brandy. Supposing the Verdegris has already been used, and the part finished, you may then glaze it thinly with this dissolved Aloe, and it will produce a very fine colour. This Aloe may be ground also in oil by itself, or with the Verdegris, or any other colour, at pleasure.

CHAP. CCXXX.
HOW TO PAINT A PICTURE THAT WILL LAST ALMOST FOR EVER.

After you have made a drawing of your intended picture, prepare a good and thick priming with pitch and brickdust well pounded; after which give it a second coat of white lead and Naples yellow; then, having traced your drawing upon it, and painted your picture, varnish it with clear and thick old oil, and stick it to a flat glass, or crystal, with a clear varnish. Another method, which may be better, is, instead of the priming of pitch and brickdust, take a flat tile well vitrified, then apply the coat of white and Naples yellow, and all the rest as before. But before the glass is applied to it, the painting must be perfectly dried in a stove, and varnished with nut oil and amber, or else with purified nut oil alone, thickened in the sun[263].

CHAP. CCXXXI.

THE MODE OF PAINTING ON CANVASS, OR LINEN CLOTH[264].

STRETCH your canvass upon a frame, then give it a coat of weak size, let it dry, and draw your outlines upon it. Paint the flesh colours first; and while it is still fresh or moist, paint also the shadows, well softened and blended together. The flesh colour may be made with white, lake, and Naples yellow. The shades with black, umber, and a little lake; you may, if you please, use black chalk. After you have softened this first coat, or dead colour, and let it dry, you may retouch over it with lake and other colours, and gum water that has been a long while made and kept liquid, because in that state it becomes better, and does not leave any gloss.

Again, to make the shades darker, take the lake and gum as above, and ink[265]; and with this you may shade or glaze many colours, because it is transparent; such as azure, lake, and several others. As for the lights, you may retouch or glaze them slightly with gum water and pure lake, particularly vermilion.

CHAP. CCXXXII.

OF LIVELY AND BEAUTIFUL COLOURS.

FOR those colours which you mean should appear beautiful, prepare a ground of pure white. This is meant only for transparent colours: as for those that have a body, and are opake, it matters not what ground they have, and a white one is of no use. This is exemplified by painted glasses; when placed between the eye and clear air, they exhibit most excellent and beautiful colours, which is not the case, when they have thick air, or some opake body behind them.

---

[263] The French translation of 1716 has a note on this chapter, saying, that the invention of enamel painting found out since the time of Leonardo da Vinci, would better answer to the title of this chapter, and also be a better method of painting. I must beg leave, however, to dissent from this opinion, as the two kinds of painting are so different, that they cannot be compared. Leonardo treats of oil painting, but the other is vitrification. Leonardo is known to have spent a great deal of time in experiments, of which this is a specimen, and it may appear ridiculous to the practitioners of more modern date, as he does not enter more fully into a minute description of the materials, or the mode of employing them. The principle laid down in the text appears to me to be simply this: to make the oil entirely evaporate from the colours by the action of fire, and afterwards to prevent the action of the air by the means of a glass, which in itself is an excellent principle, but not applicable, any more than enamel painting to large works.

[264] It is evident that distemper or size painting is here meant.

[265] Indian ink.

CHAP. CCXXXIII.

OF TRANSPARENT COLOURS.

WHEN a transparent colour is laid upon another of a different nature, it produces a mixed colour, different from either of the simple ones which compose it. This is observed in the smoke coming out of a chimney, which, when passing before the black soot, appears blueish, but as it ascends against the blue of the sky, it changes its appearance into a reddish brown. So the colour lake laid on blue will turn it to a violet colour; yellow upon blue turns to green; saffron upon white becomes yellow; white scumbled upon a dark ground appears blue, and is more or less beautiful, as the white and the ground are more or less pure.

CHAP. CCXXXIV.

IN WHAT PART A COLOUR WILL APPEAR IN ITS GREATEST BEAUTY.

WE are to consider here in what part any colour will shew itself in its most perfect purity; whether in the strongest light or deepest shadow, in the demi-tint, or in the reflex. It would be necessary to determine first, of what colour we mean to treat, because different colours differ materially in that respect. Black is most beautiful in the shades; white in the strongest light; blue and green in the half-tint; yellow and red in the principal light; gold in the reflexes; and lake in the half-tint.

CHAP. CCXXXV.

HOW ANY COLOUR WITHOUT GLOSS, IS MORE BEAUTIFUL IN THE LIGHTS THAN IN THE SHADES.

ALL objects which have no gloss, shew their colours better in the light than in the shadow, because the light vivifies and gives a true knowledge of the nature of the colour, while the shadows lower, and destroy its beauty, preventing the discovery of its nature. If, on the contrary, black be more beautiful in the shadows, it is because black is not a colour.

CHAP. CCXXXVI.

OF THE APPEARANCE OF COLOURS.

THE lighter a colour is in its nature, the more so it will appear when removed to some distance; but with dark colours it is quite the reverse.

CHAP. CCXXXVII.

WHAT PART OF A COLOUR IS TO BE THE MOST BEAUTI-FUL.

IF A be the light, and B the object receiving it in a direct line, E cannot receive that light, but only the reflexion from B, which we shall suppose to be red. In that case, the light it produces being red, it will tinge with red the object E; and if E happen to be also red before, you will see that colour increase in beauty, and appear redder than B; but if E were yellow, you will see a new colour, participating of the red and the yellow.

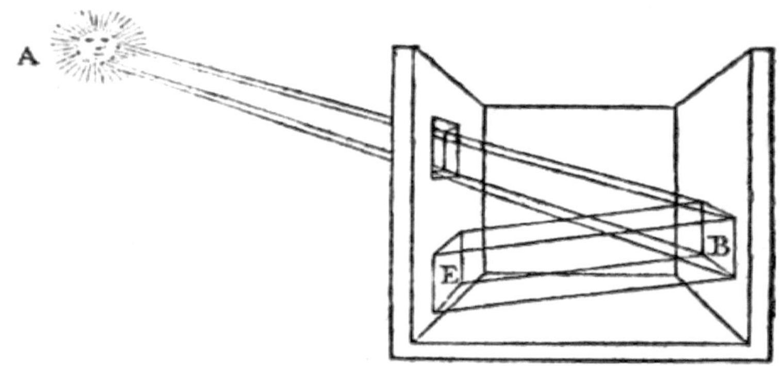

CHAP. CCXXXVIII.

THAT THE BEAUTY OF A COLOUR IS TO BE FOUND IN THE LIGHTS.

As the quality of colours is discovered to the eye by the light, it is natural to conclude, that where there is most light, there also the true quality of the colour is to be seen; and where there is most shadow the colour will participate of, and be tinged with the colour of that shadow. Remember then to shew the true quality of the colour in the light parts only[266].

CHAP. CCXXXIX.

OF COLOURS.

THE colour which is between the light and the shadow will not be so beautiful as that which is in the full light. Therefore the chief beauty of colours will be found in the principal lights[267].

---

[266] This rule is not without exception: see chap. ccxxxiv.
[267] See chap. ccxxxviii.

CHAP. CCXL.

NO OBJECT APPEARS IN ITS TRUE COLOUR, UNLESS THE LIGHT WHICH STRIKES UPON IT BE OF THE SAME CO-LOUR.

THIS is very observable in draperies, where the light folds casting a reflexion, and throwing a light on other folds opposite to them, make them appear in their natural colour. The same effect is produced by gold leaves casting their light reciprocally on each other. The effect is quite contrary if the light be received from an object of a different colour[268].

CHAP. CCXLI.

OF THE COLOUR OF SHADOWS.

THE colour of the shadows of an object can never be pure if the body which is opposed to these shadows be not of the same colour as that on which they are produced. For instance, if in a room, the walls of which are green, I place a figure clothed in blue, and receiving the light from another blue object, the light part of that figure will be of a beautiful blue, but the shadows of it will become dingy, and not like a true shade of that beautiful blue, because it will be corrupted by the reflexions from the green wall; and it would be still worse if the walls were of a darkish brown.

CHAP. CCXLII.

OF COLOURS.

COLOURS placed in shadow will preserve more or less of their original beauty, as they are more or less immersed in the shade. But colours situated in a light space will shew their natural beauty in proportion to the brightness of that light. Some say, that there is as great variety in the colours of shadows, as in the colours of objects shaded by them. It may be answered, that colours placed in shadow will shew less variety amongst themselves as the shadows are darker. We shall soon convince ourselves of this truth, if, from a large square, we look through the open door of a church, where pictures, though enriched with a variety of colours, appear all clothed in darkness.

CHAP. CCXLIII.

WHETHER IT BE POSSIBLE FOR ALL COLOURS TO AP-PEAR ALIKE BY MEANS OF THE SAME SHADOW.

IT is very possible that all the different colours may be changed into that of a general shadow: as is manifest in the darkness of a cloudy night, in which neither

[268] See chap. ccxxxvii.

the shape nor colour of bodies is distinguished. Total darkness being nothing but a privation of the primitive and reflected lights, by which the form and colour of bodies are seen; it is evident, that the cause being removed the effect ceases, and the objects are entirely lost to the sight.

CHAP. CCXLIV.

WHY WHITE IS NOT RECKONED AMONG THE COLOURS.

WHITE is not a colour, but has the power of receiving all the other colours. When it is placed in a high situation in the country, all its shades are azure; according to the fourth proposition[269], which says, that the surface of any opake body participates of the colour of any other body sending the light to it. Therefore white being deprived of the light of the sun by the interposition of any other body, will remain white; if exposed to the sun on one side, and to the open air on the other, it will participate both of the colour of the sun and of the air. That side which is not opposed to the sun, will be shaded of the colour of the air. And if this white were not surrounded by green fields all the way to the horizon, nor could receive any light from that horizon, without doubt it would appear of one simple and uniform colour, viz. that of the air.

CHAP. CCXLV.

OF COLOURS.

THE light of the fire tinges every thing of a reddish yellow; but this will hardly appear evident, if we do not make the comparison with the daylight. Towards the close of the evening this is easily done; but more certainly after the morning twilight; and the difference will be clearly distinguished in a dark room, when a little glimpse of daylight strikes upon any part of the room, and there still remains a candle burning. Without such a trial the difference is hardly perceivable, particularly in those colours which have most similarity; such as white and yellow, light green and light blue; because the light which strikes the blue, being yellow, will naturally turn it green; as we have said in another place[270], that a mixture of blue and yellow produces green. And if to a green colour you add some yellow, it will make it of a more beautiful green.

CHAP. CCXLVI.

OF THE COLOURING OF REMOTE OBJECTS.

THE painter, who is to represent objects at some distance from the eye, ought

---

[269] See chapters ccxlvii. cclxxiv. in the present work. Probably they were intended to form a part of a distinct treatise, and to have been ranged as propositions in that, but at present they are not so placed.

[270] See chap. ccxlviii.

merely to convey the idea of general undetermined masses, making choice, for that purpose, of cloudy weather, or towards the evening, and avoiding, as was said before, to mark the lights and shadows too strong on the extremities; because they would in that case appear like spots of difficult execution, and without grace. He ought to remember, that the shadows are never to be of such a quality, as to obliterate the proper colour, in which they originated; if the situation of the coloured body be not in total darkness. He ought to mark no outline, not to make the hair stringy, and not to touch with pure white, any but those things which in themselves are white; in short, the lightest touch upon any particular object ought to denote the beauty of its proper and natural colour.

CHAP. CCXLVII.

THE SURFACE OF ALL OPAKE BODIES PARTICIPATES OF THE COLOUR OF THE SURROUNDING OBJECTS.

THE painter ought to know, that if any white object is placed between two walls, one of which is also white, and the other black, there will be found between the shady side of that object and the light side, a similar proportion to that of the two walls; and if that object be blue, the effect will be the same. Having therefore to paint this object, take some black, similar to that of the wall from which the reflexes come; and to proceed by a certain and scientific method, do as follows. When you paint the wall, take a small spoon to measure exactly the quantity of colour you mean to employ in mixing your tints; for instance, if you have put in the shading of this wall three spoonfuls of pure black, and one of white, you have, without any doubt, a mixture of a certain and precise quality. Now having painted one of the walls white, and the other dark, if you mean to place a blue object between them with shades suitable to that colour, place first on your pallet the light blue, such as you mean it to be, without any mixture of shade, and it will do for the lightest part of your object. After which take three spoonfuls of black, and one of this light blue, for your darkest shades. Then observe whether your object be round or square: if it be square, these two extreme tints of light and shade will be close to each other, cutting sharply at the angle; but if it be round, draw lines from the extremities of the walls to the centre of the object, and put the darkest shade between equal angles, where the lines intersect upon the superficies of it; then begin to make them lighter and lighter gradually to the point N O, lessening the strength of the shadows as much as that place participates of the light A D, and mixing that colour with the darkest shade A B, in the same proportion.

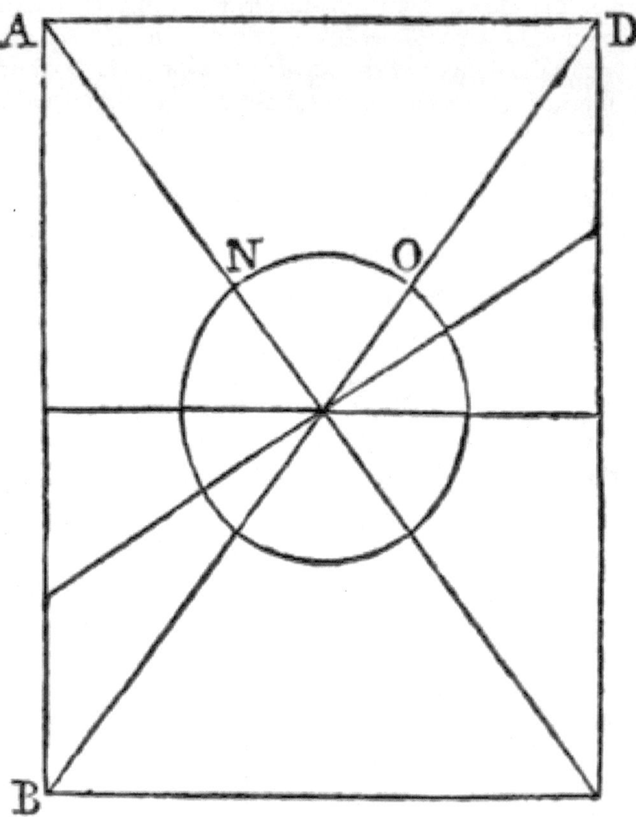

CHAP. CCXLVIII.

GENERAL REMARKS ON COLOURS.

BLUE and green are not simple colours in their nature, for blue is composed of light and darkness; such is the azure of the sky, viz. perfect black and perfect white. Green is composed of a simple and a mixed colour, being produced by blue and yellow.

Any object seen in a mirror, will participate of the colour of that body which serves as a mirror; and the mirror in its turn is tinged in part by the colour of the object it represents; they partake more or less of each other as the colour of the object seen is more or less strong than the colour of the mirror. That object will appear of the strongest and most lively colour in the mirror, which has the most affinity to the colour of the mirror itself.

Of coloured bodies, the purest white will be seen at the greatest distance, therefore the darker the colour, the less it will bear distance.

Of different bodies equal in whiteness, and in distance from the eye, that which is surrounded by the greatest darkness will appear the whitest; and on the contrary, that shadow will appear the darkest that has the brightest white round it.

Of different colours, equally perfect, that will appear most excellent, which is seen near its direct contrary. A pale colour against red, a black upon white (though neither the one nor the other are colours), blue near a yellow; green near red; because each colour is more distinctly seen, when opposed to its contrary, than to any other similar to it.

Any thing white seen in a dense air full of vapours, will appear larger than it is in reality.

The air, between the eye and the object seen, will change the colour of that object into its own; so will the azure of the air change the distant mountains into blue masses. Through a red glass every thing appears red; the light round the stars is dimmed by the darkness of the air, which fills the space between the eye and the planets.

The true colour of any object whatever will be seen in those parts which are not occupied by any kind of shade, and have not any gloss (if it be a polished surface).

I say, that white terminating abruptly upon a dark ground, will cause that part where it terminates to appear darker, and the white whiter.

COLOURS IN REGARD TO LIGHT AND SHADOW.

CHAP. CCXLIX.

OF THE LIGHT PROPER FOR PAINTING FLESH COLOUR FROM NATURE.

Your window must be open to the sky, and the walls painted of a reddish colour. The summertime is the best, when the clouds conceal the sun, or else your walls on the south side of the room must be so high, as that the sun-beams cannot strike on the opposite side, in order that the reflexion of those beams may not destroy the shadows.

CHAP. CCL.

OF THE PAINTER'S WINDOW.

The window which gives light to a painting-room, ought to be made of oiled paper, without any cross bar, or projecting edge at the opening, or any sharp angle in the inside of the wall, but should be slanting by degrees the whole thickness of it; and the sides be painted black.

CHAP. CCLI.

THE SHADOWS OF COLOURS.

The shadows of any colour whatever must participate of that colour more or less, as it is nearer to, or more remote from the mass of shadows; and also in proportion to its distance from, or proximity to the mass of light.

CHAP. CCLII.

OF THE SHADOWS OF WHITE.

To any white body receiving the light from the sun, or the air, the shadows should be of a blueish cast; because white is no colour, but a receiver of all colours; and as by the fourth proposition[271] we learn, that the surface of any object partic-

[271] See chap. cclxxiv.

ipates of the colours of other objects near it, it is evident that a white surface will participate of the colour of the air by which it is surrounded.

CHAP. CCLIII.

WHICH OF THE COLOURS WILL PRODUCE THE DARKEST SHADE.

THAT shade will be the darkest which is produced by the whitest surface; this also will have a greater propensity to variety than any other surface; because white is not properly a colour, but a receiver of colours, and its surface will participate strongly of the colour of surrounding objects, but principally of black or any other dark colour, which being the most opposite to its nature, produces the most sensible difference between the shadows and the lights.

CHAP. CCLIV.

HOW TO MANAGE, WHEN A WHITE TERMINATES UPON ANOTHER WHITE.

WHEN one white body terminates on another of the same colour, the white of these two bodies will be either alike or not. If they be alike, that object which of the two is nearest to the eye, should be made a little darker than the other, upon the rounding of the outline; but if the object which serves as a ground to the other be not quite so white, the latter will detach of itself, without the help of any darker termination.

CHAP. CCLV.

ON THE BACK-GROUNDS OF FIGURES.

OF two objects equally light, one will appear less so if seen upon a whiter ground; and, on the contrary, it will appear a great deal lighter if upon a space of a darker shade. So flesh colour will appear pale upon a red ground, and a pale colour will appear redder upon a yellow ground. In short, colours will appear what they are not, according to the ground which surrounds them.

CHAP. CCLVI.

THE MODE OF COMPOSING HISTORY.

AMONGST the figures which compose an historical picture, those which are meant to appear the nearest to the eye, must have the greatest force; according to the second proposition[272] of the third book, which says, that colour will be seen

[272] Although the author seems to have designed that this, and many other propositions to which he refers, should have formed a part of some regular work, and he has ac-

in the greatest perfection which has less air interposed between it and the eye of the beholder; and for that reason the shadows (by which we express the relievo of bodies) appear darker when near than when at a distance, being then deadened by the air which interposes. This does not happen to those shadows which are near the eye, where they will produce the greatest relievo when they are darkest.

CHAP. CCLVII.

REMARKS CONCERNING LIGHTS AND SHADOWS.

OBSERVE, that where the shadows end, there be always a kind of half-shadow to blend them with the lights. The shadow derived from any object will mix more with the light at its termination, in proportion as it is more distant from that object. But the colour of the shadow will never be simple: this is proved by the ninth proposition[273], which says, that the superficies of any object participates of the colours of other bodies, by which it is surrounded, although it were transparent, such as water, air, and the like: because the air receives its light from the sun, and darkness is produced by the privation of it. But as the air has no colour in itself any more than water, it receives all the colours that are between the object and the eye. The vapours mixing with the air in the lower regions near the earth, render it thick, and apt to reflect the sun's rays on all sides, while the air above remains dark; and because light (that is, white) and darkness (that is, black), mixed together, compose the azure that becomes the colour of the sky, which is lighter or darker in proportion as the air is more or less mixed with damp vapours.

---

cordingly referred to them whenever he has mentioned them, by their intended numerical situation in that work, whatever it might be, it does not appear that he ever carried this design into execution. There are, however, several chapters in the present work, viz. ccxciii. cclxxxix. cclxxxv. ccxcv. in which the principle in the text is recognised, and which probably would have been transferred into the projected treatise, if he had ever drawn it up.

[273] The note on the preceding chapter is in a great measure applicable to this, and the proposition mentioned in the text is also to be found in chapter ccxlvii. of the present work.

CHAP. CCLVIII.

WHY THE SHADOWS OF BODIES UPON A WHITE WALL ARE BLUEISH TOWARDS EVENING.

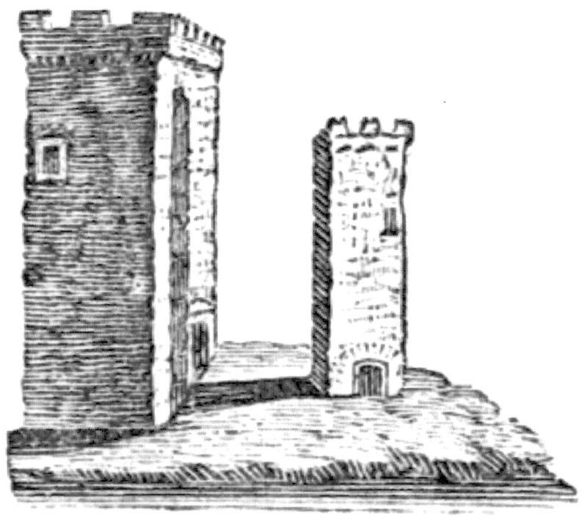
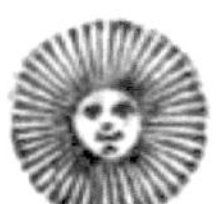

THE shadows of bodies produced by the redness of the setting sun, will always be blueish. This is accounted for by the eleventh proposition[274], which says, that the superficies of any opake body participates of the colour of the object from which it receives the light; therefore the white wall being deprived entirely of colour, is tinged by the colour of those bodies from which it receives the light, which in this case are the sun and the sky. But because the sun is red towards the evening, and the sky is blue, the shadow on the wall not being enlightened by the sun, receives only the reflexion of the sky, and therefore will appear blue; and the rest of the wall, receiving light immediately from the sun, will participate of its red colour.

CHAP. CCLIX.

OF THE COLOUR OF FACES.

THE colour of any object will appear more or less distinct in proportion to the extent of its surface. This proportion is proved, by observing that a face appears dark at a small distance, because, being composed of many small parts, it produces a great number of shadows; and the lights being the smallest part of it, are soonest lost to the sight, leaving only the shadows, which being in a greater quantity, the whole of the face appears dark, and the more so if that face has on the head, or at the back, something whiter.

---

[274] See the note on the chapter next but one preceding. The proposition in the text occurs in chap. ccxlvii. of the present work.

CHAP. CCLX.

A PRECEPT RELATING TO PAINTING.

WHERE the shadows terminate upon the lights, observe well what parts of them are lighter than the others, and where they are more or less softened and blended; but above all remember, that young people have no sharp shadings: their flesh is transparent, something like what we observe when we put our hand between the sun and eyes; it appears reddish, and of a transparent brightness. If you wish to know what kind of shadow will suit the flesh colour you are painting, place one of your fingers close to your picture, so as to cast a shadow upon it, and according as you wish it either lighter or darker, put it nearer or farther from it, and imitate it.

CHAP. CCLXI.

OF COLOURS IN SHADOW.

IT happens very often that the shadows of an opake body do not retain the same colour as the lights. Sometimes they will be greenish, while the lights are reddish, although this opake body be all over of one uniform colour. This happens when the light falls upon the object (we will suppose from the East), and tinges that side with its own colour. In the West we will suppose another opake body of a colour different from the first, but receiving the same light. This last will reflect its colour towards the East, and strike the first with its rays on the opposite side, where they will be stopped, and remain with their full colour and brightness. We often see a white object with red lights, and the shades of a blueish cast; this we observe particularly in mountains covered with snow, at sun-set, when the effulgence of its rays makes the horizon appear all on fire.

CHAP. CCLXII.

OF THE CHOICE OF LIGHTS.

WHATEVER object you intend to represent is to be supposed situated in a particular light, and that entirely of your own choosing. If you imagine such objects to be in the country, and the sun be overcast, they will be surrounded by a great quantity of general light. If the sun strikes upon those objects, then the shadows will be very dark, in proportion to the lights, and will be determined and sharp; the primitive as well as the secondary ones. These shadows will vary from the lights in colour, because on that side the object receives a reflected light hue from the azure of the air, which tinges that part; and this is particularly observable in white objects. That side which receives the light from the sun, participates also of the colour of that. This may be particularly observed in the evening, when the sun is setting between the clouds, which it reddens; those clouds being tinged with the colour of the body illuminating them, the red colour of the clouds, with that of the sun, casts a hue on those parts which receive the light from them. On the contrary, those parts which are not turned towards that side of the sky, remain of the colour of the air, so that the former and the latter are of two different colours. This we must not lose sight of, that, knowing the cause of those lights and shades, it be made apparent in the effect, or else the work will be false and absurd. But if a figure be situated within a house, and seen from without, such figure will have its shadows very soft; and if the beholder stands in the line of the light, it will acquire grace, and do credit to the painter, as it will have great relief in the lights, and soft and well-blended shadows, particularly in those parts where the inside of the room appears less obscure, because there the shadows are almost imperceptible: the cause of which we shall explain in its proper place.

COLOURS IN REGARD TO BACK-GROUNDS.

CHAP. CCLXIII.
OF AVOIDING HARD OUTLINES.

Do not make the boundaries of your figures with any other colour than that of the back-ground, on which they are placed; that is, avoid making dark outlines.

CHAP. CCLXIV.
OF OUTLINES.

THE extremities of objects which are at some distance, are not seen so distinctly as if they were nearer. Therefore the painter ought to regulate the strength of his outlines, or extremities, according to the distance.

The boundaries which separate one body from another, are of the nature of mathematical lines, but not of real lines. The end of any colour is only the beginning of another, and it ought not to be called a line, for nothing interposes between them, except the termination of the one against the other, which being nothing in itself, cannot be perceivable; therefore the painter ought not to pronounce it in distant objects.

CHAP. CCLXV.
OF BACK-GROUNDS.

ONE of the principal parts of painting is the nature and quality of back-grounds, upon which the extremities of any convex or solid body will always detach and be distinguished in nature, though the colour of such objects, and that of the ground, be exactly the same. This happens, because the convex sides of solid bodies do not receive the light in the same manner with the ground, for such sides or extremities are often lighter or darker than the ground. But if such extremities were to be of the same colour as the ground, and in the same degree of light, they certainly could not be distinguished. Therefore such a choice in painting ought to be avoided by all intelligent and judicious painters; since the intention is to make the objects appear as it were out of the ground. The above case would produce the contrary effect, not only in painting, but also in objects of real relievo.

CHAP. CCLXVI.

HOW TO DETACH FIGURES FROM THE GROUND.

ALL solid bodies will appear to have a greater relief, and to come more out of the canvass, on a ground of an undetermined colour, with the greatest variety of lights and shades against the confines of such bodies (as will be demonstrated in its place), provided a proper diminution of lights in the white tints, and of darkness in the shades, be judiciously observed.

CHAP. CCLXVII.

OF UNIFORMITY AND VARIETY OF COLOURS UPON PLAIN SURFACES.

THE back-grounds of any flat surfaces which are uniform in colour and quantity of light, will never appear separated from each other; *vice versâ*, they will appear separated if they are of different colours or lights.

CHAP. CCLXVIII.

OF BACK-GROUNDS SUITABLE BOTH TO SHADOWS AND LIGHTS.

THE shadows or lights which surround figures, or any other objects, will help the more to detach them the more they differ from the objects; that is, if a dark colour does not terminate upon another dark colour, but upon a very different one; as white, or partaking of white, but lowered, and approximated to the dark shade.

CHAP. CCLXIX.

THE APPARENT VARIATION OF COLOURS, OCCASIONED BY THE CONTRASTE OF THE GROUND UPON WHICH THEY ARE PLACED.

No colour appears uniform and equal in all its parts unless it terminate on a ground of the same colour. This is very apparent when a black terminates on a white ground, where the contraste of colour gives more strength and richness to the extremities than to the middle.

CONTRASTE, HARMONY, AND REFLEXES, IN REGARD TO COLOURS.

CHAP. CCLXX.

GRADATION IN PAINTING.

WHAT is fine is not always beautiful and good: I address this to such painters as are so attached to the beauty of colours, that they regret being obliged to give them almost imperceptible shadows, not considering the beautiful relief which figures acquire by a proper gradation and strength of shadows. Such persons may be compared to those speakers who in conversation make use of many fine words without meaning, which altogether scarcely form one good sentence.

CHAP. CCLXXI.

HOW TO ASSORT COLOURS IN SUCH A MANNER AS THAT THEY MAY ADD BEAUTY TO EACH OTHER.

IF you mean that the proximity of one colour should give beauty to another that terminates near it, observe the rays of the sun in the composition of the rainbow, the colours of which are generated by the falling rain, when each drop in its descent takes every colour of that bow, as is demonstrated in its place[275].

If you mean to represent great darkness, it must be done by contrasting it with great light; on the contrary, if you want to produce great brightness, you must oppose to it a very dark shade: so a pale yellow will cause red to appear more beautiful than if opposed to a purple colour.

There is another rule, by observing which, though you do not increase the natural beauty of the colours, yet by bringing them together they may give additional grace to each other, as green placed near red, while the effect would be quite the reverse, if placed near blue.

Harmony and grace are also produced by a judicious arrangement of colours, such as blue with pale yellow or white, and the like; as will be noticed in its place.

---

[275] Not in this work.

CHAP. CCLXXII.
OF DETACHING THE FIGURES.

LET the colours of which the draperies of your figures are composed, be such as to form a pleasing variety, to distinguish one from the other; and although, for the sake of harmony, they should be of the same nature[276], they must not stick together, but vary in point of light, according to the distance and interposition of the air between them. By the same rule, the outlines are to be more precise, or lost, in proportion to their distance or proximity.

CHAP. CCLXXIII
OF THE COLOUR OF REFLEXES.

ALL reflected colours are less brilliant and strong, than those which receive a direct light, in the same proportion as there is between the light of a body and the cause of that light.

CHAP. CCLXXIV.
WHAT BODY WILL BE THE MOST STRONGLY TINGED WITH THE COLOUR OF ANY OTHER OBJECT.

AN opake surface will partake most of the genuine colour of the body nearest to it, because a great quantity of the species of colour will be conveyed to it; whereas such colour would be broken and disturbed if coming from a more distant object.

CHAP. CCLXXV.
OF REFLEXES.

REFLEXES will partake, more or less, both of the colour of the object which produces them, and of the colour of that object on which they are produced, in proportion as this latter body is of a smoother or more polished surface, than that by which they are produced.

---

[276] I do not know a better comment on this passage than Felibien's Examination of Le Brun's Picture of the Tent of Darius. From this (which has been reprinted with an English translation, by Colonel Parsons in 1700, in folio) it will clearly appear, what the chain of connexion is between every colour there used, and its nearest neighbour, and consequently a rule may be formed from it with more certainty and precision than where the student is left to develope it for himself, from the mere inspection of different examples of colouring.

CHAP. CCLXXVI.

OF THE SURFACE OF ALL SHADOWED BODIES.

THE surface of any opake body placed in shadow, will participate of the colour of any other object which reflects the light upon it. This is very evident; for if such bodies were deprived of light in the space between them and the other bodies, they could not shew either shape or colour. We shall conclude then, that if the opake body be yellow, and that which reflects the light blue, the part reflected will be green, because green is composed of blue and yellow.

CHAP. CCLXXVII.

THAT NO REFLECTED COLOUR IS SIMPLE, BUT IS MIXED WITH THE NATURE OF THE OTHER COLOURS.

No colour reflected upon the surface of another body, will tinge that surface with its own colour alone, but will be mixed by the concurrence of other colours also reflected on the same spot. Let us suppose A to be of a yellow colour, which is reflected on the convex C O E, and that the blue colour B be reflected on the same place. I say that a mixture of the blue and yellow colours will tinge the convex surface; and that, if the ground be white, it will produce a green reflexion, because it is proved that a mixture of blue and yellow produces a very fine green.

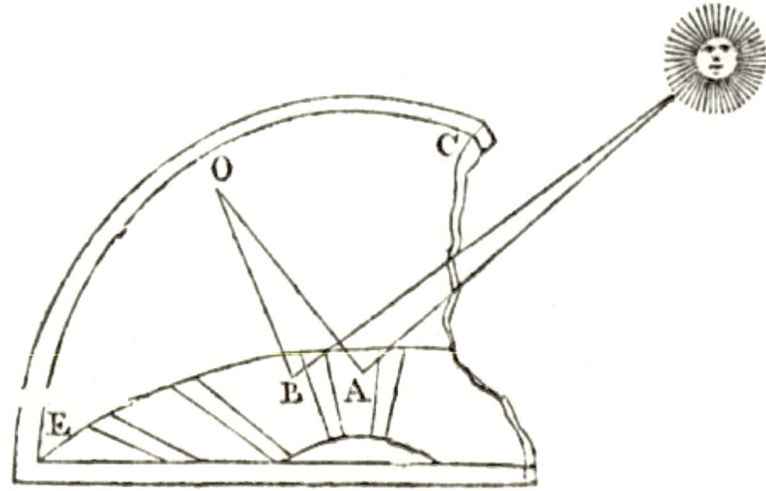

CHAP. CCLXXVIII.

OF THE COLOUR OF LIGHTS AND REFLEXES.

WHEN two lights strike upon an opake body, they can vary only in two ways; either they are equal in strength, or they are not. If they be equal, they may still vary in two other ways, that is, by the equality or inequality of their brightness; they will be equal, if their distance be the same; and unequal, if it be otherwise. The object placed at an equal distance, between two equal lights, in point both of colour and brightness, may still be enlightened by them in two different ways, either equally on each side, or unequally. It will be equally enlightened by them, when the space which remains round the lights shall be equal in colour, in degree of shade, and in brightness. It will be unequally enlightened by them when the spaces happen to be of different degrees of darkness.

CHAP. CCLXXIX.

WHY REFLECTED COLOURS SELDOM PARTAKE OF THE COLOUR OF THE BODY WHERE THEY MEET.

It happens very seldom that the reflexes are of the same colour with the body from which they proceed, or with that upon which they meet. To exemplify this, let the convex body D F G E be of a yellow colour, and the body B C, which reflects its colour on it, blue; the part of the convex surface which is struck by that reflected light, will take a green tinge, being B C, acted on by the natural light of the air, or the sun.

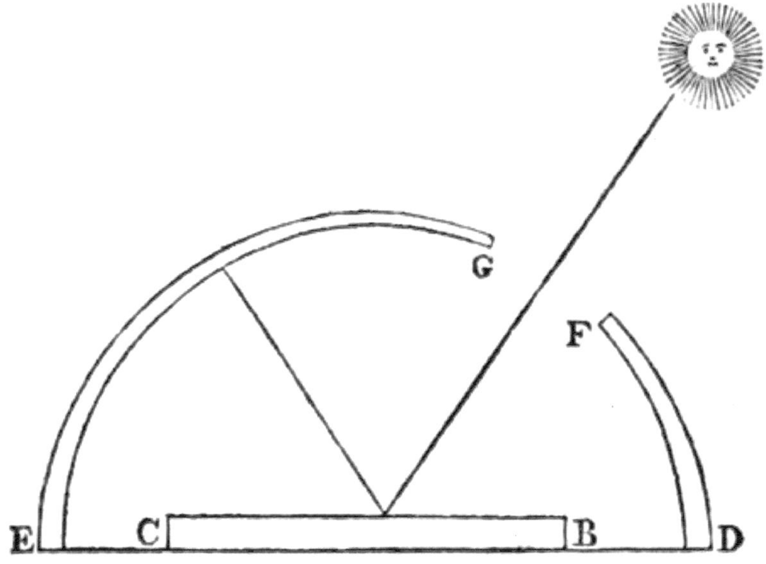

CHAP. CCLXXX.

THE REFLEXES OF FLESH COLOURS.

The lights upon the flesh colours, which are reflected by the light striking upon another flesh-coloured body, are redder and more lively than any other part of the human figure; and that happens according to the third proposition of the second book[277], which says, the surface of any opake body participates of the colour of the object which reflects the light, in proportion as it is near to or remote from it, and also in proportion to the size of it; because, being large, it prevents the variety of colours in smaller objects round it, from interfering with, and discomposing the principal colour, which is nearer. Nevertheless it does not prevent its participating more of the colour of a small object near it, than of a large one more remote. See the sixth proposition[278] of perspective, which says, that large objects may be situated at such a distance as to appear less than small ones that are near.

CHAP. CCLXXXI.

OF THE NATURE OF COMPARISON.

BLACK draperies will make the flesh of the human figure appear whiter than in reality it is[279]; and white draperies, on the contrary, will make it appear darker. Yellow will render it higher coloured, while red will make it pale.

CHAP. CCLXXXII.

WHERE THE REFLEXES ARE SEEN.

OF all reflexions of the same shape, size, and strength, that will be more or less strong, which terminates on a ground more or less dark.

The surface of those bodies will partake most of the colour of the object that reflects it, which receive that reflexion by the most nearly equal angles.

Of the colours of objects reflected upon any opposite surface by equal angles, that will be the most distinct which has its reflecting ray the shortest.

Of all colours, reflected under equal angles, and at equal distance upon the opposite body, those will be the strongest, which come reflected by the lightest coloured body.

That object will reflect its own colour most precisely on the opposite object, which has not round it any colour that clashes with its own; and consequently that reflected colour will be most confused which takes its origin from a variety of bodies of different colours.

That colour which is nearest the opposed object, will tinge it the most strongly; and *vice versâ*: let the painter, therefore, in his reflexes on the human body, par-

---

[277] See chap. ccxxiii. ccxxxvii. cclxxiv. cclxxxii. of the present work. We have before remarked, that the propositions so frequently referred to by the author, were never reduced into form, though apparently he intended a regular work in which they were to be included.

[278] No where in this work.

[279] This is evident in many of Vandyke's portraits, particularly of ladies, many of whom are dressed in black velvet; and this remark will in some measure account for the delicate fairness which he frequently gives to the female complexion.

ticularly on the flesh colour, mix some of the colour of the drapery which comes nearest to it; but not pronounce it too distinctly, if there be not good reason for it.

PERSPECTIVE OF COLOURS.

CHAP. CCLXXXIII.
A PRECEPT OF PERSPECTIVE IN REGARD TO PAINTING.

When, on account of some particular quality of the air, you can no longer distinguish the difference between the lights and shadows of objects, you may reject the perspective of shadows, and make use only of the linear perspective, and the diminution of colours, to lessen the knowledge of the objects opposed to the eye; and this, that is to say, the loss of the knowledge of the figure of each object, will make the same object appear more remote.

The eye can never arrive at a perfect knowledge of the interval between two objects variously distant, by means of the linear perspective alone, if not assisted by the perspective of colours.

CHAP. CCLXXXIV.
OF THE PERSPECTIVE OF COLOURS.

The air will participate less of the azure of the sky, in proportion as it comes nearer to the horizon, as it is proved by the third and ninth proposition[280], that pure and subtile bodies (such as compose the air) will be less illuminated by the sun than those of thicker and grosser substance: and as it is certain that the air which is remote from the earth, is thinner than that which is near it, it will follow, that the latter will be more impregnated with the rays of the sun, which giving light at the same time to an infinity of atoms floating in this air, renders it more sensible to the eye. So that the air will appear lighter towards the horizon, and darker as well as bluer in looking up to the sky; because there is more of the thick air between our eyes and the horizon, than between our eyes and that part of the sky above our heads.

---

[280] These propositions, any more than the others mentioned in different parts of this work, were never digested into a regular treatise, as was evidently intended by the author, and consequently are not to be found, except perhaps in some of the volumes of the author's manuscript collections.

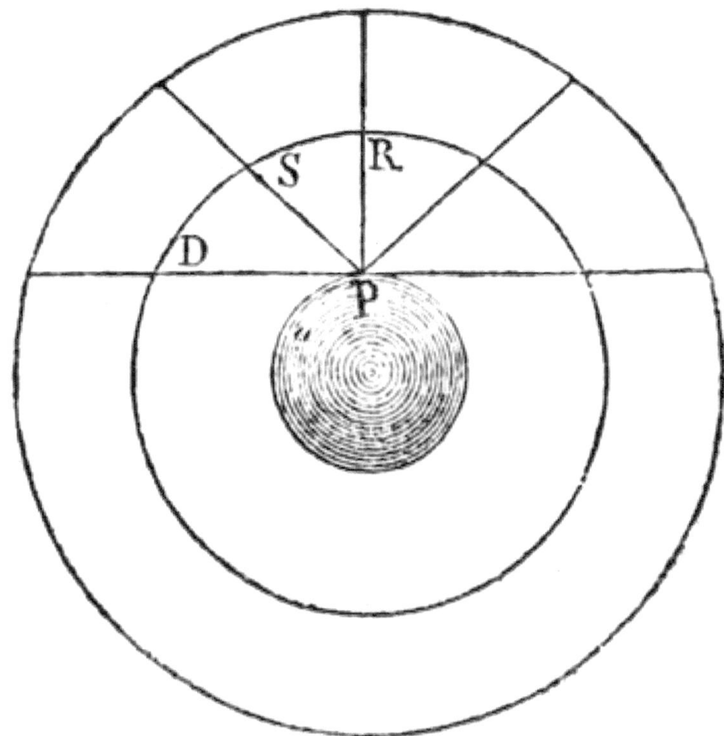

For instance: if the eye placed in P, looks through the air along the line P R, and then lowers itself a little along P S, the air will begin to appear a little whiter, because there is more of the thick air in this space than in the first. And if it be still removed lower, so as to look straight at the horizon, no more of that blue sky will be perceived which was observable along the first line P R, because there is a much greater quantity of thick air along the horizontal line P D, than along the oblique P S, or the perpendicular P R.

CHAP. CCLXXXV.

THE CAUSE OF THE DIMINUTION OF COLOURS.

THE natural colour of any visible object will be diminished in proportion to the density of any other substance which interposes between that object and the eye.

CHAP. CCLXXXVI.

OF THE DIMINUTION OF COLOURS AND OBJECTS.

LET the colours vanish in proportion as the objects diminish in size, according to the distance.

CHAP. CCLXXXVII.

OF THE VARIETY OBSERVABLE IN COLOURS, ACCORDING TO THEIR DISTANCE, OR PROXIMITY.

The local colour of such objects as are darker than the air, will appear less dark as they are more remote; and, on the contrary, objects lighter than the air will lose their brightness in proportion to their distance from the eye. In general, all objects that are darker or lighter than the air, are discoloured by distance, which changes their quality, so that the lighter appears darker, and the darker lighter.

CHAP. CCLXXXVIII.

AT WHAT DISTANCE COLOURS ARE ENTIRELY LOST.

Local colours are entirely lost at a greater or less distance, according as the eye and the object are more or less elevated from the earth. This is proved by the seventh proposition[281], which says, the air is more or less pure, as it is near to, or remote from the earth. If the eye then, and the object are near the earth, the thickness of the air which interposes, will in a great measure confuse the colour of that object to the eye. But if the eye and the object are placed high above the earth, the air will disturb the natural colour of that object very little. In short, the various gradations of colour depend not only on the various distances, in which they may be lost; but also on the variety of lights, which change according to the different hours of the day, and the thickness or purity of the air, through which the colour of the object is conveyed to the eye.

CHAP. CCLXXXIX.

OF THE CHANGE OBSERVABLE IN THE SAME COLOUR, ACCORDING TO ITS DISTANCE FROM THE EYE.

Among several colours of the same nature, that which is the nearest to the eye will alter the least; because the air which interposes between the eye and the object seen, envelopes, in some measure, that object. If the air, which interposes, be in great quantity, the object seen will be strongly tinged with the colour of that air; but if the air be thin, then the view of that object, and its colour, will be very little obstructed.

CHAP. CCXC.

OF THE BLUEISH APPEARANCE OF REMOTE OBJECTS IN A LANDSCAPE.

Whatever be the colour of distant objects, the darkest, whether natural or accidental, will appear the most tinged with azure. By the natural darkness is meant

[281] See chap. ccxciii. cccvii. cccviii.

the proper colour of the object; the accidental one is produced by the shadow of some other body.

CHAP. CCXCI.

OF THE QUALITIES IN THE SURFACE WHICH FIRST LOSE THEMSELVES BY DISTANCE.

THE first part of any colour which is lost by the distance, is the gloss, being the smallest part of it, as a light within a light. The second that diminishes by being farther removed, is the light, because it is less in quantity than the shadow. The third is the principal shadows, nothing remaining at last but a kind of middling obscurity.

CHAP. CCXCII.

FROM WHAT CAUSE THE AZURE OF THE AIR PROCEEDS.

THE azure of the sky is produced by the transparent body of the air, illumined by the sun, and interposed between the darkness of the expanse above, and the earth below. The air in itself has no quality of smell, taste, or colour, but is easily impregnated with the quality of other matter surrounding it; and will appear bluer in proportion to the darkness of the space behind it, as may be observed against the shady sides of mountains, which are darker than any other object. In this instance the air appears of the most beautiful azure, while on the other side that receives the light, it shews through that more of the natural colour of the mountain.

CHAP. CCXCIII.

OF THE PERSPECTIVE OF COLOURS.

THE same colour being placed at various distances and equal elevation, the force and effect of its colouring will be according to the proportion of the distance which there is from each of these colours to the eye. It is proved thus: let C B E D be one and the same colour. The first, E, is placed at two degrees of distance from the eye A; the second, B, shall be four degrees, the third, C, six degrees, and the fourth, D, eight degrees; as appears by the circles which terminate upon and intersect the line A R. Let us suppose that the space A R, S P, is one degree of thin air, and S P E T another degree of thicker air. It will follow, that the first colour, E, will pass to the eye through one degree of thick air, E S, and through another degree, S A, of thinner air. And B will send its colour to the eye in A, through two degrees of thick air, and through two others of the thinner sort. C will send it through three degrees of the thin, and three of the thick sort, while D goes through four degrees of the one, and four of the other. This demonstrates, that the gradation of colours is in proportion to their distance from the eye[282]. But this happens only

[282] See chap. cclxxxvii.

to those colours which are on a level with the eye; as for those which happen to be at unequal elevations, we cannot observe the same rule, because they are in that case situated in different qualities of air, which alter and diminish these colours in various manners.

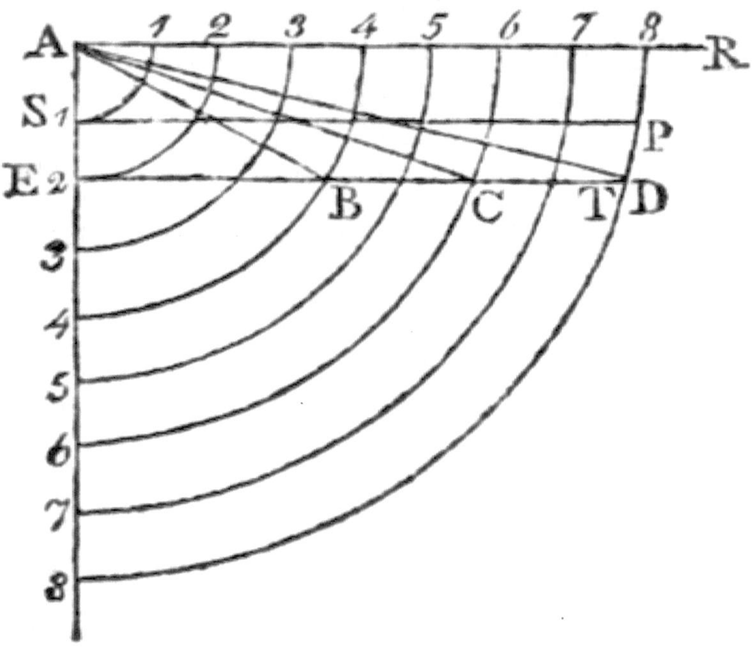

CHAP. CCXCIV.

OF THE PERSPECTIVE OF COLOURS IN DARK PLACES.

In any place where the light diminishes in a gradual proportion till it terminates in total darkness, the colours also will lose themselves and be dissolved in proportion as they recede from the eye.

CHAP. CCXCV.

OF THE PERSPECTIVE OF COLOURS.

The principal colours, or those nearest to the eye, should be pure and simple; and the degree of their diminution should be in proportion to their distance, viz. the nearer they are to the principal point, the more they will possess of the purity of those colours, and they will partake of the colour of the horizon in proportion as they approach to it.

CHAP. CCXCVI.

OF COLOURS.

OF all the colours which are not blue, those that are nearest to black will, when distant, partake most of the azure; and, on the contrary, those will preserve their proper colour at the greatest distance, that are most dissimilar to black.

The green therefore of the fields will change sooner into blue than yellow, or white, which will preserve their natural colour at a greater distance than that, or even red.

CHAP. CCXCVII.

HOW IT HAPPENS THAT COLOURS DO NOT CHANGE, THOUGH PLACED IN DIFFERENT QUALITIES OF AIR.

THE colour will not be subject to any alteration when the distance and the quality of air have a reciprocal proportion. What it loses by the distance it regains by the purity of the air, viz. if we suppose the first or lowest air to have four degrees of thickness, and the colour to be at one degree from the eye, and the second air above to have three degrees. The air having lost one degree of thickness, the colour will acquire one degree upon the distance. And when the air still higher shall have lost two degrees of thickness, the colour will acquire as many upon the distance; and in that case the colour will be the same at three degrees as at one. But to be brief, if the colour be raised so high as to enter that quality of air which has lost three degrees of thickness, and acquired three degrees of distance, then you may be certain that that colour which is high and remote, has lost no more than the colour which is below and nearer; because in rising it has acquired those three degrees which it was losing by the same distance from the eye; and this is what was meant to be proved.

CHAP. CCXCVIII.

WHY COLOURS EXPERIENCE NO APPARENT CHANGE, THOUGH PLACED IN DIFFERENT QUALITIES OF AIR.

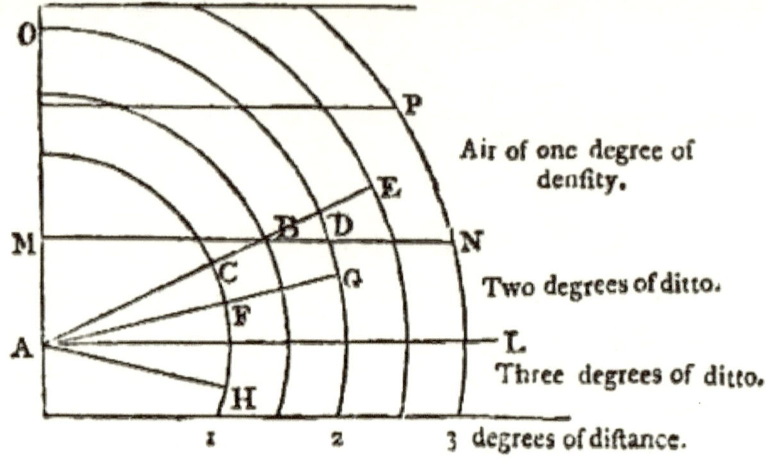

IT may happen that a colour does not alter, though placed at different distances, when the thickness of the air and the distance are in the same inverse proportion. It is proved thus: let A be the eye, and H any colour whatever, placed at one degree of distance from the eye, in a quality of air of four degrees of thickness; but because the second degree above, A M N L, contains a thinner air by one half, which air conveys this colour, it follows that this colour will appear as if removed double the distance it was at before, viz. at two degrees of distance, A F and F G, from the eye; and it will be placed in G. If that is raised to the second degree of air A M N L, and to the degree O M, P N, it will necessarily be placed at E, and will be removed from the eye the whole length of the line A E, which will be proved in this manner to be equal in thickness to the distance A G. If in the same quality of air the distance A G interposed between the eye and the colour occupies two degrees, and A E occupies two degrees and a half, it is sufficient to preserve the colour G, when raised to E, from any change, because the degree A C and the degree A F being the same in thickness, are equal and alike, and the degree C D, though equal in length to the degree F G, is not alike in point of thickness of air; because half of it is situated in a degree of air of double the thickness of the air above: this half degree of distance occupies as much of the colour as one whole degree of the air above would, which air above is twice as thin as the air below, with which it terminates; so that by calculating the thickness of the air, and the distances, you will find that the colours have changed places without undergoing any alteration in their beauty. And we shall prove it thus: reckoning first the thickness of air, the colour H is placed in four degrees of thickness, the colour G in two degrees, and E at one degree. Now let us see whether the distances are in an equal inverse proportion; the colour E is at two degrees and a half of distance, G at two degrees, and H at one degree. But as this distance has not an exact proportion with the thickness of air, it is necessary to make a third calculation in this manner: A C is perfectly like and equal to A F; the half degree, C B, is like but not equal to A F, because it is only half a degree in length, which is equal to a whole degree of the quality of the air above; so that by this calculation we shall solve the question. For A C is equal to two degrees of thickness of the air above, and the half degree C B is equal to a whole degree of the same air above; and one degree more is to be taken in, viz. B E, which makes the fourth. A H has four degrees of thickness of air, A G also four, viz. A F two in value, and F G also two, which taken together make four. A E has also four, because A C contains two, and C D one, which is the half of A C, and in the same quality of air; and there is a whole degree above in the thin air, which all together make four. So that if A E is not double the distance A G, nor four times the distance A H, it is made equivalent by the half degree C B of thick air, which is equal to a whole degree of thin air above. This proves the truth of the proposition, that the colour H G E does not undergo any alteration by these different distances.

CHAP. CCXCIX.

CONTRARY OPINIONS IN REGARD TO OBJECTS SEEN AFAR OFF.

Many painters will represent the objects darker, in proportion as they are removed from the eye; but this cannot be true, unless the objects seen be white; as shall be examined in the next chapter.

CHAP. CCC.

OF THE COLOUR OF OBJECTS REMOTE FROM THE EYE.

The air tinges objects with its own colour more or less in proportion to the quantity of intervening air between it and the eye, so that a dark object at the distance of two miles (or a density of air equal to such distance), will be more tinged with its colour than if only one mile distant.

It is said, that, in a landscape, trees of the same species appear darker in the distance than near; this cannot be true, if they be of equal size, and divided by equal spaces. But it will be so if the first trees are scattered, and the light of the fields is seen through and between them, while the others which are farther off, are thick together, as is often the case near some river or other piece of water: in this case no space of light fields can be perceived, but the trees appear thick together, accumulating the shadow on each other. It also happens, that as the shady parts of plants are much broader than the light ones, the colour of the plants becoming darker by the multiplied shadows, is preserved, and conveyed to the eye more strongly than that of the other parts; these masses, therefore, will carry the strongest parts of their colour to a greater distance.

CHAP. CCCI.

OF THE COLOUR OF MOUNTAINS.

THE darker the mountain is in itself, the bluer it will appear at a great distance. The highest part will be the darkest, as being more woody; because woods cover a great many shrubs, and other plants, which never receive any light. The wild plants of those woods are also naturally of a darker hue than cultivated plants; for oak, beech, fir, cypress, and pine trees are much darker than olive and other domestic plants. Near the top of these mountains, where the air is thinner and purer, the darkness of the woods will make it appear of a deeper azure, than at the bottom, where the air is thicker. A plant will detach very little from the ground it stands upon, if that ground be of a colour something similar to its own; and, *vice versâ*, that part of any white object which is nearest to a dark one, will appear the whitest, and the less so as it is removed from it; and any dark object will appear darker, the nearer it is to a white one; and less so, if removed from it.

CHAP. CCCII.

WHY THE COLOUR AND SHAPE OF OBJECTS ARE LOST IN SOME SITUATIONS APPARENTLY DARK, THOUGH NOT SO IN REALITY.

THERE are some situations which, though light, appear dark, and in which objects are deprived both of form and colour. This is caused by the great light which pervades the intervening air; as is observable by looking in through a window at some distance from the eye, when nothing is seen but an uniform darkish shade; but if we enter the house, we shall find that room to be full of light, and soon distinguish every small object contained within that window. This difference of effect is produced by the great brightness of the air, which contracts considerably the pupil of the eye, and by so doing diminishes its power. But in dark places the pupil is enlarged, and acquires as much in strength, as it increases in size. This is proved in my second proposition of perspective[283].

CHAP. CCCIII.

VARIOUS PRECEPTS IN PAINTING.

THE termination and shape of the parts in general are very little seen, either in great masses of light, or of shadows; but those which are situated between the extremes of light and shade are the most distinct.

Perspective, as far as it extends in regard to painting, is divided into three principal parts; the first consists in the diminution of size, according to distance; the second concerns the diminution of colours in such objects; and the third treats of the diminution of the perception altogether of those objects, and of the degree

---

[283] This book on perspective was never drawn up.

of precision they ought to exhibit at various distances.

The azure of the sky is produced by a mixture composed of light and darkness[284]; I say of light, because of the moist particles floating in the air, which reflect the light. By darkness, I mean the pure air, which has none of these extraneous particles to stop and reflect the rays. Of this we see an example in the air interposed between the eye and some dark mountains, rendered so by the shadows of an innumerable quantity of trees; or else shaded on one side by the natural privation of the rays of the sun; this air becomes azure, but not so on the side of the mountain which is light, particularly when it is covered with snow.

Among objects of equal darkness and equal distance, those will appear darker that terminate upon a lighter ground, and *vice versâ*[285].

That object which is painted with the most white and the most black, will shew greater relief than any other; for that reason I would recommend to painters to colour and dress their figures with the brightest and most lively colours; for if they are painted of a dull or obscure colour, they will detach but little, and not be much seen, when the picture is placed at some distance; because the colour of every object is obscured in the shades; and if it be represented as originally so all over, there will be but little difference between the lights and the shades, while lively colours will shew a striking difference.

----

[284] See chap. ccxcii.

[285] See chap. ccxii. ccxlviii. cclv.

AERIAL PERSPECTIVE.

CHAP. CCCIV.
AERIAL PERSPECTIVE.

THERE is another kind of perspective called aerial, because by the difference of the air it is easy to determine the distance of different objects, though seen on the same line; such, for instance, as buildings behind a wall, and appearing all of the same height above it. If in your picture you want to have one appear more distant than another, you must first suppose the air somewhat thick, because, as we have said before, in such a kind of air the objects seen at a great distance, as mountains are, appear blueish like the air, by means of the great quantity of air that interposes between the eye and such mountains. You will then paint the first building behind that wall of its proper colour; the next in point of distance, less distinct in the outline, and participating, in a greater degree, of the blueish colour of the air; another which you wish to send off as much farther, should be painted as much bluer; and if you wish one of them to appear five times farther removed beyond the wall, it must have five times more of the azure. By this rule these buildings which appeared all of the same size, and upon the same line, will be distinctly perceived to be of different dimensions, and at different distances.

CHAP. CCCV.
THE PARTS OF THE SMALLEST OBJECTS WILL FIRST DISAPPEAR IN PAINTING.

OF objects receding from the eye the smallest will be the first lost to the sight; from which it follows, that the largest will be the last to disappear. The painter, therefore, ought not to finish the parts of those objects which are very far off, but follow the rule given in the sixth book[286].

How many, in the representation of towns, and other objects remote from the eye, express every part of the buildings in the same manner as if they were very near. It is not so in nature, because there is no sight so powerful as to perceive distinctly at any great distance the precise form of parts or extremities of objects. The painter therefore who pronounces the outlines, and the minute distinction of parts, as several have done, will not give the representation of distant objects, but

[286] There is no work of this author to which this can at present refer, but the principle is laid down in chapters cclxxxiv. cccvi. of the present treatise.

by this error will make them appear exceedingly near. Again, the angles of buildings in distant towns are not to be expressed (for they cannot be seen), considering that angles are formed by the concurrence of two lines into one point, and that a point has no parts; it is therefore invisible.

CHAP. CCCVI.

SMALL FIGURES OUGHT NOT TO BE TOO MUCH FINISHED.

OBJECTS appear smaller than they really are when they are distant from the eye, and because there is a great deal of air interposed, which weakens the appearance of forms, and, by a natural consequence, prevents our seeing distinctly the minute parts of such objects. It behoves the painter therefore to touch those parts slightly, in an unfinished manner; otherwise it would be against the effect of Nature, whom he has chosen for his guide. For, as we said before, objects appear small on account of their great distance from the eye; that distance includes a great quantity of air, which, forming a dense body, obstructs the light, and prevents our seeing the minute parts of the objects.

CHAP. CCCVII.

WHY THE AIR IS TO APPEAR WHITER AS IT APPROACHES NEARER TO THE EARTH.

As the air is thicker nearer the earth, and becomes thinner as it rises, look, when the sun is in the east, towards the west, between the north and south, and you will perceive that the thickest and lowest air will receive more light from the sun than the thinner air, because its beams meet with more resistance.

If the sky terminate low, at the end of a plain, that part of it nearest to the horizon, being seen only through the thick air, will alter and break its natural colour, and will appear whiter than over your head, where the visual ray does not pass through so much of that gross air, corrupted by earthy vapours. But if you turn towards the east, the air will be darker the nearer it approaches the earth; for the air being thicker, does not admit the light of the sun to pass so freely.

CHAP. CCCVIII.

HOW TO PAINT THE DISTANT PART OF A LANDSCAPE.

IT is evident that the air is in some parts thicker and grosser than in others, particularly that nearest to the earth; and as it rises higher, it becomes thinner and more transparent. The objects which are high and large, from which you are at some distance, will be less apparent in the lower parts; because the visual ray which perceives them, passes through a long space of dense air; and it is easy to prove that the upper parts are seen by a line, which, though on the side of the eye it originates in a thick air, nevertheless, as it ascends to the highest summit of its object, terminates in an air much thinner than that of the lower parts; and for that reason the more that line or visual ray advances from the eye, it becomes, in its progress from one point to another, thinner and thinner, passing from a pure air into another which is purer; so that a painter who has mountains to represent in a landscape, ought to observe, that from one hill to another, the tops will appear always clearer than the bases. In proportion as the distance from one to another is greater, the top will be clearer; and the higher they are, the more they will shew their variety of form and colour.

CHAP. CCCIX.

OF PRECISE AND CONFUSED OBJECTS.

The parts that are near in the fore-ground should be finished in a bold determined manner; but those in the distance must be unfinished, and confused in their outlines.

CHAP. CCCX.

OF DISTANT OBJECTS.

That part of any object which is nearest to the luminary from which it receives the light, will be the lightest.

The representation of an object in every degree of distance, loses degrees of its strength; that is, in proportion as the object is more remote from the eye it will be less perceivable through the air in its representation.

CHAP. CCCXI.

OF BUILDINGS SEEN IN A THICK AIR.

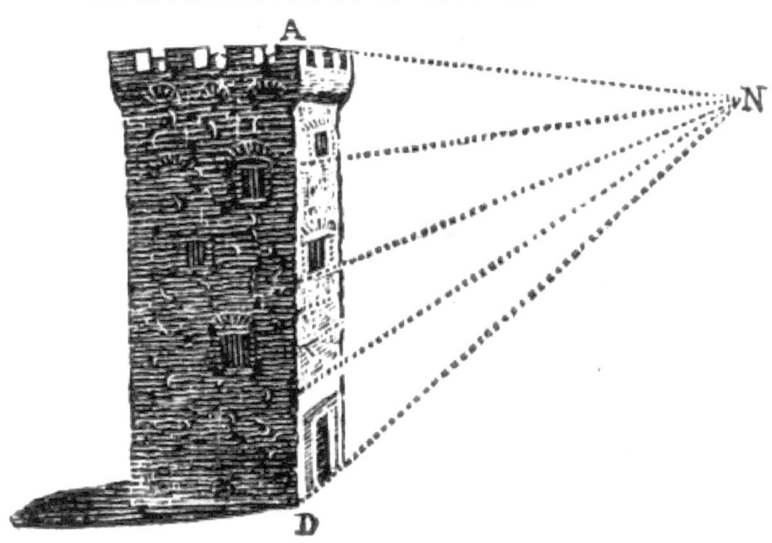

THAT part of a building seen through a thick air, will appear less distinct than another part seen through a thinner air. Therefore the eye, N, looking at the tower A D, will see it more confusedly in the lower degrees, but at the same time lighter; and as it ascends to the other degrees it will appear more distinct, but somewhat darker.

CHAP. CCCXII.

OF TOWNS AND OTHER OBJECTS SEEN THROUGH A THICK AIR.

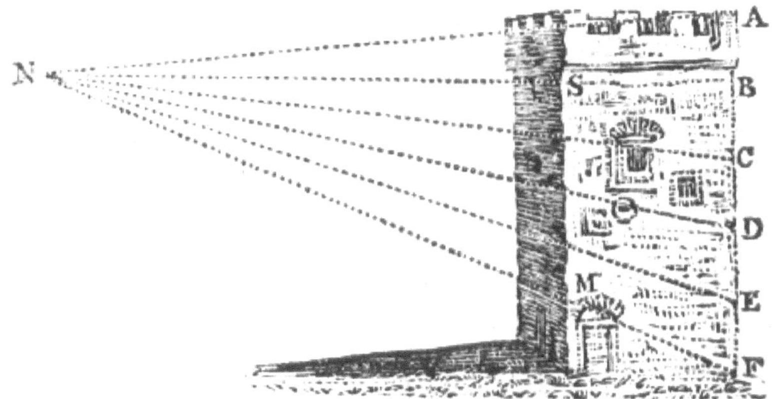

BUILDINGS or towns seen through a fog, or the air made thick by smoke or other vapours, will appear less distinct the lower they are; and, *vice versâ*, they will be sharper and more visible in proportion as they are higher. We have said, in Chapter cccxxi. that the air is thicker the lower it is, and thinner as it is higher. It is demonstrated also by the cut, where the tower, A F, is seen by the eye N, in a thick air, from B to F, which is divided into four degrees, growing thicker as they are nearer the bottom. The less the quantity of air interposed between the eye and its object is, the less also will the colour of the object participate of the colour of that air. It follows, that the greater the quantity of the air interposed between the eye and the object seen, is, the more this object will participate of the colour of the air. It is demonstrated thus: N being the eye looking at the five parts of the tower A F, viz. A B C D E, I say, that if the air were of the same thickness, there would be the same proportion between the colour of the air at the bottom of the tower and the colour of the air that the same tower has at the place B, as there is in length between the line M and F. As, however, we have supposed that the air is not of equal thickness, but, on the contrary, thicker as it is lower, it follows, that the proportion by which the air tinges the different elevations of the tower B C F, exceeds the proportion of the lines; because the line M F, besides its being longer than the line S B, passes by unequal degrees through a quality of air which is unequal in thickness.

CHAP. CCCXIII.

OF THE INFERIOR EXTREMITIES OF DISTANT OBJECTS.

THE inferior or lower extremities of distant objects are not so apparent as the upper extremities. This is observable in mountains and hills, the tops of which detach from the sides of other mountains behind. We see the tops of these more determined and distinctly than their bases; because the upper extremities are darker, being less encompassed by thick air, which always remains in the lower regions, and makes them appear dim and confused. It is the same with trees, buildings, and other objects high up. From this effect it often happens that a high tower, seen at a great distance, will appear broad at top, and narrow at bottom; because the thin air towards the top does not prevent the angles on the sides and other different parts of the tower from being seen, as the thick air does at bottom. This is demonstrated by the seventh proposition[287], which says, that the thick air interposed between the eye and the sun, is lighter below than above, and where the air is whiteish, it confuses the dark objects more than if such air were blueish or thinner, as it is higher up. The battlements of a fortress have the spaces between equal to the breadth of the battlement, and yet the space will appear wider; at a great distance the battlements will appear very much diminished, and being removed still farther, will disappear entirely, and the fort shew only the straight wall, as if there were no battlements.

---

[287] See chapters cccvii. cccxxii.

CHAP. CCCXIV.

WHICH PARTS OF OBJECTS DISAPPEAR FIRST BY BEING REMOVED FARTHER FROM THE EYE, AND WHICH PRESERVE THEIR APPEARANCE.

THE smallest parts are those which, by being removed, lose their appearance first; this may be observed in the gloss upon spherical bodies, or columns, and the slender parts of animals; as in a stag, the first sight of which does not discover its legs and horns so soon as its body, which, being broader, will be perceived from a greater distance. But the parts which disappear the very first, are the lines which describe the members, and terminate the surface and shape of bodies.

CHAP. CCCXV.

WHY OBJECTS ARE LESS DISTINGUISHED IN PROPORTION AS THEY ARE FARTHER REMOVED FROM THE EYE.

THIS happens because the smallest parts are lost first; the second, in point of size, are also lost at a somewhat greater distance, and so on successively; the parts by degrees melting away, the perception of the object is diminished; and at last all the parts, and the whole, are entirely lost to the sight[288]. Colours also disappear on account of the density of the air interposed between the eye and the object.

CHAP. CCCXVI.
WHY FACES APPEAR DARK AT A DISTANCE.

IT is evident that the similitude of all objects placed before us, large as well as small, is perceptible to our senses through the iris of the eye. If through so small an entrance the immensity of the sky and of the earth is admitted, the faces of men (which are scarcely any thing in comparison of such large objects), being still diminished by the distance, will occupy so little of the eye, that they become almost imperceptible. Besides, having to pass through a dark medium from the surface to the *Retina* in the inside, where the impression is made, the colour of faces (not being very strong, and rendered still more obscure by the darkness of the tube) when arrived at the focus appears dark. No other reason can be given on that point, except that the speck in the middle of the apple of the eye is black, and, being full of a transparent fluid like air, performs the same office as a hole in a board, which on looking into it appears black; and that those things which are seen through both a light and dark air, become confused and obscure.

---

[288] See chap. cxvi. cxxi. cccv.

CHAP. CCCXVII.

OF TOWNS AND OTHER BUILDINGS SEEN THROUGH A FOG IN THE MORNING OR EVENING.

Buildings seen afar off in the morning or in the evening, when there is a fog, or thick air, shew only those parts distinctly which are enlightened by the sun towards the horizon; and the parts of those buildings which are not turned towards the sun remain confused and almost of the colour of the fog.

CHAP. CCCXVIII.

OF THE HEIGHT OF BUILDINGS SEEN IN A FOG.

Of a building near the eye the top parts will appear more confused than the bottom, because there is more fog between the eye and the top than at the base. And a square tower, seen at a great distance through a fog, will appear narrower at the base than at the summit. This is accounted for in Chapter cccxiii. which says, that the fog will appear whiter and thicker as it approaches the ground; and as it is said before[289], that a dark object will appear smaller in proportion as it is placed on a whiter ground. Therefore the fog being whiter at bottom than at top, it follows that the tower (being darkish) will appear narrower at the base than at the summit.

CHAP. CCCXIX.

WHY OBJECTS WHICH ARE HIGH, APPEAR DARKER AT A DISTANCE THAN THOSE WHICH ARE LOW, THOUGH THE FOG BE UNIFORM, AND OF EQUAL THICKNESS.

Amongst objects situated in a fog, thick air, vapour, smoke, or at a distance, the highest will be the most distinctly seen: and amongst objects equal in height, that placed in the darkest fog, will be most confused and dark. As it happens to the eye H, looking at A B C, three towers of equal height; it sees the top C as low as R, in two degrees of thickness; and the top B, in one degree only; therefore the top C will appear darker than the top of the tower B.

---

[289] See chap. cccxiii. and cccxxiii.

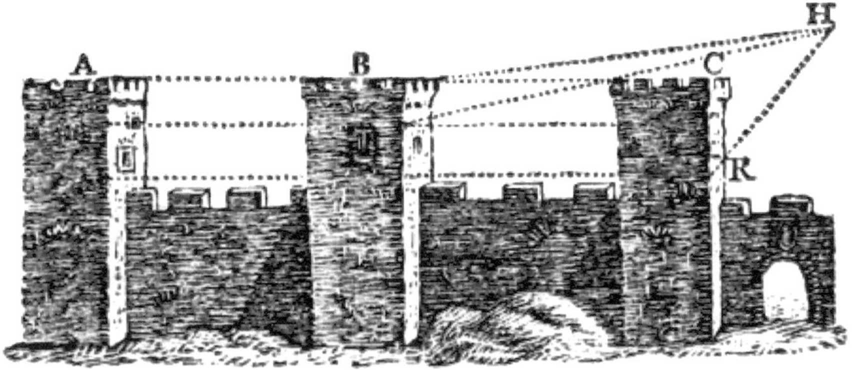

CHAP. CCCXX.

OF OBJECTS SEEN IN A FOG.

OBJECTS seen through a fog will appear larger than they are in reality, because the aerial perspective does not agree with the linear, viz. the colour does not agree with the magnitude of the object[290]; such a fog being similar to the thickness of air interposed between the eye and the horizon in fine weather. But in this case the fog is near the eye, and though the object be also near, it makes it appear as if it were as far off as the horizon; where a great tower would appear no bigger than a man placed near the eye.

CHAP. CCCXXI.

OF THOSE OBJECTS WHICH THE EYES PERCEIVE THROUGH A MIST OR THICK AIR.

THE nearer the air is to water, or to the ground, the thicker it becomes. It is proved by the nineteenth proposition of the second book[291], that bodies rise in

[290] To our obtaining a correct idea of the magnitude and distance of any object seen from afar, it is necessary that we consider how much of distinctness an object loses at a distance (from the mere interposition of the air), as well as what it loses in size; and these two considerations must unite before we can decidedly pronounce as to its distance or magnitude. This calculation, as to distinctness, must be made upon the idea that the air is clear, as, if by any accident it is otherwise, we shall (knowing the proportion in which clear air dims a prospect) be led to conclude this farther off than it is, and, to justify that conclusion, shall suppose its real magnitude correspondent with the distance, at which from its degree of distinctness it appears to be. In the circumstance remarked in the text there is, however, a great deception; the fact is, that the colour and the minute parts of the object are lost in the fog, while the size of it is not diminished in proportion; and the eye being accustomed to see objects diminished in size at a great distance, supposes this to be farther off than it is, and consequently imagines it larger.

[291] This proposition, though undoubtedly intended to form a part of some future

proportion to their weight; and it follows, that a light body will rise higher than another which is heavy.

CHAP. CCCXXII.

MISCELLANEOUS OBSERVATIONS.

Of different objects equal in magnitude, form, shade, and distance from the eye, those will appear the smaller that are placed on the lighter ground. This is exemplified by observing the sun when seen behind a tree without leaves; all the ramifications seen against that great light are so diminished that they remain almost invisible. The same may be observed of a pole placed between the sun and the eye.

Parallel bodies placed upright, and seen through a fog, will appear larger at top than at bottom. This is proved by the ninth proposition[292], which says, that a fog, or thick air, penetrated by the rays of the sun, will appear whiter the lower they are.

Things seen afar off will appear out of proportion, because the parts which are the lightest will send their image with stronger rays than the parts which are darkest. I have seen a woman dressed in black, with a white veil over her head, which appeared twice as large as her shoulders covered with black.

---

work, which never was drawn up, makes no part of the present.
[292] See chap. cccvii.

MISCELLANEOUS OBSERVATIONS.

LANDSCAPE.

CHAP. CCCXXIII.
OF OBJECTS SEEN AT A DISTANCE.

Any dark object will appear lighter when removed to some distance from the eye. It follows, by the contrary reason, that a dark object will appear still darker when brought nearer to the eye. Therefore the inferior parts of any object whatever, placed in thick air, will appear farther from the eye at the bottom than at the top; for that reason the lower parts of a mountain appear farther off than its top, which is in reality the farthest.

CHAP. CCCXXIV.
OF A TOWN SEEN THROUGH A THICK AIR.

The eye which, looking downwards, sees a town immersed in very thick air, will perceive the top of the buildings darker, but more distinct than the bottom. The tops detach against a light ground, because they are seen against the low and thick air which is beyond them. This is a consequence of what has been explained in the preceding chapter.

CHAP. CCCXXV.
HOW TO DRAW A LANDSCAPE.

Contrive that the trees in your landscape be half in shadow and half in the light. It is better to represent them as when the sun is veiled with thin clouds, because in that case the trees receive a general light from the sky, and are darkest in those parts which are nearest to the earth.

CHAP. CCCXXVI.
OF THE GREEN OF THE COUNTRY.

Of the greens seen in the country, that of trees and other plants will appear darker than that of fields and meadows, though they may happen to be of the same quality.

CHAP. CCCXXVII.

WHAT GREENS WILL APPEAR MOST OF A BLUEISH CAST.

Those greens will appear to approach nearest to blue which are of the darkest shade when remote. This is proved by the seventh proposition[293], which says, that blue is composed of black and white seen at a great distance.

CHAP. CCCXXVIII.

THE COLOUR OF THE SEA FROM DIFFERENT ASPECTS.

When the sea is a little ruffled it has no sameness of colour; for whoever looks at it from the shore, will see it of a dark colour, in a greater degree as it approaches towards the horizon, and will perceive also certain lights moving slowly on the surface like a flock of sheep. Whoever looks at the sea from on board a ship, at a distance from the land, sees it blue. Near the shore it appears darkish, on account of the colour of the earth reflected by the water, as in a looking-glass; but at sea the azure of the air is reflected to the eye by the waves in the same manner.

CHAP. CCCXXIX.

WHY THE SAME PROSPECT APPEARS LARGER AT SOME TIMES THAN AT OTHERS.

Objects in the country appear sometimes larger and sometimes smaller than they actually are, from the circumstance of the air interposed between the eye and the horizon, happening to be either thicker or thinner than usual.

Of two horizons equally distant from the eye, that which is seen through the thicker air will appear farther removed; and the other will seem nearer, being seen through a thinner air.

Objects of unequal size, but equally distant, will appear equal if the air which is between them and the eye be of proportionable inequality of thickness, viz. if the thickest air be interposed between the eye and the smallest of the objects. This is proved by the perspective of colours[294], which is so deceitful that a mountain which would appear small by the compasses, will seem larger than a small hill near the eye; as a finger placed near the eye will cover a large mountain far off.

CHAP. CCCXXX.

OF SMOKE.

Smoke is more transparent, though darker towards the extremities of its waves than in the middle.

[293] Vide chap. ccxcii. ccciii.
[294] See chapter ccxcviii.

It moves in a more oblique direction in proportion to the force of the wind which impels it.

Different kinds of smoke vary in colour, as the causes that produce them are various.

Smoke never produces determined shadows, and the extremities are lost as they recede from their primary cause. Objects behind it are less apparent in proportion to the thickness of the smoke. It is whiter nearer its origin, and bluer towards its termination.

Fire appears darker, the more smoke there is interposed between it and the eye.

Where smoke is farther distant, the objects are less confused by it.

It encumbers and dims all the landscape like a fog. Smoke is seen to issue from different places, with flames at the origin, and the most dense part of it. The tops of mountains will be more seen than the lower parts, as in a fog.

CHAP. CCCXXXI.

IN WHAT PART SMOKE IS LIGHTEST.

Smoke which is seen between the sun and the eye will be lighter and more transparent than any other in the landscape. The same is observed of dust, and of fog; while, if you place yourself between the sun and those objects, they will appear dark.

CHAP. CCCXXXII.

OF THE SUN-BEAMS PASSING THROUGH THE OPENINGS OF CLOUDS.

The sun-beams which penetrate the openings interposed between clouds of various density and form, illuminate all the places over which they pass, and tinge with their own colour all the dark places that are behind: which dark places are only seen in the intervals between the rays.

CHAP. CCCXXXIII.

OF THE BEGINNING OF RAIN.

When the rain begins to fall, it tarnishes and darkens the air, giving it a dull colour, but receives still on one side a faint light from the sun, and is shaded on the other side, as we observe in clouds; till at last it darkens also the earth, depriving it entirely of the light of the sun. Objects seen through the rain appear confused and of undetermined shape, but those which are near will be more distinct. It is observable, that on the side where the rain is shaded, objects will be more clearly distinguished than where it receives the light; because on the shady side they lose only their principal lights, whilst on the other they lose both their lights and shadows, the lights mixing with the light part of the rain, and the shadows are also considerably weakened by it.

CHAP. CCCXXXIV.
THE SEASONS ARE TO BE OBSERVED.

In Autumn you will represent the objects according as it is more or less advanced. At the beginning of it the leaves of the oldest branches only begin to fade, more or less, however, according as the plant is situated in a fertile or barren country; and do not imitate those who represent trees of every kind (though at equal distance) with the same quality of green. Endeavour to vary the colour of meadows, stones, trunks of trees, and all other objects, as much as possible, for Nature abounds in variety *ad infinitum*.

CHAP. CCCXXXV.
THE DIFFERENCE OF CLIMATES TO BE OBSERVED.

Near the sea-shore, and in southern parts, you will be careful not to represent the Winter season by the appearance of trees and fields, as you would do in places more inland, and in northern countries, except when these are covered with ever-greens, which shoot afresh all the year round.

CHAP. CCCXXXVI.
OF DUST.

Dust becomes lighter the higher it rises, and appears darker the less it is raised, when it is seen between the eye and the sun.

CHAP. CCCXXXVII.
HOW TO REPRESENT THE WIND.

In representing the effect of the wind, besides the bending of trees, and leaves twisting the wrong side upwards, you will also express the small dust whirling upwards till it mixes in a confused manner with the air.

CHAP. CCCXXXVIII.
OF A WILDERNESS.

Those trees and shrubs which are by their nature more loaded with small branches, ought to be touched smartly in the shadows, but those which have larger foliage, will cause broader shadows.

CHAP. CCCXXXIX.

OF THE HORIZON SEEN IN THE WATER.

By the sixth proposition[295], the horizon will be seen in the water as in a looking-glass, on that side which is opposite the eye. And if the painter has to represent a spot covered with water, let him remember that the colour of it cannot be either lighter or darker than that of the neighbouring objects.

CHAP. CCCXL.

OF THE SHADOW OF BRIDGES ON THE SURFACE OF THE WATER.

The shadows of bridges can never be seen on the surface of the water, unless it should have lost its transparent and reflecting quality, and become troubled and muddy; because clear water being polished and smooth on its surface, the image of the bridge is formed in it as in a looking-glass, and reflected in all the points situated between the eye and the bridge at equal angles; and even the air is seen under the arches. These circumstances cannot happen when the water is muddy, because it does not reflect the objects any longer, but receives the shadow of the bridge in the same manner as a dusty road would receive it.

CHAP. CCCXLI.

HOW A PAINTER OUGHT TO PUT IN PRACTICE THE PERSPECTIVE OF COLOURS.

To put in practice that perspective which teaches the alteration, the lessening, and even the entire loss of the very essence of colours, you must take some points in the country at the distance of about sixty-five yards[296] from each other; as trees, men, or some other remarkable objects. In regard to the first tree, you will take a glass, and having fixed that well, and also your eye, draw upon it, with the greatest accuracy, the tree you see through it; then put it a little on one side, and compare it closely with the natural one, and colour it, so that in shape and colour it may resemble the original, and that by shutting one eye they may both appear painted, and at the same distance. The same rule may be applied to the second and third tree at the distance you have fixed. These studies will be very useful if managed with judgment, where they may be wanted in the offscape of a picture. I have

[295] This was probably to have been a part of some other work, but it does not occur in this.

[296] Cento braccia, or cubits. The Florence braccio is one foot ten inches seven eighths, English measure.

observed that the second tree is less by four fifths than the first, at the distance of thirteen yards.

CHAP. CCCXLII.

VARIOUS PRECEPTS IN PAINTING.

THE superficies of any opake body participates of the colour of the transparent medium interposed between the eye and such body, in a greater or less degree, in proportion to the density of such medium and the space it occupies.

The outlines of opake bodies will be less apparent in proportion as those bodies are farther distant from the eye.

That part of the opake body will be the most shaded, or lightest, which is nearest to the body that shades it, or gives it light.

The surface of any opake body participates more or less of the colour of that body which gives it light, in proportion as the latter is more or less remote, or more or less strong.

Objects seen between lights and shadows will appear to have greater relievo than those which are placed wholly in the light, or wholly in shadow.

When you give strength and precision to objects seen at a great distance, they will appear as if they were very near. Endeavour that your imitation be such as to give a just idea of distances. If the object in nature appear confused in the outlines, let the same be observed in your picture.

The outlines of distant objects appear undetermined and confused, for two reasons: the first is, that they come to the eye by so small an angle, and are therefore so much diminished, that they strike the sight no more than small objects do, which though near can hardly be distinguished, such as the nails of the fingers, insects, and other similar things: the second is, that between the eye and the distant objects there is so much air interposed, that it becomes thick; and, like a veil, tinges the shadows with its own whiteness, and turns them from a dark colour to another between black and white, such as azure.

Although, by reason of the great distance, the appearance of many things is lost, yet those things which receive the light from the sun will be more discernible, while the rest remain enveloped in confused shadows. And because the air is thicker near the ground, the things which are lower will appear confused; and *vice versâ*.

When the sun tinges the clouds on the horizon with red, those objects which, on account of their distance, appear blueish, will participate of that redness, and will produce a mixture between the azure and red, which renders the prospect lively and pleasant; all the opake bodies which receive that light will appear distinct, and of a reddish colour, and the air, being transparent, will be impregnated with it, and appear of the colour of lilies[297].

------

[297] Probably the Author here means yellow lilies, or fleurs de lis.

The air which is between the earth and the sun when it rises or sets, will always dim the objects it surrounds, more than the air any where else, because it is whiter.

It is not necessary to mark strongly the outlines of any object which is placed upon another. It ought to detach of itself.

If the outline or extremity of a white and curved surface terminate upon another white body, it will have a shade at that extremity, darker than any part of the light; but if against a dark object, such outline, or extremity, will be lighter than any part of the light.

Those objects which are most different in colour, will appear the most detached from each other.

Those parts of objects which first disappear in the distance, are extremities similar in colour, and ending one upon the other, as the extremities of an oak tree upon another oak similar to it. The next to disappear at a greater distance are, objects of mixed colours, when they terminate one upon the other, as trees, ploughed fields, walls, heaps of rubbish, or of stones. The last extremities of bodies that vanish are those which, being light, terminate upon a dark ground; or being dark, upon a light ground.

Of objects situated above the eye, at equal heights, the farthest removed from the eye will appear the lowest; and if situated below the eye, the nearest to it will appear the lowest. The parallel lines situated sidewise will concur to one point[298].

Those objects which are near a river, or a lake, in the distant part of a landscape, are less apparent and distinct than those that are remote from them.

Of bodies of equal density, those that are nearest to the eye will appear thinnest, and the most remote thickest.

A large eye-ball will see objects larger than a small one. The experiment may be made by looking at any of the celestial bodies, through a pin-hole, which being capable of admitting but a portion of its light, it seems to diminish and lose of its size in the same proportion as the pin-hole is smaller than the usual apparent size of the object.

A thick air interposed between the eye and any object, will render the outlines of such object undetermined and confused, and make it appear of a larger size than it is in reality; because the linear perspective does not diminish the angle which conveys the object to the eye. The aerial perspective carries it farther off, so that the one removes it from the eye, while the other preserves its magnitude[299].

When the sun is in the West the vapours of the earth fall down again and thicken the air, so that objects not enlightened by the sun remain dark and confused, but those which receive its light will be tinged yellow and red, according to the sun's appearance on the horizon. Again, those that receive its light are very

---

[298] That point is always found in the horizon, and is called the point of sight, or the vanishing point.
[299] See chap. cccxx.

distinct, particularly public buildings and houses in towns and villages, because their shadows are dark, and it seems as if those parts which are plainly seen were coming out of confused and undetermined foundations, because at that time every thing is of one and the same colour, except what is enlightened by the sun[300].

Any object receiving the light from the sun, receives also the general light; so that two kinds of shadows are produced: the darkest of the two is that which happens to have its central line directed towards the centre of the sun. The central lines of the primitive and secondary lights are the same as the central lines of the primitive and secondary shadows.

The setting sun is a beautiful and magnificent object when it tinges with its colour all the great buildings of towns, villages, and the top of high trees in the country. All below is confused and almost lost in a tender and general mass; for, being only enlightened by the air, the difference between the shadows and the lights is small, and for that reason it is not much detached. But those that are high are touched by the rays of the sun, and, as was said before, are tinged with its colour; the painter therefore ought to take the same colour with which he has painted the sun, and employ it in all those parts of his work which receive its light.

It also happens very often, that a cloud will appear dark without receiving any shadow from a separate cloud, according to the situation of the eye; because it will see only the shady part of the one, while it sees both the enlightened and shady parts of the other.

Of two objects at equal height, that which is the farthest off will appear the lowest. Observe the first cloud in the cut, though it is lower than the second, it appears as if it were higher. This is demonstrated by the section of the pyramidical rays of the low cloud at M A, and the second (which is higher) at N M, below M A. This happens also when, on account of the rays of the setting or rising sun, a dark cloud appears higher than another which is light.

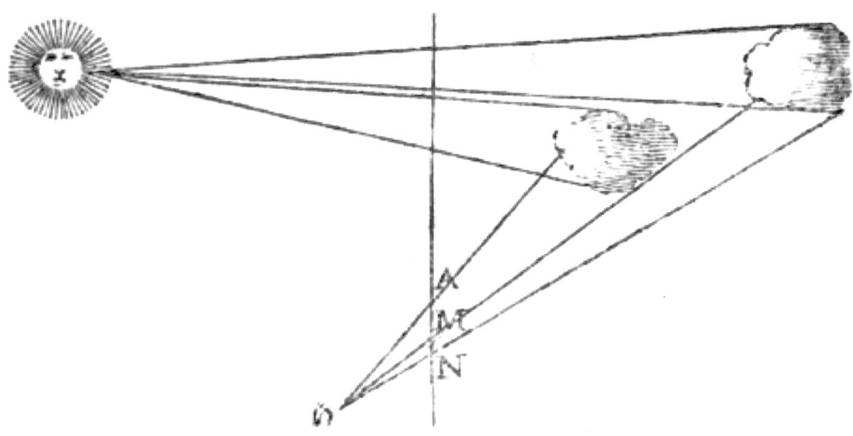

---

[300] See chap. cccxvii.

CHAP. CCCXLIII.

THE BRILLIANCY OF A LANDSCAPE.

THE vivacity and brightness of colours in a landscape will never bear any comparison with a landscape in nature when illumined by the sun, unless the picture be placed so as to receive the same light from the sun itself.

MISCELLANEOUS OBSERVATIONS.

CHAP. CCCXLIV.

WHY A PAINTED OBJECT DOES NOT APPEAR SO FAR DISTANT AS A REAL ONE, THOUGH THEY BE CONVEYED TO THE EYE BY EQUAL ANGLES.

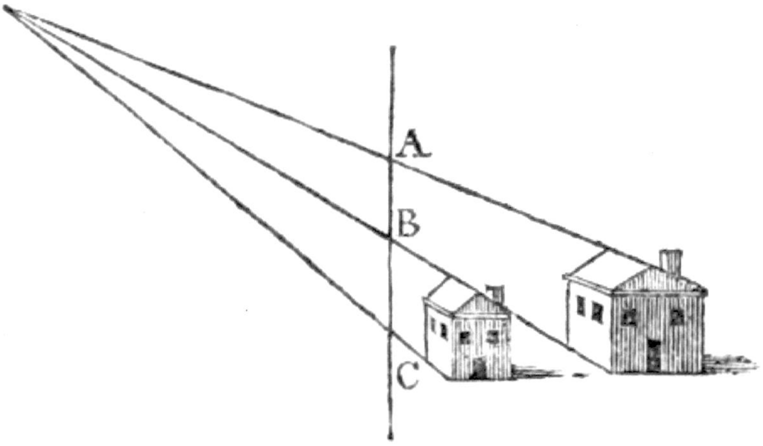

If a house be painted on the pannel B C, at the apparent distance of one mile, and by the side of it a real one be perceived at the true distance of one mile also; which objects are so disposed, that the pannel, or picture, A C, intersects the pyramidical rays with the same opening of angles; yet these two objects will never appear of the same size, nor at the same distance, if seen with both eyes[301].

---

[301] This position has been already laid down in chapter cxxiv. (and will also be found in chapter cccxlviii.); and the reader is referred to the note on that passage, which will also explain that in the text, for further illustration. It may, however, be proper to remark, that though the author has here supposed both objects conveyed to the eye by an angle of the same extent, they cannot, in fact, be so seen, unless one eye be shut; and the reason is this: if viewed with both eyes, there will be two points of sight, one in the centre of each eye; and the rays from each of these to the objects must of course be different, and will consequently form different angles.

CHAP. CCCXLV.

HOW TO DRAW A FIGURE STANDING UPON ITS FEET, TO APPEAR FORTY BRACCIA[302] HIGH, IN A SPACE OF TWEN-TY BRACCIA, WITH PROPORTIONATE MEMBERS.

In this, as in any other case, the painter is not to mind what kind of surface he has to work upon; particularly if his painting is to be seen from a determined point, such as a window, or any other opening. Because the eye is not to attend to the evenness or roughness of the wall, but only to what is to be represented as beyond that wall; such as a landscape, or any thing else. Nevertheless a curved surface, such as F R G, would be the best, because it has no angles.

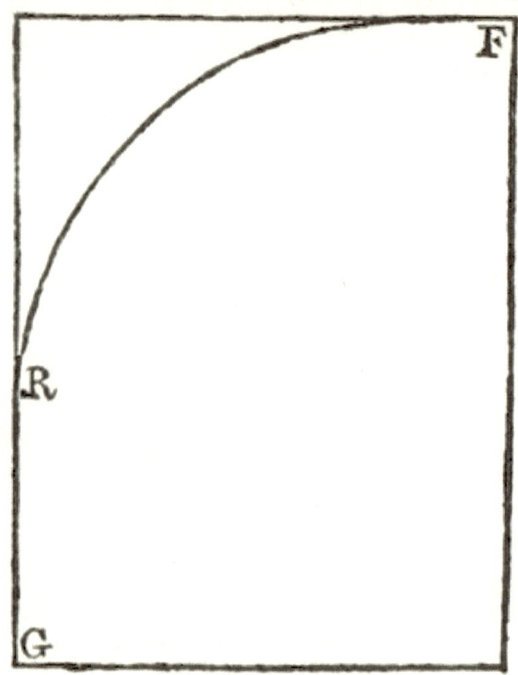

CHAP. CCCXLVI.

HOW TO DRAW A FIGURE TWENTY-FOUR BRACCIA HIGH, UPON A WALL TWELVE BRACCIA HIGH. PLATE XXII.

Draw upon part of the wall M N, half the figure you mean to represent; and the other half upon the cove above, M R. But before that, it will be necessary to draw upon a flat board, or a paper, the profile of the wall and cove, of the same shape and dimension, as that upon which you are to paint. Then draw also the profile of your figure, of whatever size you please, by the side of it; draw all the lines to the point F, and where they intersect the profile M R, you will have the

[302] The braccio is one foot ten inches and seven eighths English measure.

dimensions of your figure as they ought to be drawn upon the real spot. You will find, that on the straight part of the wall M N, it will come of its proper form, because the going off perpendicularly will diminish it naturally; but that part which comes upon the curve will be diminished upon your drawing. The whole must be traced afterwards upon the real spot, which is similar to M N. This is a good and safe method.

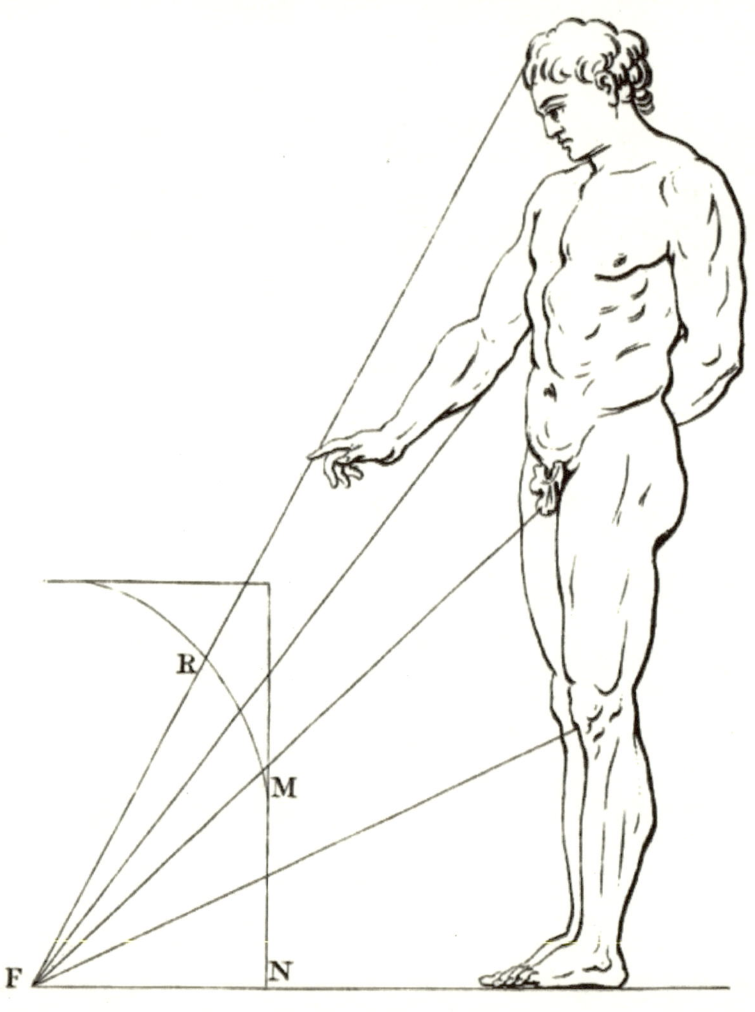

Page 158.

Chap. 346.

PLATE 22.

CHAP. CCCXLVII.

WHY, ON MEASURING A FACE, AND THEN PAINTING IT OF THE SAME SIZE, IT WILL APPEAR LARGER THAN THE NATURAL ONE.

A B is the breadth of the space, or of the head, and it is placed on the paper at the distance C F, where the cheeks are, and it would have to stand back all A C, and then the temples would be carried to the distance O R of the lines A F, B F; so that there is the difference C O and R D. It follows that the line C F, and the line D F, in order to become shorter[303], have to go and find the paper where the whole height is drawn, that is to say, the lines F A, and F B, where the true size is; and so it makes the difference, as I have said, of C O, and R D.

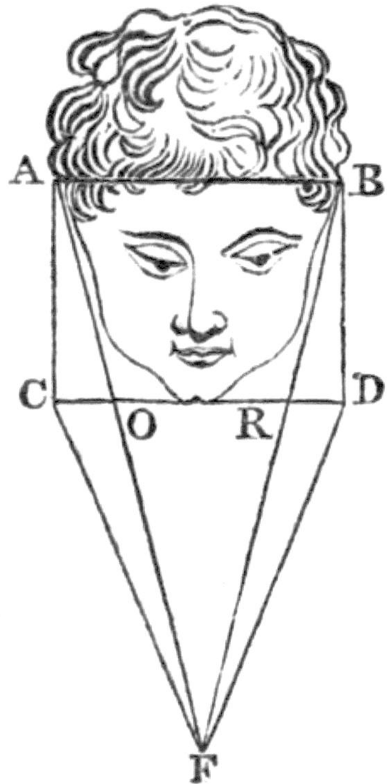

---

[303] i.e. To be abridged according to the rules of perspective.

CHAP. CCCXLVIII.

WHY THE MOST PERFECT IMITATION OF NATURE WILL NOT APPEAR TO HAVE THE SAME RELIEF AS NATURE IT-SELF.

IF nature is seen with two eyes, it will be impossible to imitate it upon a picture so as to appear with the same relief, though the lines, the lights, shades, and colour, be perfectly imitated[304]. It is proved thus: let the eyes A B, look at the object C, with the concurrence of both the central visual rays A C and B C. I say, that the sides of the visual angles (which contain these central rays) will see the space G D, behind the object C. The eye A will see all the space FD, and the eye B all the space G E. Therefore the two eyes will see behind the object C all the space F E; for which reason that object C becomes as it were transparent, according to the definition of transparent bodies, behind which nothing is hidden. This cannot happen if an object were seen with one eye only, provided it be larger than the eye. From all that has been said, we may conclude, that a painted object, occupying all the space it has behind, leaves no possible way to see any part of the ground, which it covers entirely by its own circumference[305].

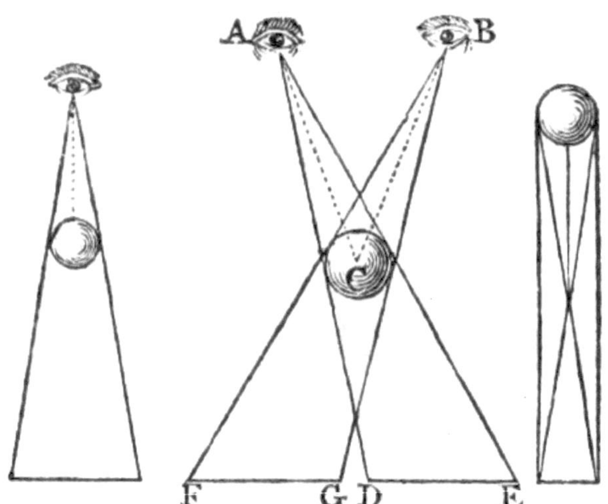

---

[304] See chap. cxxii.

[305] The whole of this chapter, like the next but one preceding, depends on the circumstance of there being in fact two points of sight, one in the centre of each eye, when an object is viewed with both eyes. In natural objects the effect which this circumstance produces is, that the rays from each point of sight, diverging as they extend towards the object, take in not only that, but some part also of the distance behind it, till at length, at a certain distance behind it, they cross each other; whereas, in a painted representation, there being no real distance behind the object, but the whole being a flat surface, it is impossible that the rays from the points of sight should pass beyond that flat surface; and as the object itself is on that flat surface, which is the real extremity of the view, the eyes cannot acquire a sight of any thing beyond.

CHAP. CCCXLIX.

UNIVERSALITY OF PAINTING; A PRECEPT.

A PAINTER cannot be said to aim at universality in the art, unless he love equally every species of that art. For instance, if he delight only in landscape, his can be esteemed only as a simple investigation; and, as our friend Botticello[306] remarks, is but a vain study; since, by throwing a sponge impregnated with various colours against a wall, it leaves some spots upon it, which may appear like a landscape. It is true also, that a variety of compositions may be seen in such spots, according to the disposition of mind with which they are considered; such as heads of men, various animals, battles, rocky scenes, seas, clouds, woods, and the like. It may be compared to the sound of bells, which may seem to say whatever we choose to imagine. In the same manner also, those spots may furnish hints for compositions, though they do not teach us how to finish any particular part; and the imitators of them are but sorry landscape-painters.

CHAP. CCCL.

IN WHAT MANNER THE MIRROR IS THE TRUE MASTER OF PAINTERS.

WHEN you wish to know if your picture be like the object you mean to represent, have a flat looking-glass, and place it so as to reflect the object you have imitated, and compare carefully the original with the copy. You see upon a flat mirror the representation of things which appear real; Painting is the same. They are both an even superficies, and both give the idea of something beyond their superficies. Since you are persuaded that the looking-glass, by means of lines and shades, gives you the representation of things as if they were real; you being in possession of colours which in their different lights and shades are stronger than those of the looking-glass, may certainly, if you employ the rules with judgment, give to your picture the same appearance of Nature as you admire in the looking-glass. Or rather, your picture will be like Nature itself seen in a large looking-glass.

This looking-glass (being your master) will shew you the lights and shades of any object whatever. Amongst your colours there are some lighter than the lightest part of your model, and also some darker than the strongest shades; from which it follows, that you ought to represent Nature as seen in your looking-glass, when you look at it with one eye only; because both eyes surround the objects too much, particularly when they are small[307].

---

[306] A well-known painter at Florence, contemporary with Leonardo da Vinci, who painted several altar-pieces and other public works.

[307] See chap. cxxiv. and cccxlviii.

CHAP. CCCLI.

WHICH PAINTING IS TO BE ESTEEMED THE BEST.

THAT painting is the most commendable which has the greatest conformity to what is meant to be imitated. This kind of comparison will often put to shame a certain description of painters, who pretend they can mend the works of Nature; as they do, for instance, when they pretend to represent a child twelve months old, giving him eight heads in height, when Nature in its best proportion admits but five. The breadth of the shoulders also, which is equal to the head, they make double, giving to a child a year old, the proportions of a man of thirty. They have so often practised, and seen others practise these errors, that they have converted them into habit, which has taken so deep a root in their corrupted judgment, that they persuade themselves that Nature and her imitators are wrong in not following their own practice[308].

CHAP. CCCLII.

OF THE JUDGMENT TO BE MADE OF A PAINTER'S WORK.

THE first thing to be considered is, whether the figures have their proper relief, according to their respective situations, and the light they are in: that the shadows be not the same at the extremities of the groups, as in the middle; because being surrounded by shadows, or shaded only on one side, produce very different effects. The groups in the middle are surrounded by shadows from the other figures, which are between them and the light. Those which are at the extremities have the shadows only on one side, and receive the light on the other. The strongest and smartest touches of shadows are to be in the interstice between the figures of the principal group where the light cannot penetrate[309].

Secondly, that by the order and disposition of the figures they appear to be accommodated to the subject, and the true representation of the history in question.

Thirdly, that the figures appear alive to the occasion which brought them together, with expressions suited to their attitudes.

CHAP. CCCLIII.

HOW TO MAKE AN IMAGINARY ANIMAL APPEAR NATURAL.

IT is evident that it will be impossible to invent any animal without giving it members, and these members must individually resemble those of some known animal.

If you wish, therefore, to make a chimera, or imaginary animal, appear natural (let us suppose a serpent); take the head of a mastiff, the eyes of a cat, the ears of

[308] See chap. x.
[309] See chap. cci.

a porcupine, the mouth of a hare, the brows of a lion, the temples of an old cock, and the neck of a sea tortoise[310].

CHAP. CCCLIV.
PAINTERS ARE NOT TO IMITATE ONE ANOTHER.

ONE painter ought never to imitate the manner of any other; because in that case he cannot be called the child of Nature, but the grandchild. It is always best to have recourse to Nature, which is replete with such abundance of objects, than to the productions of other masters, who learnt every thing from her.

CHAP. CCCLV.
HOW TO JUDGE OF ONE'S OWN WORK.

IT is an acknowledged fact, that we perceive errors in the works of others more readily than in our own. A painter, therefore, ought to be well instructed in perspective, and acquire a perfect knowledge of the dimensions of the human body; he should also be a good architect, at least as far as concerns the outward shape of buildings, with their different parts; and where he is deficient, he ought not to neglect taking drawings from Nature.

It will be well also to have a looking-glass by him, when he paints, to look often at his work in it, which being seen the contrary way, will appear as the work of another hand, and will better shew his faults. It will be useful also to quit his work often, and take some relaxation, that his judgment may be clearer at his return; for too great application and sitting still is sometimes the cause of many gross errors.

CHAP. CCCLVI.
OF CORRECTING ERRORS WHICH YOU DISCOVER.

REMEMBER, that when, by the exercise of your own judgment, or the observation of others, you discover any errors in your work, you immediately set about correcting them, lest, in exposing your works to the public, you expose your defects also. Admit not any self-excuse, by persuading yourself that you shall retrieve your character, and that by some succeeding work you shall make amends for your shameful negligence; for your work does not perish as soon as it is out of your hands, like the sound of music, but remains a standing monument of your ignorance. If you excuse yourself by saying that you have not time for the study necessary to form a great painter, having to struggle against necessity, you yourself are only to blame; for the study of what is excellent is food both for mind and body. How many philosophers, born to great riches, have given them away, that they might not be retarded in their pursuits!

[310] Leonardo da Vinci was remarkably fond of this kind of invention, and is accused of having lost a great deal of time that way.

CHAP. CCCLVII.

THE BEST PLACE FOR LOOKING AT A PICTURE.

Let us suppose, that A B is the picture, receiving the light from D; I say, that whoever is placed between C and E, will see the picture very badly, particularly if it be painted in oil, or varnished; because it will shine, and will appear almost of the nature of a looking-glass. For these reasons, the nearer you go towards C, the less you will be able to see, because of the light from the window upon the picture, sending its reflection to that point. But if you place yourself between E D, you may conveniently see the picture, and the more so as you draw nearer to the point D, because that place is less liable to be struck by the reflected rays.

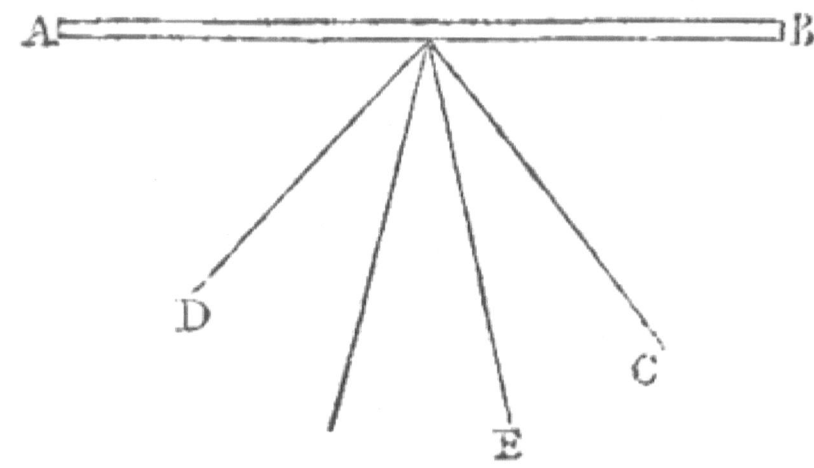

CHAP. CCCLVIII.

OF JUDGMENT.

There is nothing more apt to deceive us than our own judgment, in deciding on our own works; and we should derive more advantage from having our faults pointed out by our enemies, than by hearing the opinions of our friends, because they are too much like ourselves, and may deceive us as much as our own judgment.

CHAP. CCCLIX.

OF EMPLOYMENT ANXIOUSLY WISHED FOR BY PAINT-ERS.

And you, painter, who are desirous of great practice, understand, that if you do not rest it on the good foundation of Nature, you will labour with little honour and less profit; and if you do it on a good ground your works will be many and good, to your great honour and advantage.

CHAP. CCCLX.
ADVICE TO PAINTERS.

A PAINTER ought to study universal Nature, and reason much within himself on all he sees, making use of the most excellent parts that compose the species of every object before him. His mind will by this method be like a mirror, reflecting truly every object placed before it, and become, as it were, a second Nature.

CHAP. CCCLXI.
OF STATUARY.

To execute a figure in marble, you must first make a model of it in clay, or plaster, and when it is finished, place it in a square case, equally capable of receiving the block of marble intended to be shaped like it. Have some peg-like sticks to pass through holes made in the sides, and all round the case; push them in till every one touches the model, marking what remains of the sticks outwards with ink, and making a countermark to every stick and its hole, so that you may at pleasure replace them again. Then having taken out the model, and placed the block of marble in its stead, take so much out of it, till all the pegs go in at the same holes to the marks you had made. To facilitate the work, contrive your frame so that every part of it, separately, or all together, may be lifted up, except the bottom, which must remain under the marble. By this method you may chop it off with great facility[311].

CHAP. CCCLXII.
ON THE MEASUREMENT AND DIVISION OF STATUES INTO PARTS.

DIVIDE the head into twelve parts, each part into twelve degrees, each degree into twelve minutes, and these minutes into seconds[312].

---

[311] The method here recommended, was the general and common practice at that time, and continued so with little, if any variation, till lately. But about thirty years ago, the late Mr. Bacon invented an entirely new method, which, as better answering the purpose, he constantly used, and from him others have also adopted it into practice.

[312] This may be a good method of dividing the figure for the purpose of reducing from large to small, or *vice versâ*; but it not being the method generally used by the painters

CHAP. CCCLXIII.

A PRECEPT FOR THE PAINTER.

The painter who entertains no doubt of his own ability, will attain very little. When the work succeeds beyond the judgment, the artist acquires nothing; but when the judgment is superior to the work, he never ceases improving, if the love of gain do not retard his progress.

CHAP. CCCLXIV.

ON THE JUDGMENT OF PAINTERS.

When the work is equal to the knowledge and judgment of the painter, it is a bad sign; and when it surpasses the judgment, it is still worse, as is the case with those who wonder at having succeeded so well. But when the judgment surpasses the work, it is a perfectly good sign; and the young painter who possesses that rare disposition, will, no doubt, arrive at great perfection. He will produce few works, but they will be such as to fix the admiration of every beholder.

CHAP. CCCLXV.

THAT A MAN OUGHT NOT TO TRUST TO HIMSELF, BUT OUGHT TO CONSULT NATURE.

Whoever flatters himself that he can retain in his memory all the effects of Nature, is deceived, for our memory is not so capacious; therefore consult Nature for every thing.

THE END.

---

for measuring their figures, as being too minute, this chapter was not introduced amongst those of general proportions.

Lector House believes that a society develops through a two-fold approach of continuous learning and adaptation, which is derived from the study of classic literary works spread across the historic timeline of literature records. Therefore, we aim at reviving, repairing and redeveloping all those inaccessible or damaged but historically as well as culturally important literature across subjects so that the future generations may have an opportunity to study and learn from past works to embark upon a journey of creating a better future.

This book is a result of an effort made by Lector House towards making a contribution to the preservation and repair of original ancient works which might hold historical significance to the approach of continuous learning across subjects.

HAPPY READING & LEARNING!

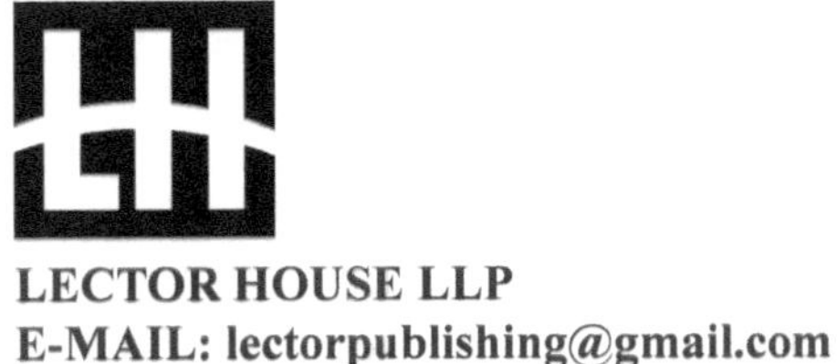

LECTOR HOUSE LLP
E-MAIL: lectorpublishing@gmail.com